The Taoist Manual
An Illustrated Guide
Applying Taoism to Daily Life

Temple Roof — Heng Muntain — Hunan Province

The Taoist Manual

道教手冊

An Illustrated Guide
Applying Taoism to Daily Life

Brock Silvers

Sacred Mountain Press
2005

SACRED MOUNTAIN PRESS
http://www.smpress.com
smp@smpress.com

Copyright © 2005 Brock Silvers

All rights reserved

Book and cover design by Robert Curto

Library of Congress Catalog-in-Publication Data

Silvers, Brock.

The Taoist manual : an illustrated guide : applying Taoism to daily life / Brock Silvers. — 1st ed. — Honolulu, HI : Sacred Mountain Press, 2005.

p. ; cm.

Includes bibliographical references.
ISBN: 0-9677948-1-1
1. Taoism. 2. Spiritual life—Taoism. I. Title.

BL1923 .S55 2004   2004093528
299.5/14—dc22   0501

Printed in India on acid-free paper

Celestial Master Temple — Qingcheng Mountain — Sichuan Province

Stone Lion — Mao Mountain—Jiangsu Province

Contents

Dedication ix
Aknowledgements x
Foreword xi

Chapter 1
Being a Taoist 1
  1.1 Taoism in the West 2
  1.2 What is Taoism? 4
  1.3 What is a Taoist? 6
  1.4 Modern Taoist History 9
  1.5 Gender, Race, & Taoism 12

Chapter 2
Taoist Worship 17
  2.1 Deities, Altars, & Devotions 18
  2.2 Pantheon 19
  2.3 Suggested Altar Deities 51
  2.4 Altar Location 54
  2.5 Purify Your Space 56
  2.6 Build a Taoist Altar 59
  2.7 'Opening' Your Altar 69
  2.8 How to Worship 74
  2.9 Religious Calendar 77
  2.10 Taoist Prayer 105
  2.11 Taoist Meditation 108
  2.12 Care of Your Altar 116

Chapter 3
Fundamental Taoist Activities 121
  3.1 Fundamental Taoist Activities 122
  3.2 The Canon 122
  3.3 Philosophy 124
  3.4 Divination 129
  3.5 Talismans 132
  3.6 Qigong 134
  3.7 Internal Martial Arts 135
  3.8 Feng Shui 137
  3.9 Taoist Medicine 139

Chapter 4
Taoist culture **145**
4.1 Taoist Culture 146
4.2 Yin & Yang 146
4.3 Five Phases 148
4.4 Sexual Relations 149
4.5 Diet 152
4.6 Artistic Expression 154
4.7 Iconography 159
4.8 Architecture 165
4.9 Nature 169
4.10 Clothing 170
4.11 Conduct 172

Chapter 5
Continued Study **177**
5.1 Continued Study 178
5.2 Selecting a Teacher 179
5.3 Reading and Internet Resources 182
5.4 Taoist Pilgrimage 189

Bibliography 210

Eight Trigrams Pavilion —Purple Sheep Palace — Sichuan Province

For Lex, Angie, & Liv
There will come a day, although you may not recognize it until long after it has passed, when you will face a silken choice: to follow your internal spirit, or to heed the enchanting call of some external siren. Choose well, with all your heart and with as little thought as possible, and never regret the path you have chosen. At the end of your journey, look for me, as I hope to be waiting for you. And we shall clap our hands and laugh and wonder aloud if we had ever really been apart.

Acknowledgements

The author humbly thanks all of those people who have provided him with valuable assistance, encouragement, and support:

Poul Anderson, Mark Csikszentmihalyi, Livia Kohn, Susan Levitt, Draja Mickaharic, Ashvina Patel, Michael Saso and *Abby Silvers* for valuable draft review and commentary;

Bob Curto, for his artistic vision and production assistance;

Ian Johnson, for his inspiration and delightful companionship, and for draft review and commentary;

Michael Mundaca and Neil Stern, for many decades of unmatched friendship and professional support;

Heidi Schumacher, for many years of research assistance and irreplaceable personal support;

Rebecca Xu, for her many years of loyal assistance, translation, and friendship;

The participants at the TRS Discussion Board, for their (sometimes raucous) delineation and elucidation of major issues;

The Taoists of China, both those who have provided me with knowledge and assistance, and all those who have otherwise accepted the unfortunately difficult task of perpetuating the ancient Taoist tradition.

Any mistakes, inaccuracies, or misrepresentations within this book are the sole responsibility of the author. If you notice any such occurrences, please alert Sacred Mountain Press so that any subsequent editions of this book may be thereby improved.

Foreword

Here at first glance is a strange book: a primer on how to live like a Taoist. Strange because many people nowadays assume that they know all about Taoism—it is the religion of going with the flow, *yin* and *yang*, and water wearing down stone. Not only do most Western bookstores have a seemingly endless array of books with the word "Tao" or "Dao" in the title, but Taoism would not seem in need of a manual—isn't it basically just about following your instincts?

The answer is "no," and the assumptions behind it explain why this book is so desperately needed. That's because few religions are as misunderstood as Taoism, which in its Chinese homeland is routinely criticized as embodying "feudal superstition" and abroad is the subject of all sorts of fantasies that we have projected upon it.

In China, the Taoist religion has been on the defensive for centuries, culminating in its very near extinction doing the Cultural Revolution. As China's only indigenous religion, it suffered arguably more than any other major religion. China's humiliation in the 19th century led to a growing insecurity about the value of its culture and traditions. Taoism took the brunt of this self-loathing, with its beliefs publicly denigrated and the subject of government campaigns against superstition. (By contrast, the other major religions practiced in China —Islam, Buddhism and Christianity— had powerful patrons in neighboring countries. The fact that they were "world religions" gave them a veneer of respectability that Taoism, which was "only" practiced in China, did not possess.) During the Cultural Revolution, all religions in China suffered, but since that time Taoism has benefited from the least outside support in its recovery and the attacks against it have received the least attention. Consider the situation today in Beijing, where half a dozen Christian churches operate officially, versus just two Taoist temples, one of which (the Fire God Temple on Finance Street) the government threatens to close every year or two. This, don't forget, is in a city of 12 million that used to have hundreds of Taoist temples before the communist takeover in 1949.

Beyond physical attacks, Taoism is often ridiculed in China as not really a religion. Educated people in China (and abroad as well) routinely say that Taoism might be a philosophy, but it's certainly not a "real" religion. As for people praying in Taoist temples, they're following folk practices, not religious precepts. What this line of argumentation neglects is that every religion spans a broad range of beliefs and practices. No one would argue that Catholic Christianity isn't a religion because it encompasses both the philosophical works of St. Augustine and the folk beliefs of rosary beads.

Outside China, Taoism is to a degree being killed by kindness. Every sort of well-meaning New Ager seems to have tried to translate the Daodejing (Tao Te Jing) or is writing a book on the tao of this or that. Many of these books are legitimate efforts at divining a difficult and at times obscure religion, but many reduce that religion to a commodity, the latest ingredient for the cultural consumer to add to the goulash of modern spiritual life.

Brock Silvers takes a different approach: he takes Taoism seriously. In other words, he treats it for what it is—a religion with roots in China but enough appeal to be relevant abroad. Instead of trying to twist Taoism into something it is not, he does what—and this is amazing when one thinks of it—no one has done before. He gives simple, clear and well-grounded explanations for how to live more like a traditional Taoist. In other words, this isn't an easy book about getting in touch with yourself; it's about the rigor necessary to do so. For, as any practitioner of a religion or spiritual practice knows, enlightenment requires discipline and structure.

On a deeper level, this book is a testament to Taoism's universality. Like any new cultural phenomenon in the West, it started as something exotic and light, a fun alternative to dreary Western religions, with their rules and regulations. Now, in a sign of its staying power in the West, it has entered a new phase: the desire for authenticity. Along with the growth of Taoist studies at universities around the world, this means that a growing (although percentage-wise still small) number of Taoist texts are being translated into Western languages, making it possible for practitioners to come into direct contact with the religion's main teachings. Now, thanks to Mr. Silvers, we have a textbook on how to practice it—the nitty gritty details of how to set up an altar, find statues and navigate the seemingly bewildering pantheons of gods and demons.

This development is good news for Taoism's expansion abroad, and maybe also for its fate back in China. To date, most of the minimal overseas support that Taoism in China has enjoyed has come from Southeast Asia. In years to come, the religion's growing popularity in the West may likewise offer a new fount of support. It might seem odd, but for Taoism in China, nothing could be more effective than for Westerners to treat Taoism seriously. If we respect Taoism, perhaps the authorities back in China will do so too.

The practice of Taoism is still in its infancy in the West and is still recovering back in China. During this crucial time, Mr. Silvers does the religion a great service by laying out the basics and making it possible for Westerners to practice Taoism in an authentic form. This isn't to say that Taoism won't change in the West—every religion changes when it encounters new cultures—but this book makes it possible for such interaction to happen without losing Taoism's essence.

Ian Johnson
July, 2004

1
Being a Taoist

1.1 Taoism in the West

Taoism is a tradition in resurgence. A few decades ago it was close to extinction, after more than a century of Chinese civil war, turmoil, and extreme government repression. Western scholars feared for the very survival of this ancient and influential religion. Recent years have brought respite, and now Taoists once again roam China's holiest mountains, and novices and practitioners crowd its Taoist temples. Parts of the broad-based Taoist tradition may unfortunately have been lost, but Taoism itself seems poised to survive well into the foreseeable future.

One important aspect of Taoism's remarkable revival is its significant influence upon Western culture. Not only are the West's Traditional Chinese Medical schools and internal martial arts schools filled to capacity, but our corporate executives read books on the tao of business, and the *yin-yang* symbol has been broadly adopted by our counter-cultural youth. We recognize the tao, and individual aspects of Taoism, all around us now. They have permeated the basic fabric of our Western society and civilization.

In such a climate, it is only natural that many people in our culture today want to achieve a deeper understanding of traditional Taoism, or to actually become Taoists. Taoism, they believe, will enhance their lives, careers, relationships, and practices, or will fill the spiritual void so prevalent throughout much of the modern West. Their instincts are right. Taoism does hold out such prizes to those who would seek it, learn it, and join it.

Unfortunately, however, becoming an authentic Taoist, or even acquiring a serious knowledge regarding Taoism, is not a simple proposition in the West. Simply put, many people in the West confuse activities beloved by Taoists for activities that define Taoists (see Chapter 1.3 – *What is a Taoist?*). A general lack of awareness concerning this distinction significantly hampers the development of Taoist communities in the West. Before serious Western Taoist communities can develop, there needs to be an acknowledgement that participation in the authentic Taoist tradition will require people to go beyond any individual practice favored by Taoists.

Complicating the problem is Taoism's purely Chinese origins. All of Taoism's source texts are written in Classical Chinese. Almost all of Taoism's religious centers and communities are located in Asia. Very few traditionally trained Taoists live in the West, so authentic teachers are as rare and hard to find as are the Taoist Peaches of Immortality. To make matters worse,

Tao

Ancient Seal Script

more than a few people have taken advantage of this dearth of opportunities for authentic Taoist study and training to pass off their own fraudulent or un-Taoist ideas upon an unsuspecting public. Many of the popular 'Taoist' books read by Westerners today are fictitious tales passed off as legitimate biography, physical exercises with no grounding in actual Taoist tradition, etc.

Unless one can speak Chinese, read Classical Chinese, and has the money, opportunity, and general hardiness to travel widely throughout remote Asia, can one become a serious student of traditional Taoism, or even become a true Taoist? As with any spiritual tradition, genuine Taoist achievement requires a willing heart, long and constant practice, and unshakable dedication. Even with those attributes, success may or may not come, depending upon the abilities and fate of the practitioner. Some Taoists work very hard for decades to achieve even the barest minimum of success, and thereby consider themselves highly blessed.

There will be some Westerners who nonetheless believe that Taoism is their destined path or their fate. They are to be admired for their desire, their courage, and their determination. For these people, this book provides an outline for basic Taoist practice. This book will discuss the practical nature of Taoism, and will provide specific, detailed suggestions for starting to practice and study many fundamental Taoist activities. This book will also go on to explain how Taoists commonly apply this training to their daily lives.

No book can lead an individual to the final goal of extensive, authentic Taoist knowledge and experience. Only a qualified Taoist teacher could help you to accomplish that life-changing task. Even then, most of the work would have to be done within the seeker's own heart and energy. Given the lack of serious training available to Western students of Taoism, however, this book hopes to fill a huge void. It will help any willing student to begin walking along a genuine Taoist path, whether that path leads to greater knowledge of Taoism or to becoming an authentic, traditional Taoist. Armed with the guidance in this book, any dedicated student will be able to proceed along a significant portion of that path, and will be able to understand and create a more Taoist lifestyle and environment for themselves. As the reader progresses, this book also provides specific suggestions regarding how to continue your journey, and how to continue to expand, refine, and elevate your Taoist practice.

You have started along an ancient path that has brought great beauty, wisdom, peace, and satisfaction to countless generations of people. May all such aspirants meet good fortune, and may the Taoist pantheon unfold our paths before us and fulfill our deepest dreams and desires! If our destinies permit and our wills are strong, may we all meet on the sacred shores of the Taoist island of Penglai!

1.2 What is Taoism?

Longevity
Shou

Ancient Bird Seal Script

During the late 19th Century, Western academia discovered Taoism. It unfortunately assumed the prejudices of early missionary scholars and translators and even those of Chinese society and government, and these prejudices helped keep academia from investigating Taoism's true nature for many decades. Buddhism was regarded as the 'high road,' while Taoism was seen as an amalgamation of superstition, folk religion, senseless magic, and ossified ritual. Academics, then and now, generally avoid subjects that their peers find to be devoid of value. Such was the unfortunate case with most of the Taoist tradition. The one part of the tradition that was thought to be sufficiently worthy of attention was Taoist philosophy. This philosophy contained none of the overt or obvious superstition, magic, or ritual that populated the rest of Taoism. So the works of authors like Laozi and Zhuangzi (and a very few others) were translated and dissected. Divorced from the remainder of the Taoist tradition, however, these works were often taken out of context. Moreover, decades of isolation from the Taoist tradition have served to give many people in the West the incorrect idea that Taoism is merely a naturalistic, quietist, non-religious philosophy!

Over the last several decades, however, scholars and academics have finally awakened to the organic whole of Taoist tradition. What does that tradition entail? Despite a wide variety of lineal, geographic, and personal variations, Taoist traditions commonly include:

- A worldview that sees everything in terms of flowing energy or *qi*. The natural, balanced, changing flow of universal *qi* is seen as the *tao*;
- The veneration of a large, diverse, and ever-changing pantheon of deities;
- A large, active infrastructure of temples, monasteries, religious institutions, and officials;
- Ritual initiation as an inviolable entrance requirement;
- A large and ancient corpus of ritual and prayer;

- Countless types of meditation and alchemy (both internal and external);
- World-renowned mystic philosophy;
- An official religious canon, last compiled in 1444-1445 during the reign of the Ming Emperor Zhengtong, consisting of thousands of volumes;
- An extensive religious calendar based upon a lunar system;
- Magic, exorcism, and similar activities;
- Internal martial arts and energy healing;
- A wide variety of cultural customs and requirements;
- And much more!

There are still people who will insist that Taoism can be divided into two schools: the Religious and the Philosophic. This is simply incorrect. While some Taoists may be especially attracted to either philosophic introspection or to religious ritual, all Taoists engage in both types of activity. Taoism holds that its religious activities are mere applications of its philosophic beliefs. It is only because of the incomplete or slanted works of early scholars and translators that the West was fooled into thinking that such a division ever existed! There was never a 'parting of the way' as earlier generations of misguided Western scholars claimed. Taoist philosophy or ritual, taken in absolute isolation, loses its connection to that tradition, and is no longer Taoist.

How then can we reconcile the seemingly non-religious message contained in a book like Laozi's *Dao De Jing* with the religious and ritual demands of the authentic Taoist tradition? The first thing to remember is that the *Dao De Jing* is only one of thousands of books that comprise the Taoist Canon (see Chapter 3.2 – *The Canon*). It would be a mistake to take any one book from within the Canon and to attempt to extrapolate from that single book general truths about Taoism as a whole. The Taoist tradition is too ancient, too great, and too broad for that. Moreover, as initiates, Taoists possess an understanding of the books within their Canon that often differs from common Taoist understandings. Such understandings are often passed through the teaching of what are called 'oral secrets' (*koujue*). Whereas non-initiates in the West often see an innocuous literary passage concerning political affairs or philosophical outlook, Taoists may often have a radically different interpretation that includes information about practices or rituals.

Koujue

For example, the *Dao De Jing* speaks of 'preserving the One,' and Taoists have understood this as the basis for a wide variety of specific and sometimes complex meditation and cultivation techniques. Non-initiated Western readers of the *Dao De Jing* will probably be unaware of these Taoist activities.

In the specific case of Laozi, it is also useful to remember that Taoists believe that Laozi was not only a man who wrote an important book, he is a deity that Taoists have worshipped since the very beginnings of Taoism. Since that time, Taoists believe they have received countless visitations and messages from the deified Laozi, all of which contribute to the general Taoist understanding of the works left to us by the temporarily human Laozi. Celestial Master Taoism was originally founded upon one of these supernatural visitations from Laozi in 142 A.D.!

The overall individual goal of Taoism is to unite the Taoist with his or her true, original nature. This can be seen in purely philosophical terms, but that would not accurately or fully depict Taoism's traditional goals. A Taoist traditionally goes through a lifetime of training in order to finally purify, transmute, and project his or her energy into a mystical union with primordial energy, a union that Westerners might commonly call 'heaven.' But to a Taoist this is not a purely psychological or philosophical exercise. It also demands that the Taoist attempt to transform himself or herself into an Immortal. The quest for such immortality is a central theme throughout all of Taoist history, and involves the Taoist undertaking a lengthy energetic transmutation allowing the Taoist to take his or her place in the Taoist heavens. This is a complicated topic, but it is enough right now to know that Taoists seek, through the purifying transmutation of their energy, to become what is termed an 'Immortal' (a *xian*), and to thus take their literal place in the Taoist heavens.

1.3 What is a Taoist?

Taoism is a religion with strict entrance requirements. Just as other religions like Catholicism and Judaism have their requisite rituals of initiation (for example, baptism and bar mitzvah, respectively), so too does Taoism. To be a Taoist, one must be initiated into a Taoist lineage. Only after such initiation is one actually a Taoist. Prior to initiation one might be regarded as a 'Student of the Tao' or a 'Taoist Practitioner,' i.e., one who seriously studies or practices Taoism, but not as a 'Taoist.'

Xian

Initiation Platform
White Cloud Monastery
Beijing City

It is important to note the implications of this terminology. Within Taoism there is no laity. Every Taoist is an initiated member of the 'clergy,' and it is the non-Taoist community of Students and Practitioners who fill the equivalent role of laity. People who worship deities, support temples, and lead lives according to Taoist principles are still not Taoists. Thus the term 'Taoist Priest' should not be taken to indicate someone within Taoism who has a special status akin to that of a Catholic Priest. It simply indicates a Taoist who fills a societal priestly function. There is no difference in status between a Taoist Priest and a Taoist; there is only a difference in social function. Likewise a Taoist Monk or a Taoist Nun is simply a male or female Taoist who lives a monastic life. These terms do not imply any sense of status, they merely indicate living conditions. In Taoism, you are either a Taoist, a Student/Practitioner, or an outsider.

During initiation the new Taoist receives Taoist 'register' or a list of spirits to be envisioned, talismans to summon them, and mantra/mudra to command them. These things are fundamentally important to the performance of ritual commonly required of Taoists. They are bestowed directly from the new Taoist's initiator, who is often the Taoist's father but in all cases is the Taoist's new 'Master.' The Master is now responsible for the education and development of the new Taoist, which also helps to ensure that the new Taoist properly utilizes his or her initiatory bequeathal. Lineage is central to Taoism.

Formal initiation into a lineage is itself only the beginning of Taoist learning. After initiation, Taoists commonly learn to meditate on the writings of Taoist philosophers, to obey the rules of Taoist ritual, to play ritual music, to sing ritual songs, and to dance ritual dances. The actual achievement of these or similar goals could take a Taoist many years (or a lifetime!) of diligent work. Until that day, however, while one is technically a Taoist, one is also no more than a humble beginner. To be a Taoist is not the same as being an expert Taoist!

Heaven
Tian

Ancient Bird Seal Script

To simply 'follow the tao' does not make one a Taoist in any meaningful or traditional sense. In fact, to 'follow the tao,' regardless of whether that entails a philosophic or mystical quest for oneness, or a heightened awareness of nature or reality, ignores Taoism's fundamental nature and structure. It is not a matter of how much goodness is in your heart or how devoutly you seek the tao in your everyday life. Although such a path may lead to tremendous spiritual advancement, it cannot replace initiation.

This concept may unfortunately upset many honest and sincere people who have dedicated their spiritual efforts to finding and following the tao. But the tao is a philosophical concept that can be applied to any situation. There is a tao to every process, and a tao to every religion. Catholic Priests, Jewish Rabbis, and Muslim Imams all try to follow the tao as they understand it. Taoism, on the other hand, is a specific, ancient, and well-defined religious tradition. To be a Taoist is to be an officially accepted (i.e., initiated) member of that religious tradition.

Some people may actually prefer a spiritual practice revolving around their personal understanding of the tao, and might prefer to ignore the dictates and traditions of Taoism. This would be a personal choice, and one that everyone, including Taoists, should respect. But after having made such a choice, one is definitely not a Taoist. A better term to describe someone who follows such a spiritual practice might be a 'tao-ist,' i.e., 'one who follows the tao,' as opposed to a 'Taoist,' which signifies an initiated member of the Taoist religion.

Many people in the West have adopted various isolated forms of Taoist practice. Again, however, learning an internal martial art, *feng shui*, acupuncture, *qigong*, or even a type of Taoist meditation does not make one a Taoist in any meaningful or traditional sense. These are all activities beloved by Taoists, but they do not define Taoists. Only initiation does so. A Buddhist who practices *taiji quan* or *qigong* is still a Buddhist and not a Taoist!

Although becoming a Taoist would require going far beyond any individual practice, you should not take this as a discouragement. Anyone who wishes to cultivate a more Taoist lifestyle will be well-served by the adoption of such practices. Moreover, the issues of initiations, registers, and titles are more appropriately reserved for very experienced practitioners. Until a very advanced stage of practice is reached it is not necessary to concern oneself with them. Most Westerners can make fantastic progress along a traditionally Taoist path for many years before these issues become important. Seekers should first focus on building a solid foundation for their continuing studies. Titles ideally reflect spiritual elevation, but never confer it.

1.4 Modern Taoist History

In order to understand the Taoism you are likely to encounter today, either in Asia or in the West, you will need to understand something of Taoism's somewhat tragic modern history. It is a history that was almost witness to the complete destruction of Taoism as a living tradition, yet has in recent decades seen a dramatic restoration of Taoist practice and spirit across the globe.

Taoism's modern history really starts in 1644 (in China modern history can start in 1644!). In that year the Ming Dynasty fell in dramatic fashion to the new Qing Dynasty. The new Qing rulers, however, were not ethnic Chinese. The Qing came from Manchuria. Not only did the people of Manchuria historically favor Buddhism, but Taoism had also taken on nationalistic overtones that were not appreciated by China's new foreign rulers. Moreover, Taoism was also associated with secret societies, and such societies had played an important role in previous dynastic revolutions. To make matters even worse, Western powers became involved in China during this period, and these colonial interests were stridently supportive of Christianity at the expense of native Chinese traditions.

For all of these reasons, Taoism found itself out of favor in Qing China. It was during the Qing Dynasty that Taoism began a centuries-long slide to the brink of extinction. The Qing Emperors' general distrust of Taoism served to lower the level of Imperial support received by Taoist communities. Amidst this process of lessened support, the Qing suffered a decade-long revolt in the mid-19th Century called the Taiping Rebellion (*taiping geming*). The revolt was led by Hong Xiuquan, who believed himself to be the younger brother of Jesus Christ.

Taiping Geming

These 'Christian' rebels controlled roughly half of China for roughly a decade. In the areas under their control, they took particular delight in destroying non-Christian infrastructure. Many Taoist communities were burnt to the ground, and many treasures were lost.

With a significantly destroyed infrastructure and reduced government support, Taoism began the difficult task of rebuilding. For the next seventy-five years or so, Taoism crawled forward as best it could, although the Qing government had become so impoverished that practically all Imperial support for Taoism had been halted.

In 1938, the Japanese Imperial Army invaded China and quickly conquered the eastern and northeastern segments of the country. This again brought terrible misfortune to Taoist communities in those areas. Many temples were destroyed in the fighting, and Japanese programs to conquer and control the Chinese populace destroyed many more. Particularly hard hit were the temples and communities around Mao Mountain in Jiangsu Province. These ancient sites were almost totally destroyed for the second time in less than a century.

After World War II ended, China was engulfed in a bitter civil war between the Nationalists and the Communists. Taoism, for a variety of reasons, was associated with the Nationalist cause. The Communists, however, won the civil war in 1949 and quickly moved to illegalize religion. According to Taiwanese researcher Shen Ping-wen, over the next ten years the number of Taoists (meaning Taoist initiates) was reduced from over five million to fewer than 50,000, a reduction of 99%! Many were sent to work camps, many were forced to renounce religious life, and many were even killed. Temples were destroyed or, at best, converted to non-religious uses. Religious life in China came to a near standstill.

If Taoism had not suffered enough already, China's Cultural Revolution (*wenhua da geming*) erupted in 1966. Originally conceived by Mao Zedong, China's supreme political leader, as a campaign to rid the government of his political enemies, it quickly turned into uncontrollable mass chaos wherein everything old or traditional was scorned. Huge gangs of teenage thugs roamed the countryside burning and looting temples as a testament to their devotion to Chairman Mao. Very little of Taoism survived this tumultuous decade, and almost all Taoists were either eliminated (killed, sent to work camps, or forced to renounce religious vows) or driven into extreme hiding.

Wenhua Da Geming

Quanzhen Pai

In 1979-80, under the new leadership of Deng Xiaoping, China ushered in a new era of relative openness and reform. The country had simply grown too tired of revolutionary chaos. This new era came as Taoism teetered on the brink of extinction. A tradition that had started in the 2nd Century A.D., and had been based upon the very roots of ancient Chinese culture, had been repressed and beaten for so long that it could not have withstood another single blow.

At that time, Western academia doubted that Taoism had survived. A great deal of Taoist tradition is oral, and must be passed from Master to student. Yet for over 30 years no students had been openly trained. A Taoist born in 1910 and apprenticed to an experienced Taoist in 1925 was just entering spiritual maturity when Taoism was outlawed in 1950. Since that time he would have led either a tortured or extremely difficult non-religious life. Now he would be an old man. Could he overcome his psychological scars? How much would he remember? Could he be convinced to return to religious life? Where would he practice, as very few temples were functioning? Would his community support his return? Would China's youth have any desire to learn his ancient secrets?

Since that time, Taoism has developed beyond the critical stage. There is a functioning group of Taoists, including a dwindling but still significant number of pre-revolutionary Taoists, who have reclaimed religious lives, temples, and communities. The Chinese government, while still exerting a great deal of repressive control over Taoism, has grudgingly allowed the tradition to recover. Taoists now practice within one of two government-defined classifications, *Zhengyi* (Orthodox Unity) and *Quanzhen* (Complete Perfection). In overly generalized terms, the former places a slightly greater emphasis on ritual and talismanic practice, while the latter places a slightly greater emphasis on meditation and internal cultivation. The important point is that Taoists, while still burdened by governmental interference, are again publicly practicing and reclaiming their traditions. Overseas Chinese communities in Hong Kong and Taiwan, assisted by international Western organizations such as the Taoist Restoration Society, have provided great assistance to Taoism in this recovery. Taoist communities have taken root outside China and in the West. Taoism is slowly being restored to its rightful place among the world's great active religions. Some parts of the Taoist tradition have undoubtedly been lost, but Taoism possesses sufficient critical mass so as to enable the tradition to repair and revive itself. Your support and interest in Taoism can only contribute to that process.

Zhengyi Pai

1.5 Gender, Race, & Taoism

I would like to make one final, important point regarding the nature of Taoism:

One's gender and race are completely unrelated to one's ability to become a wise and powerful Taoist, or to beneficially and vibrantly incorporate Taoism into one's spiritual life.

Taoism is extremely clear on this point.

The Taoist Heavens are populated by countless beings. The pantheon is exceptionally vast. If we examine ancient Taoist paintings and murals, we can plainly see that these multitudinous Heavenly Beings and Immortals are represented as having come from a wide variety of racial backgrounds. Some have dark skin, some have typical Asian skin tones, and some have skin that is whiter than white. Hair types also range from extremely curly to extremely straight. Some of the Taoist Gods even claim descent from non-Chinese deities! (See the synopses of the Taoist deities *Erlang* and *Li Nezha* in Chapter 2.2 – *Pantheon*).

Some people may even assume that one must be an ethnic Chinese in order to become a Taoist. The Chinese characteristics of Taoism, however, are cultural and not racial. Taoism was founded and primarily developed within the context of traditional Chinese culture and society. It is only natural for Taoism to retain a great deal of that influence. That does not mean that only ethnic Chinese people can be Taoists or practice Taoism. It means that whomever would do so must be comfortable and familiar with Chinese culture, not that they must be of Chinese origin.

Many of the world's great religious traditions also accord women a somewhat lesser status than is accorded men. This is not so in Taoism. In China there is a saying, 'Women hold up half the sky,' and that saying is fully endorsed by Taoism.

There are many very important female Taoist deities, including:

Guan Yin	Wei Huacun
Queen Mother of the West	Mysterious Lady of the 9th Heaven
Princess of the Azure Clouds	Mazu
Songzi Niang Niang	He Xiangu
Chang E	Sun Bu'er

and many more!

Immortal
Xian

Ancient Seal Script

Some Taoist traditions, like Complete Perfection Taoism, have a long history of female initiation. Female Taoists in that tradition are considered to be the equal of male Taoists, and have their own meditations and internal alchemical practices geared towards the female energetic system. Other traditions, like Orthodox Unity Taoism, often do not initiate females. But while there may be restrictions on female Orthodox Unity Taoists, there are no gender restrictions whatsoever in terms of Orthodox Unity Taoist practice.

Several years ago I met a female Taoist in Jiangsu Province who had devised a wonderful plan for dealing with the lineal differences regarding the status of women. She was born in an area that was historically famous as a center for Highest Purity Taoism. From the time she was a small child she dreamt of becoming a Highest Purity Taoist in the local tradition. Highest Purity Taoism, however, generally initiates only males as Taoists. So this innovative woman went away and became a Complete Perfection Taoist. She returned to her hometown, and eventually reclaimed an old, abandoned Highest Purity Taoist Monastery. She revived the old monastery as a Complete Perfection Taoist institution. In her personal practice, and in the practice she started to teach to her female disciples, she adopted as much of Highest Purity Taoism as she could. She adopted aspects of Highest Purity Taoism's pantheon, liturgies, prayers, meditations, rituals, and practices. Her practice developed, and she is now the Abbess of an ancient nunnery that is a delightful blend of Complete Perfection and Highest Purity Taoism. This Abbess applied her own ingenuity to authentic Taoist tradition as she knew it, with the result that her dreams have been fulfilled. While we should all applaud her resourcefulness and ingenuity, we must also keep in mind that a Taoist Abbess is allowed latitude in transforming Taoism, while Students, Practitioners, and outsiders are not.

Taoism is an extremely inclusive religion. Not only are all genders and nationalities fully welcomed into Taoism, some Taoist deities are also severely handicapped (See the synopsis of *Li Tieguai* in Chapter 2.2 – *Pantheon*). Moreover, many Taoist deities were once evil or previously unsuccessful people who attained spiritual greatness through Taoist application. The heights of Taoism are free to all who would claim them. The only requirement is your personal dedication.

Star Mother Temple — Purple Sheep Palace — Sichuan Province

Ci Hang Temple — Qingcheng Mountain — Sichuan Province

Three Mao Brothers Temple — Mao Mountain — Jiangsu Province

2
Taoist Worship

2.1 Deities, Altars, & Devotions

Taoism is foremost a practiced religion. Religious activity invariably includes worship, and Taoism is no exception.

The focal point of Taoist worship (and almost all Taoist activity) is the Taoist altar (*daotan*). Almost all Taoist practices occur in front of, or in relation to, an altar. Many people in the West today approach altars from a symbolic perspective. They believe that accumulating and organizing powerful symbols, in coordination with their own sincere intent, will create the energy or results that they are seeking. Although this approach may work in some cases, Taoism approaches its altars from a literal perspective, as a sanctified space where communion and interaction with Taoist deities, spirits, and energies can occur. An altar statue is thus not only a symbolic representation of a deity, but also represents the literal, actual deity.

Daotan

Taoist altars are used to venerate and communicate with a host of 'spirits,' 'gods,' or 'deities.' Taoism sees these beings as effecting changes in nature, and in the harmonious interaction of the human microcosm with those macrocosmic changes. These beings are mostly unseen, but are entirely real to the Taoist, who therefore venerates them.

Religious devotions (*baishen*) are among the primary daily activities of a Taoist. Taoists pray to open the day, and then again to close it, welcoming and thanking the Heavens for that which is greater than man. Morning and evening prayer sessions are among the most special and energetically charged times

Chaoyang Cave
Qingcheng Mountain
Sichuan Province

Baishen

at Taoist temples and monasteries. I have never met anyone who claimed to love Taoism who did not place these times among his or her absolute favorites. With daylight either beginning or ending, Taoists gather in a main hall to play their traditional instruments as thick incense carries their chanted prayers towards the Heavens. Those who do not play an instrument or perform a ritual simply kneel in respect, and lend their voices and their devotion to the groups' efforts. Our own Western society might do well to imitate this ancient custom, as would anyone who wants to cultivate a more Taoist lifestyle.

Many Taoists also utilize personal shrines in addition to these communal rituals and chanted liturgies every sunrise and sunset. This allows for a more intimate relationship with any chosen deity. While a main hall within the temple is used for communal ritual and devotion, many Taoists frequently express their veneration for their deities at their personal altars throughout the day or night, as their practices demand.

Taoist devotions, however, are not usually directed towards the tao, abstract nature, the universe, or some other similar entity. Taoists worship a broad pantheon of mostly anthropomorphic deities. There are too many deities in the Taoist pantheon to render an accurate accounting. Although there are a variety of 'major' deities who are almost universally worshipped by Taoists, specific decisions regarding which deities to venerate are generally made according to regional and lineal traditions. Only after those concerns are met would a Taoist normally exercise personal preference. Non-Taoists, however, will be unburdened by these influences, and will be free to select the focus of their devotions based upon intuition and instinct.

Taoist practices and regimens differ widely from area to area, lineage to lineage, and person to person. There are some Taoists for whom worship will play a more important role in their practice, and some for whom it will play a lesser role. But absolutely all Taoists engage in the veneration of deities.

2.2 Pantheon

Taoists conceive of their pantheon as a mirror image of traditional Chinese society. There is a clearly defined leader, a large hierarchical bureaucracy supporting that leader, and a complex system of ritual and custom that must be observed in order to create an atmosphere and energy under which this entire system can thrive. Those deities who succeed within this

Heavenly Emperor
Di

Ancient Seal Script

system may be rewarded (i.e., elevated to a higher position), while those who transgress are usually punished (i.e., possibly demoted or given redeeming tasks.).

Immortal
Xian Ren

Ancient Seal Script

Taoism's pantheon of deities is a constant work-in-progress. Occasionally, although not very often, deities fall into disuse and obscurity. More often, however, deities are added to the pantheon. How does someone or something become a deity? This happens in a variety of ways. One of the more common methods is for a famous individual person to pass away and to be acclaimed a newly minted Taoist deity by respected Taoists. These Taoists would base their acclamation upon various 'signs': perhaps the method of death, combined with the known experience and knowledge of the recently deceased Taoist; perhaps after receiving some information during meditation or via some other psychic avenue. Traditionally, a petition would then be made to government and religious authorities, who would review the case and render a decision.

Not all Taoist deities were once human beings, let alone Taoists! Some deities have only existed in the spirit realm. Another method for discovering such a deity was for someone to deliver a message while under possession by a given deity. A common sight in traditional temples was once a 'planchette,' a small sandbox with an overhanging instrument used for writing in the sand. There were Taoists who specialized in possession writing and others who specialized in the reading and interpretation of such writing. Countless Taoist deities have left messages via this method, which still continues to this day in some societies (particularly in Taiwan and in Southeast Asia). (See Chapter 3.4 – *Divination*)

Regardless of the method used, once a new deity had been discovered, or a new position for an existing deity had been discovered, the government and religious authorities were petitioned to proclaim the event. If such a petition were successful, a new deity would be formally included in the Taoist pantheon. Even without a successful petition, a discovery could gain sufficient momentum within popular religious society that the authorities would eventually be forced to relent.

Different sects, regions, and individuals view the pantheon in different manners. Not all Taoists are in exact agreement on all aspects of the pantheon. (Are all Taoists ever in exact agreement on all aspects of anything? If you ever have evidence of this, please take notes or a photo, as you will be witnessing a unique historic moment!) Taoists do have, however, a general consensus on the basic elements of the pantheon. The highest

Taoist Worship

deities are generally believed to be the *Three Purities*. The *Three Purities*, however, are so elevated that they function almost like elemental forces. They do not usually have the same interaction with the human world as do lower-ranking deities. Beneath the *Three Purities* is generally considered to be the *Great Jade Emperor*. He is more anthropomorphic than the *Three Purities*, and is a counterpart of the earthly Chinese Emperor. He is the highest authority in terms of the ongoing operation of the Taoist heavens. In modern terms, the *Three Purities* can be seen as the Chairmen of the Board, while the *Great Jade Emperor* can be seen as the Chief Executive Officer. Below the *Great Jade Emperor* are realms of different deities, most with specific functions, and many with retinues of valets and assistants.

The following are synopses of many of the more important and well-known Taoist deities. Interpretations vary amongst Taoists, and sometimes change over time, but the following are fairly standard summaries:

Bai Yuchan: See Five Southern Patriarchs

Cao Guojiu: See Eight Immortals

Chang E 嫦娥

Chang E

Chang E is the Moon Goddess. She lives on the moon, and her story is a sad one. She and her husband had been Immortals in the heavenly realm. Due to a mistaken offense by her husband, they were banished to the earth as mortals. Her husband made an arduous and dangerous trek to find the *Queen Mother of the West*. He succeeded, and begged for forgiveness. The *Queen Mother of the West* took pity on this good-hearted man and gave him a magic immortality elixir. Taken in one dose, it would elevate one person to heavenly immortality. Taken in two doses, it would give two people earthly immortality. He brought the elixir back to his wife, and waited for an auspicious day for them to reclaim earthly immortality. As he slept, however, his wife drank all the elixir! She became a heavenly Immortal, but for her greed and trickery she was banished to the cold and dark moon, where she lives in a lonely palace with a white rabbit. Because she had to face her husband's great anger at being cheated out of immortality, Cheng E is venerated by unhappy or abused wives. *Chang E* is often depicted with very white skin, to refle ct the dark, cold atmosphere of the moon. She is traditionally worshipped on the night of the Mid-Autumn Festival (15th day of the 8th lunar month).

21

Chen Tuan

Chen Nan: See **Five Southern Patriarchs**

Chen Tuan 陳摶

Chen Tuan (906 – 989 A.D.) was a famous T'ang Dynasty Taoist who was regarded as an expert in both internal and external alchemy. He spent most of his career at Hua Mountain (see Chapter 5.4 — *Taoist Pilgrimage*), and is one of the most famous Taoists ever produced by that mountain. Taoists naturally believe that *Chen Tuan's* expertise enabled him to become an Immortal upon his physical death.

Ci Hang 慈航

Ci Hang is revered as a Taoist 'Mercy God,' and is an emanation of *Taiyi Jiuku Tianzun*. His name literally translates as 'Benevolent Deliverance.' He is a member of a group called the 'Twelve Golden Immortals,' who are disciples of Taoism's absolute highest deity, *The Celestial Worthy of the Primordial Origin*, or the *Jade Purity*. *Ci Hang* seems to be most popular in southwestern China. He is commonly depicted with a thousand hands and eyes, and riding a nine-headed golden lion.

Taoist Worship

Constellation Deities

City Deities 城隍

Taoism has long recognized that every city has a protective deity (a *cheng huang*) whose responsibility is to protect the local populace, to ward off disasters, drought, etc. When helping the passage of deceased souls, Taoists often must first make a presentation to the local City Deity. The City Deity from any given location is also usually thought to be the direct supervisor of the *Land/Earth God* from that same area, and to report to the Eastern Mountain Emperor.

Constellation Deities 宿星君

Taoists long ago divided the ancient Chinese sky into twenty-eight zones or constellations, with seven in each of the four directions. Taoists further believed that each such division was ruled over by a particular deity. These very ancient stellar deities are thought to have an important role in regulating heavenly movements and energies, and in their interaction with earthly counterparts.

Dark Emperor of th e North 眞武大帝

Great Emperor Xuanwu is variously called *Great Emperor Zhenwu* (due to an imperial proscription against using the word '*xuan*'), *Dark Emperor of the North, Great Emperor of Perfected Martiality, North Lord Xuanwu, Lord Black, Lord of Black Martiality,* etc. He is one of the most widely revered Gods of traditional China, ranking in popularity behind only *Guan Yin* and *Guan Gong*. The God is usually depicted in black robes, holding a sword and sometimes wearing a jade belt. His long black hair flows freely down his back (Most Taoist deities are only shown wearing a hat or with bound hair). *Great Emperor Zhenwu* is always depicted with a tortoise and a snake, sometimes beneath one of his feet. He is revered as a powerful God, able to control the elements (worshipped by those wishing to avoid fires), and capable of great magic. He is particularly revered by martial artists, and is the 'patron saint' of Wudang Mountain in China's Hubei Province, where he allegedly attained immortality. The name 'Wudang' roughly translates as 'only *Zhenwu* deserves it.' *Great Emperor Zhenwu*'s birthday is celebrated on the 3rd day of the 3rd lunar month, and his ascen-

Dark Emperor of the North

sion as a Taoist immortal is celebrated on the 9th day of the 9th lunar month.

Dragon Kings 龍王

Taoists believe there are a large number of *Dragon Kings*, with some saying there are 185. The primary *Dragon Kings* are the *Dragon Kings of the Four Seas*, and the *Dragon Kings of the Five Directions*. In addition to these *Dragon Kings*, any locality or body of water may have its own *Dragon King*. The main responsibility of the *Dragon Kings* is to regulate waterways and rainfall, and in doing so to take orders only from the *Jade Emperor* himself. Taoists will still pray to the *Dragon Kings* during times of drought. Taoist complexes may have separate temples dedicated to *Dragon Kings*, but *Dragon Kings* may also be relegated to outdoor shrines located near temple wells or nearby rivers. *Dragon King Shrines* are also some of the few Taoist shrines that are commonly without statuary or other physical representations. Perhaps the *Dragon Kings*, like the tao itself, are indescribable.

Dragon King

Du Guangting 杜光庭

Du Guangting (850 – 933) was a Taoist during the last years of the Tang Dynasty and into the Five Dynasties era. He was a Confucian scholar who undertook a roaming Taoist lifestyle upon failing the Imperial examinations for governmental service. His first stop was Mount Tiantai, where he undertook initiation and gained national fame for his Taoist knowledge. Later in life Du moved to Qingcheng Mountain in Sichuan and spent his remaining time in deep canonical study. He was the leading figure in a major recodification of the Numinous Treasure Taoism liturgy, and his work became reflected in almost all subsequent forms of Taoist ritual. His brilliant canonical synthesis provided a great contribution to the spread of Taoism. Du wrote many famous Taoist books, the most famous of which is the *Life of the Man with Curly Sideburns*.

Eastern Mountain Emperor 東岳大帝

Tai Mountain, as the easternmost of Taoism's five holy mountains, is commonly known the Eastern Mountain. Tai Mountain is considered the holiest of the five mountains, and the celestial *Eastern Mountain Emperor* is thus considered to be

Eastern Mountain Emperor Temple Imperial Front Gate

the most important of the *Lords of the Five Mountains*. Subservient only to the *Jade Emperor* himself, the *Eastern Mountain Emperor* is considered by Taoists to be responsible for determining a person's time of birth and death. Among the many deities who are directly responsible to the Eastern Mountain Emperor are the local *City Deities*. Tai Mountain is also sometimes considered as the place for disembodied souls, and the *Eastern Mountain Emperor* is thus sometimes regarded as a deity of the dead. Taoists also regard the *Eastern Mountain Emperor* to be the father of the *Princess of the Azure Clouds*.

Eight Immortals 八仙人

Cao Guojiu

The *Eight Immortals* are mixed group of deities, each with their own characteristics. Although mostly thought of as a group, three members *(Zhang Guolao, Lü Dongbin, and Li Tieguai)* are sometimes worshipped independently. The eight are among the most well known members of the Taoist pantheon. They are famous for gathering in large, sometimes drunken banquets. A mortal who happens upon such an affair will usually suffer some extreme jolt to their sense of reality, after which he or she will know (often only after the fact) that they had stumbled upon the *Eight Immortals*.

Cao Guojiu 曹國舅

Taoists believe *Cao Guojiu* was once a high-ranking member of the Imperial court, and that he had a vicious streak to his personality. He was an admitted murderer, albeit a reformed one. He usually carries an Imperial tablet of recommendation, although he is sometimes depicted with castanets. *Cao* gives hope to all that there is a chance for any individual to reach immortality.

Han Xiangzi 韓湘子

Han Xiangzi

Han Xianzi is the romantic ideal of the Taoist recluse. He loves the mountains, and prefers quiet and solitude. He is a skilled poet and musician. He usually carries a long jade flute as a symbol of his typical Taoist artistry. He is a lover of the universe, and seems completely at ease with himself.

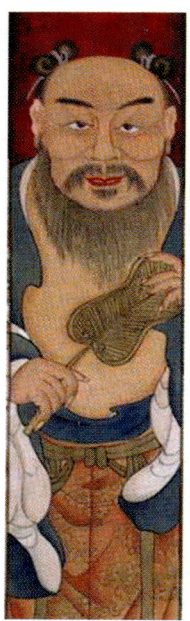

Han Zhongli

Han Zhongli 漢鍾離

Also known as *Zhongli Quan*, *Han Zhongli* was a Han Dynasty (207 B.C. – 220 A.D.) high ranking military official. He may have graduated from a military official to a political one. He is regarded as a tremendous alchemist, capable of producing immortality pills. Taoists believe that *Han* was a disciple of *Wang Xuanpu*, and is thereby regarded as one of the *Five Northern Patriarchs* of Complete Perfection Taoism (one of the largest active sects in China), Roughly 1,000 years after his mortal death, *Han* is credited with visiting *Lü Dongbin* and teaching him the secrets of Taoism and immortality. He remained a very popular figure for those seeking immortality or even longevity. *Han Zhongli* usually carries the Taoist Peaches of Immortality or an immortality pill of his own making, or sometimes a feather-like fan with which he controls the seas.

Lan Caihe

He Xiangu 何仙姑

He Xiangu is the only full-time female among the eight immortals. Her strident ascetic lifestyle won her immortality. She typically carries a lotus blossom, which symbolizes the ability to rise above situation and circumstance in beauty. It is no accident that a woman (or two? See *Lan Caihe*) has made it into this august group.

Lan Caihe 籃采和

Lan Caihe is among the least understood of the *Eight Immortals*. At times *Lan* is represented as a female, and at other time as a male. *Lan's* style of dress and hair is similarly ambivalent. *Lan* represents someone who has been touched by the divine, and is thereafter beyond the understanding of 'normal' society. He/She typically carries a basket of flowers, which symbolize his/her love of life and beauty.

Li Tieguai 李鐵拐

Li Tieguai ('Iron Crutch Li') is the second most popular of the *Eight Immortals*. One day while medi-

He Xiangu

Li Tieguai

tating *Li* had an out-of-body experience. While he was flying around the ethers, however, he forgot to ritually or magically secure his body, and wild animals ate it. Upon *Li's* return, he saw that his body had been ruined, and he was forced to search for another. The best he could do was to find the body of a recently deceased, crippled beggar. Thus *Li* is always depicted as a cripple with a cane or crutch. He is regarded as potent in medical affairs, although he is also thought to possess an angry temper. To those brave enough to confront *Li*, he may also lend his magical or exorcistic help.

Lü Dongbin 呂洞賓

Lü Dongbin is the most famous of the *Eight Immortals*. He is regarded as one of the *Five Northern Patriarchs* of Complete Perfection Taoism (one of the largest active sects in China). The most common historical tale claims that *Lü Dongbin* was a mortal in the Tang Dynasty from China's Shanxi Province. He was a failed candidate for government service, and was unaccomplished until he was 64. At that time he met the Taoist Immortal *Han Zhongli*, who explained Taoism to him. From that time he dedicated himself to Taoist cultivation and eventually became an Immortal. Among his many disciples are *Liu Haichan* and *Wang Chongyang* (see *Five Northern Patriarchs*). Despite his relatively high status in the Taoist hierarchy, *Lü Dongbin* remains an accessible figure. He is credited with frequent travels among the people to provide healing, exorcise demons, resolve disputes, and promote Taoist cultivation. *Lü Dongbin* is almost always depicted wearing a hat that is flat and slopes downward past his forehead. He usually carries a double-edged sword, and sometimes a shield, with which he can capture and tame all evil spirits if he is correctly invoked. *Lü* often carries a flywhisk, the symbol of one who can fly at will. His birthday is generally celebrated on the 14th day of the 4th lunar month.

Lü Dongbin

Zhang Guolao 張果老

Zhang Guolao is the third most popular of this group, and only these three are sometimes independently worshipped. *Zhang* is usually riding a magical donkey, and frequently rides backwards on the donkey. He is associated with Heng Mountain in Shanxi Province, which Taoists believe still bears hoof prints from *Zhang's* magic donkey. He usually carries a musical instrument made of bamboo, which has several tubes sticking out of the top. *Zhang* is credited with being able to bring children to childless couples, especially male children.

Zhang Guolao

Erlang 二郎

Erlang (literally, 'second son') is a famous albeit slightly confusing deity associated with the taming of floods and the fighting of pestilence. One version of *Erlang* claims that over two thousand years ago during the Qin Dynasty a man named *Li Bing* was appointed the Governor of Sichuan. His son, *Erlang*, helped him to overcome flooding problems. During the course of their duties, *Erlang* and seven of his friends came upon a dragon demanding a human child as a sacrificial offering. The eight men fought the dragon over many, many miles, until they were able to subdue it. Taoists believe the area was thereafter free from flooding. Many *Erlang* temples contain a wooden plaque depicting *Erlang* and his seven friends helping *Li Bing* to subdue a monster. *Erlang* himself usually carries a three-pointed, double-edged sword. At least two other historical people were also credited with being *Erlang,* although both fought dragons and tamed floods with the help of double-edged swords. There is another Taoist legend that *Erlang* was the second son of an Indian deity, the *Vaisravana Heavenly King*. Equally interesting is that the third son of this Indian deity is sometimes regarded to be *Li Nezha*, another famous Taoist deity. *Erlang* is also commonly depicted along with a *Celestial Dog,* who assists *Erlang* in his hunts for calamity-causing dragons and other evil demons. *Erlang's* birthday is celebrated on the 28th day of the 8th lunar month.

Fengdu Emperor

Fengdu Emperor 豐都大帝

Taoists consider the *Fengdu Emperor* to be the ruler of Hell and to thereby control all spirits of deceased people. Upon mortal death all spirits must go to *Fengdu*, a mythical place in the north where there are mountains many thousands of miles high and wide. There they are judged by the *Fengdu Emperor* or by one of his subordinates. Taoists often pray or make offerings to the *Fengdu Emperor* upon the death of a family member or loved one, in an attempt to convince the *Fengdu Emperor* to overlook or to forgive any sins committed by the recently deceased.

Fire God 火神

Taoists believe the *Fire God,* also called the *Red Emperor,* was a proto-historical Emperor named *Zhu Rong* who knew the secret methods of starting, preserving, and using fire. For this, the *Yellow Emperor* entitled him as the Fire Administrator.

Fire God

Emperors of the Five Directions

Upon his physical death (suffered during a battle defeat), the Yellow Emperor appointed *Zhu Rong* to Southern Heng Mountain, where he was to protect China's southern lands. The *Fire God*, who is still worshipped at Heng Mountain to this day, is often depicted as a large man with broad shoulders, a red face, and an excited temperament. His birthday is celebrated on the 8th day of the 1st lunar month.

Five Directions, Emperors of the 五方帝君

These five deities, usually depicted together, rule the five directions (including the center). They are the focal point of very complex mandalas that can be constructed according to 5 Phase Theory (Chapter 4.3 – *Five Phases*). These deities are often considered to be identical to the *Lords of the Five Mountains*.

Five Northern Patriarchs 北五祖

The *Five Northern Patriarchs* comprise the formative lineage of Complete Perfection Taoism's 'Northern School'. Complete Perfection Taoism holds that heaven transmitted important lessons to *Wang Xuanpu*, who passed his knowledge on to *Han Zhongli*. *Han* became the teacher of *Lü Dongbin*, who in turn taught *Liu Haichan* and *Wang Chongyang*. *Liu Haichan* eventually passed his lineage to to *Zhang Boduan*, the first of the *Five Southern Patriarchs*, while *Wang Chongyang* passed his lineage to the *Seven Perfected Beings*, who popularized Complete Perfection Taoism's teachings throughout northern China.

Wang Xuanpu 王玄甫

Wang Xuanpu was a Jin Dynasty Taoist (d. 345 A.D.) who came to be known as the first of the *Five Northern Patriarchs*. Taoists believe *Wang* secured a lineage of Taoist teachings directly from heaven (though the *Queen Mother of the West* and others), and to have attained great supernatural powers such as the ability to eat stone and to see human organs within the bodies of living people. *Wang* is believed to have taught alchemy and marital arts to his disciple *Han Zhongli*. *Wang's* ascension is celebrated on the 15th day of the 1st lunar month.

Han Zhongli: See Eight Immortals

Lü Dongbin: See Eight Immortals

Wang Chongyang

Liu Haichan 劉海蟾

Liu Haichan was a high-ranking government minister who one day met a Taoist and renounced his position in order to seek Taoist knowledge. He later became a student of *Lü Dongbin*. *Liu* often appears as a beggar, and one day he caught a three-legged toad from a well. This toad gave *Liu* the power to travel great distances in an instant, and *Liu* is typically depicted with a toad on his back or shoulder (*Haichan* literally means 'sea toad').

Wang Chongyang 王重陽

Taoists believe that *Wang Chongyang* met two of the *Eight Immortals*, *Lü Dongbin* and *Han Zhongli*, in 1159 A.D. and received myriad teachings from them. Wang went on to found a school in Shandong Province that produced the *Seven Perfected Beings*. This school went on to become Complete Perfection Taoism, and *Wang* is regarded as one of its founders. Complete Perfection Taoism blends aspects of Confucianism and Buddhism into Taoism. Taoists believe that *Wang* attained immortality at the time of his mortal death.

Five Southern Patriarchs 南五祖

The *Five Southern Patriarchs* comprise the formative lineage of Complete Perfection Taoism's 'Southern School'. Complete Perfection Taoism holds that *Liu Haichan*, one of the *Five Northern Patriarchs*, transmitted Taoist lessons to *Zhang*

Liu Haichan

Taoist Worship

Bai Yuchan

Boduan, who passed his knowledge on to *Shi Tai*. *Shi* became the teacher of *Xue Shi*, who in turn taught *Chen Nan*. *Chen* eventually passed his lineage to to *Bai Yuchan*, the last of the *Five Southern Patriarchs*. Complete Perfection Taoism's 'Southern School', while not as famous in the West as its 'Northern' counterpart, is nonetheless a historically important Taoist tradition.

Zhang Boduan 張伯端

Zhang Boduan (984 to 1082) was a Northern Song Dynasty official who left his government sinecure in order to pursue Taoism. Taoists believe that *Zhang* was a disciple of *Liu Haichan*, and that with *Liu's* assistance he succeeded in creating a golden pill of immortality thirteen years prior to *Zhang's* death. *Zhang* improperly passed on his alchemical knowledge three times, and each time he suffered a personal disaster. *Zhang's* alchemical writings and ideas nonetheless became extremely influential throughout the whole of Taoism.

Shi Tai 石泰

Shi Tai lived at the end of the Northern Song Dynasty (960-1127) and the beginning of the Southern Song Dynasty (1127-1279). He was a tailor who loved to travel to Taoist sites. He eventually became a student of *Zhang Boduan*, and went on to write an important alchemical text entitled *The Tablet on Reversion to the Origin* (*Huanyuan Pian*). *Zhang* reportedly lived to be 137 before he ascended to immortality.

Central Mountain Emperor
Zhong Tian

Xue Shi 薛式

Xue Shi was originally a Buddhist Monk during the Northern Song Dynasty (960-1127), until he met *Shi Tai* in 1106 and received an alchemical formula. He thereafter became a Taoist and earned great fame for his knowledge.

Chen Nan 陳楠

Chen Nan was a barrel maker during the Southern Song Dynasty (1127-1279), who after a period of wandering and studying with various masters became a Taoist. He earned great fame as a healer and exorcist, and for his use of 'thunder magic.' He eventually accepted *Bai Yuchan* as a disciple in 1212.

Fuxi, Pangu and Shennong

Bai Yuchan 白玉蟾

Bai Yuchan lived during the Southern Song Dynasty (1127-1279), and showed great early promise as an imperial bureaucrat. He killed a man in an act of chivalry, however, and thereafter took refuge in the wilderness of the mountains. He became a Taoist disciple of *Chen Nan* for nine years. After *Chen's* death *Bai* developed the appearance of a madman, and eventually became known as a great scholar of Taoism and alchemy.

Five Mountains, Lords of the 五嶽帝君

Taoism has five traditional holy mountains: Tai Mountain in the east, Heng Mountain in the north, Hua Mountain in the west, Heng Mountain in the south, and Song Mountain in the center. Each mountain is ruled by a deity (variously called 'Lord', 'King,' or 'Emperor'). Each of the Lords not only rules that particular mountain, but also rules that particular direction. The *Lord of the East* (See *Eastern Mountain Emperor*), called *Emperor Tian Qi,* wears a green/blue robe and is associated with the element wood. The *Lord of the North*, called *Emperor An Tian,* wear a wears a black/purple robe and is associated with the element water. The *Lord of the West*, called *Emperor Jin Tian,* wears a white robe and is associated with the element metal. The *Lord of the South*, called *Emperor Si Tian,* wears a red robe and is associated with the element fire. The *Lord of the Center*, called *Emperor Zhong Tian,* wears a yellow robe and is associ-

Ge Hong

Taoist Worship

ated with the element earth (and is sometimes considered to be the *Yellow Emperor*). The five mountains are thought by Taoists to contain passageways to the underworld, and these deities are often invoked for rituals and ceremonies involving such matters.

Four Divine Marshals 四大元師

The *Four Divine Marshals* are immortalized historical figures whom Taoists believe to have been deified in light of their outstanding virtue. They are *Ma Sheng*, *Yue Fei*, *Wen Qiong*, and *Zhao Gongming*. The *Divine Marshals* are considered to be primarily concerned with loyalty, military service, justice, and law. They are seen standing at attention alongside Taoist altars as an honor guard for the deities worshipped at those altars.

God of Wealth

Fu Xi 伏羲

Fu Xi was the first of China's proto-historical Emperors. Taoists believe that he reigned around 3000 B.C.! He is credited with many inventions, including music, the eight trigrams, and divination via yarrow stalks. He is almost always represented along with the eight trigrams, and sometimes has the body of a snake.

Ge Hong 葛洪

Ge Hong, the great-nephew of Taoist Immortal *Ge Xuan*, was famous as a 4th Century Taoist with a tremendous dedication to alchemical practices. A former Confucian and dedicated classicist, he wrote one of Taoism's most revered alchemical treatises, the *Bao Pu Zi* (The Master Who Embraces Simplicity). This book, which adds a moral dimension to the search for immortality, is still used and revered by Taoists today. Taoists believe *Ge Hong* to have entered into immortality upon his mortal death in 364 A.D.

Ge Xuan 葛玄

Ge Xuan (220 – 280), the great-uncle of Taoist Immortal *Ge Hong*, was a Three Kingdoms era Taoist who was a renowned alchemist. As teenager he decided to pursue a Taoist life after both of his parents passed away. *Ge* received through transmission from several deities a wide variety of Taoist texts, and his personal application

Ge Xuan

33

of those texts gained him wide fame as a healer and exorcist. Taoists believe that *Ge* told his disciple the exact day when he would depart the world. When the predicted day arrived, *Ge* laid down and stopped breathing. His disciple watched over his body for three days and nights, until a large wind came and *Ge's* physical body disappeared, leaving only his empty clothes on the bed.

God of Wealth 財神

The *God of Wealth* was one of the most popular Taoist Gods in traditional China. All individuals in historically poor China worshipped this wealth-giving deity. In modern China people continue to worship the *God of Wealth,* and businesses across East Asia routinely maintain an altar in his honor. Every Lunar New Year the *God of Wealth* descends from heaven to inspect his followers. Chinese people across Asia eat dumplings on this day, as they are thought to resemble ancient ingots of precious metal. He is depicted in many images, but most include a long white or black beard, and a smiling countenance. He also frequently wears a broad, heavy belt and a hat that includes protruding rectangular earpieces.

Lady of Good Eyesight

Good Eyesight, Lady of 眼光娘娘

An assistant to the *Princess of the Azure Clouds,* the *Lady of Good Eyesight* is thought by Taoists to bestow good eyesight upon her supplicants, and especially to small children.

Golden Lad 金童

Golden Lad, commonly mentioned along with *Jade Maiden,* is a generic name for a type of heavenly assistant. They frequently appear, sometimes in a child-like and rather androgynous form, alongside of better-known deities as servants.

Guan Gong 關公

Guan Gong, or *Guan Yu,* was the object of the second most prevalent Taoist cult in traditional China (behind the cult dedicated to *Guan Yin*). He was a highly decorated military general during China's Warring States Period (220 A.D. - 280 A.D.), and was regarded as a strong and able military officer who possessed an outstanding degree of loyalty. Despite his military abilities, and due to his unwavering loyalty, *Guan Gong* was killed in battle. He was almost immediately revered as an Immortal, and throughout many succeeding centuries people con-

Guan Gong

Guan Yin

tinued to believe in *Guan Gong's* celestial promotions. *Guan Gong* is typically depicted as a large man with a long black beard. He is either standing or seated at a desk. His countenance is always stern, and his face is red. Standing behind *Guan Gong* are always his assistants, *General Zhou Cang* and the white-faced *General Guan Ping* (*Guan Gong's* son). *Guan Gong* always holds his long-handled, double-edged broadsword. *Guan Gong* is venerated by those concerned with such things as loyalty, military affairs, commerce, giving birth to sons, or exorcising spirits.

Guan Ping, General 關平

General Guan Ping is the son of *Guan Gong*, and serves as his assistant. He is regarded as an excellent martial artist. *Guan Ping* is typically depicted with an extremely white countenance, and is rarely seen independent of his more famous father.

Guan Yin 觀音

Guan Yin (the Hearer of the Cries of the World) is undoubtedly the most popular of all Chinese deities. China was once littered with Temples dedicated to *Guan Yin,* as she was worshipped by both Buddhists and Taoists, by men and women, by rich and poor people. *Guan Yin* has been depicted at times as a man and at times as a woman, but the female image has proven more popular in modern times. She is commonly depicted as a young, pretty woman, with red lips, often wearing a lace or brocade robe, carrying a willow branch (right hand) and a vase (left hand). She is regarded as a savior from all types of misfortune, one who would uphold justice and provide fortune to the needy. She is also regarded as a bestower of children for infertile or childless women.

Han Xiangzi: See Eight Immortals
Han Zhongli: See Eight Immortals
He Xiangu: See Eight Immortals
Hua Tuo 華陀

Hua Tuo was a famous Taoist physician of the 2nd – 3rd Centuries. He is credited with originating myriad *qigong* exercises, including the famous *Five Animal Frolics*. Taoists believe that *Hua Tuo,* with such a well-developed understanding of human energy and Taoist cultivation, became an Immortal upon his physical death and his remains were buried at Hua Mountain.

Golden Lad

Jade Emperor, Great 玉皇大帝

The *Great Jade Emperor* is the highest ruler in the Taoist Heavens. He does rank beneath the *Three Purities*, but they act more as elemental forces and less like ruling deities. Usually depicted sitting on a throne with an impassive countenance partially obscured by strings of pearls hanging from the front brim of his hat, the *Great Jade Emperor* often holds a pointed slab of jade in his hands as a symbol of his authority. The *Great Jade Emperor's* birthday is typically celebrated on the 9th day of the 1st lunar month, which corresponds roughly to the annual rebirth of *yang* energy leading to spring and the traditional time of renewal and rebirth. Under normal circumstances only high ranking deities, such as the *Eastern Mountain Emperor*, report directly to the *Great Jade Emperor*.

Great Jade Emperor

Jade Maiden 玉女

Jade Maiden, commonly mentioned along with *Golden Lad*, is a generic name for a type of heavenly assistant. They frequently appear, sometimes in a rather child-like and androgynous form, alongside of better-known deities as handmaidens.

Jiang Taigong 姜太公

Jiang Taigong is considered to be the official in charge of granting titles to deities in the Taoist heavens, and is thus accorded a relatively high status. *Jiang* was a historical figure and prominent political figure in the founding of the Western Zhou Dynasty. Taoists believe that he became an Immortal, and *Jiang* was the central figure in a popular book called the *Romance of the Canonized Gods*. He was once popularly regarded on par with Confucius, and his image is often used to chase away spirits.

King of Ghosts 鬼王

The *King of Ghosts* is an emanation of *Taiyi Jiuku Tiancun* who resides in hell and provides respite to those souls he judges to be worthy. He is always depicted as a demonic figure with upswept red hair on the sides of his head.

Kitchen God 灶君

The *Kitchen God* is a deity worshipped by practically all families who believe in Taoism. The *Kitchen God* has a particular interest in and responsibility for issues concerning hearth,

King of Ghosts

Jade Maiden

food, and fuel. Every year on the 24th day of the 12th lunar month the *Kitchen God* must report to the *Great Jade Emperor* regarding the merits or sins of every household. The *Great Jade Emperor* then punishes or rewards families throughout the coming year. Therefore on the day of reporting, families who believe in Taoism hold a banquet for the *Kitchen God*, who is served a variety of meat dishes and wine. Some people traditionally have a feast in honor of the *Kitchen God* the next day as well, at which all manner of sweet things are served. The purpose is to make sure the message from the *Kitchen God* to the *Great Jade Emperor* is a sweet one. At all other times of the year, the bureaucratically insignificant *Kitchen God* reports only to the local *Land/Earth God*.

Kou Qianzhi 寇謙之

Kou Qianzhi (365 – 448) was a Celestial Master Taoist who was living as a hermit on Song Mountain in Henan Province in 415 when he received the first of a series of revelations from the deified *Laozi*. In 424 he accepted a position at court, and eventually became the powerful head of a state-sponsored Taoism. In 440, the Emperor himself underwent Taoist initiation at the hands of *Kou*. Taoists believe that *Kou* ascended into immortality eight years later.

Lan Caihe: See Eight Immortals

Land/Earth God 土地公

Land/Earth God

In traditional China, every village had a shrine to the local *Land/Earth God*. It was this god who was in charge of administering the affairs of a particular village. In traditional times, village concerns were primarily agricultural or weather-related. This god was not all-powerful, but was a modest celestial bureaucrat to whom individual villagers could turn in times of need, famine, or drought. He generally is thought to be under the direct responsibility of the local *City Deity* and is thought to be the direct superior of the local *Kitchen God*. This God is often called *Grandpa*, which reflects his close relationship to the common people. He often wears a black hat and a red robe, which signify his position as a celestial bureaucrat but his appearance has many variations. His birthday is commonly celebrated on the 2nd day of the 2nd lunar month.

Laozi (Lao Tzu) 老子

Laozi is perhaps the most famous of all Taoist deities. According to Taoist legend, he was an older contemporary of Confucius who was born as an old man. He came from a minor aristocratic family, and gradually developed a system of Taoist mysticism and philosophy. As *Laozi* finally rejected society and rode off to the 'uncivilized' west, he was stopped and persuaded to write down his thoughts. Taoists believe that *Laozi* was the human incarnation of a powerful deity called *Taishang Laojun*, and that *Laozi's* success in personal cultivation reflected this background. Popular Taoism sometimes also holds that *Laozi* is one of the *Three Purities – The Celestial Worthy of the Dao and its Virtues*.

Laozi

Li Nezha 李哪吒

Sometimes called the *Boy Immortal*, *Li Nezha* is always depicted as a young, playful boy. He is sometimes described as the son of an Indian deity *Vaisravana* and the younger brother of *Erlang*, and sometimes as the third son of the Taoist *Li Jing*. *Li Nezha* is able to ride the waves of the sea on wind-powered wheels of fire, and he carries a golden ring of fire that he uses to strike those who offend him, as well as a fire-tipped spear. He is an important figure in the well-known book *Journey to the West*, and is particularly popular today in Southeast Asia.

Li Tieguai: See **Eight Immortals**

Liu Haichan: See **Five Northern Patriarchs**

Lu Ban 鲁班

Lu Ban is a historical figure (507– 444 B.C.) regarded as a legendary craftsman, inventor, weapon-maker, and bridge-builder. Taoists revere *Lu Ban* as the archetype of the craftsmen described by *Zhuangzi* as being able to achieve great success by losing themselves in the tao. *Lu Ban* is a 'patron saint' for all tradesmen.

Lü Dongbin: See **Eight Immortals**

Li Nezha

Lu Xiujing 陸修靜

Three Mao Brothers

Lu Xiujing (406-477) was a famous Taoist of the Southern Dynasties. He abandoned his family as an adult in order to study Taoism in remote places and search for Immortals. This was a time of great social chaos in China, and *Lu* became famous as a Taoist codifier and traditionalist. He vilified Taoist self-initiation and helped to create a Taoist hierarchical system of rank. He strongly advocated fasting and ritual as fundamental Taoist activities within the orthodox lineages of his day. He was also responsible for a significant reorganization of the Taoist Canon into a system of three 'grottoes' and relevant sub-sections, as well as helping to systematize the liturgies of the Numinous Treasure Taoism.

Ma Sheng: See Four Divine Marshals

Mao Brothers 三茅眞君

Mao Ying, Mao Gu, and *Mao Zhong* were brothers born at Jun Qu Mountain in Jiangsu Province from 150 -141 B.C. When *Mao Ying* was 18, he ran away to Heng Mountain in Shanxi Province in order to practice Taoist cultivation. After 31 years he returned to Jun Qu Mountain with miraculous healing powers. *Mao Ying's* brothers, who were government officials at the time, saw *Mao Ying's* level of cultivation and decided to dedicate themselves to Taoism. The three became very famous as mystics and healers, and are each believed to have ascended to immortality. After the Mao Brothers' physical deaths Jun Qu Mountain was renamed *Mao Mountain* in their honor.

Mazu 媽祖

Mazu

Also called *Tianhou* (Goddess of Heaven) or the *Goddess of the South China Sea, Mazu* was originally a young peasant girl who lived in Fujian Province in the 10th Century. Fujian is a coastal province, and *Mazu* became famous for her efforts to save ships and seafarers having trouble on rough seas. She drowned during one attempt. Since that time Taoists believe that *Mazu* has continued to perform many miracles. She is credited with great supernatural powers, and people pray to her for prosperity, for the birth of children, for health, and for protection. She is especially revered in China's coastal communities, and her birthday is celebrated on the 23rd day of the 3rd lunar month.

Medicine King 藥王

Sun Simiao (581-682) was a real physician and herbalist whom Taoists believe to have entered the pantheon as the *Medicine King (Yao Wang)* upon his mortal death. Invited by three Emperors of the Sui and Tang Dynasties to serve at the Imperial court, *Sun* declined in order to spend his life as a wandering physician. He is usually depicted as a ruddy-cheeked old man wearing a wide-sleeved robe and a flattish headdress. Two young male assistants carry his medical gear, while a nearby tiger with a white forehead is his daily companion.

Mysterious Lady of the 9th Heaven, The
九天玄女娘娘

The *Mysterious Lady of the 9th Heaven (Jiu Tian Xuan Nü Niang Niang)* is an ancient and powerful deity venerated mostly (but not solely) by Orthodox Unity Taoists. Often depicted with the head of a bird (or, in more sedate depictions, with a small bird on top of her anthropomorphic head), the *Mysterious Lady of the 9th Heaven* is thought to bestow upon her favorites various psychic abilities and success in meditation or cultivation practices. She is also sometimes considered as a deity named *Nüwa*, and as such is venerated as the patron of matchmakers.

The Mysterious Lady of the 9th Heaven

Northern Dipper, True Lord of: See **Seven Star Lords of the Northern Dipper**

Pan Gu 盤古

Taoists worship *Pan Gu* as the first human being, and as a creator of the earth as we know it. Primordial chaos originally split into *yin* and *yang* dominated halves, which then formed the earth and heaven, respectively. *Pan Gu*, the first human, filled the ever-growing space between the two realms. When he died, his constituent body parts became the mountains, rivers, trees, etc. He is normally depicted along with the *taiji* symbol (also known as a *yin-yang* symbol).

Princess of the Azure Clouds 碧霞

Taoists consider *The Princess of the Azure Clouds (Bi Xia)* to be the daughter of the *Eastern Mountain Emperor*. She is the protectress of women and children, and may bring healthy children to childless couples. She often works with two major assistants: *Songzi Niang Niang* and the *Lady of Good Eyesight*. The

Pan Gu

Qui Chuji

three of them are often depicted along with six other assistants, and the nine of them are often venerated as a group.

Qing Yang 擎羊

Qing Yang is a female deity who is the representative of the deified planet Uranus.

Qiu Chuji 邱處濟

Qiu Chuji (1148-1227) was a famous monk in the Jin and Yuan Dynasties. Born into a peasant family, *Qiu* went to Shandong as a teenager to study Taoism. *Wang Chongyang*, the founder of Complete Perfection Taoism, was then teaching Taoism in Shandong, and *Qiu* eventually became one of Wang's seven students —the *Seven Perfected Beings*. After Wang's passing, *Qiu* founded the *Longmen* (Dragon Gate) tradition of Complete Perfection Taoism. *Qiu's* close relationship with the Mongol Emperors ensured governmental support of Taoism, and enabled *Qiu* to found Beijing's White Cloud Monastery. When *Qiu* became an Immortal, his physical body was buried underneath a temple in the White Cloud Monastery. *Qiu's* birthday is celebrated on the 19th day of the 1st lunar month.

Queen Mother of the West 西王母

Sometimes considered the wife of the *Jade Emperor*, the *Queen Mother of the West* (*Xi Wangmu*) is the leading deity in charge of the register of female deities. She is almost always surrounded by a retinue of female assistants, who are typically shown delivering babies or curing childhood diseases like measles. People pray to her for good luck, longevity, and for any issue relating to children. The *Queen Mother of the West* is also regarded as being in charge of the Taoist Peaches of Immortality (a special and restricted fruit that confers immortality upon anyone who partakes of it).

Sa Shoujian 薩守堅

Sa Shoujian

Sa Shoujian is the Taoist Immortal credited with being the primary teacher of *Wang the Spirit Protector*. He is often depicted, along with *Wang*, as a protection deity and is commonly seen at Temple entrances and alongside higher-ranking deities. *Sa* was himself a student of *Wang Wenqing*.

Seven Perfected Beings 七眞人

The students of *Wang Chongyang*, the *Seven Perfected Beings* are: *Ma Danyang, Sun Bu'er, Qiu Chuji, Liu Changsheng, Tan Changzhen, Hao Taigu,* and *Wang Yuyang*. These students joined *Wang Chongyang* in Shandong Province, and each one survived unique challenges on the path to becoming an Immortal. *Sun Bu'er* is the lone female in the group. Except for *Qiu Chuji*, the members of this group are rarely worshipped independently, and are usually thought of as one group.

Seven Star Lords of the Northern Dipper 北斗星君

These seven deities reside in the stars of the Northern Dipper, and serve as assistants to the *Jade Emperor*. They frequently relay messages to and from the *Jade Emperor*. These deities are commonly depicted along with two guardians, and are collectively referred to as the *Nine Kings of the Northern Dipper*. They are sometimes thought of as a single entity, the *True Lord of the Northern Dipper (beidou zhenjun)*. Each person's health and longevity is controlled by one of the *Seven Star Lords*. One the 1st and 15th of each lunar month, the *Seven Star Lords* report to the *Jade Emperor* regarding their charges. On the first seven days of the ninth lunar month, the *Seven Star Lords* come to earth to proclaim the judgments of the *Jade Emperor*. These deities are associated with the element of water, with *yin* energy, and with human death. The *Seven Star Lords of the Northern Dipper* commonly dispatch *Tuo Luo* as a representative. On a popular level, people often believe that prayers to *Seven Star Lords of the Northern Dipper* can cause them to remove the supplicant's name from the records of people scheduled for death, and that their lives will be thusly prolonged.

Seven Star Lords of the Northern Dipper

Shen Nong 神農

A proto-historical Chinese Emperor, *Shen Nong* is credited with the invention of the plow and the practices of agriculture and herbal medicine. He is also sometimes credited with being the *God of Wind*, and as such has long served as an idealized model of personified wild nature.

Shi Tai: See Five Southern Patriarchs

Shen Nong

Sima Chengzhen 司馬成眞

The Tang Dynasty (618-907) was one of the high points of ancient Chinese culture, and certainly represents a period of Taoism's greatest influence on Chinese culture and society. *Sima Chengzhen* (647-735) is among the most highly regarded Taoists of that era. A friend of important scholars, poets, and Emperors, *Sima* originally studied Taoism on Song Mountain, and eventually became the leader of Highest Purity Taoism. As one of China's best-known religious leaders, *Sima* was repeatedly called upon by various Emperors to assist in the management of Taoist affairs. *Sima* was an influential Taoist thinker and writer, and his calligraphy was highly prized.

Six Star Lords of the Southern Dipper

Six Star Lords of the Southern Dipper 南斗星君

These six deities, less famous than their northern counterparts, are associated with prosperity and with human birth. Each person's level of prosperity is governed by one of these six deities. Taoists believe them to be somewhat hot-tempered and uncompromising. The Six Star Lords are commonly depicted with one attendant. These deities are associated with the element fire and with *yang* energy. They are sometimes conceived of as a single entity, the *True Lord of the Southern Dipper (nandou zhenjun)*.

Sixty-Year Cycle Gods 六十甲子本命神

Many people mistakenly believe that Chinese astrology is based upon a simple 12-year animal cycle. Taoism's calendrical system is actually quite complex, with an overlapping rotation of ten 'heavenly stems' with twelve 'earthly branches.' The result is a 60-year cycle, with a particular deity ruling each year. The ruling deity in your birth year is your 'guide' or 'guardian angel.' The 'children' of any of these deities will exhibit particular and similar characteristics. Taoists consider the *Star Mother* to be in charge of the administration of this system.

Songzi Niang Niang 送子娘娘

Songzi Niang Niang is an ancient Taoist Goddess generally thought to manage issues of childbirth. She is also usually thought of as an assistant to the *Princess of the Azure Clouds*. Traditionally, if a woman could not become pregnant after several years of marriage, she went to pray at a temple to *Songzi Niang Niang*. One traditional method was for the supplicant to

Songzi Niang Niang

43

take some ash from an incense burner at a *Songzi Niang Niang* temple, and to mix the ash in water and drink it. This would bring the power of the Goddess into the woman's body and resolve her problem. Men would traditionally also pray to *Songzi Niang Niang* to grant them sons, although some *Songzi Niang Niang* temples are off-limits to males (being reserved for female energy).

Southern Dipper, True Lord of: See Six Star Lords of the Southern Dipper

Star Deities of the Three Terraces 三台星君

These three deities (one for each terrace) are thought to regulate issues of life and death for humans.

Star Deities of the Three Terraces

Star Mother 斗母

Star Mother (*Dou Mu*) is the *Mother of the Plough* (the seven stars of the Northern Dipper). She is generally depicted with three eyes in each of her four faces (one in each major direction). She has four arms on each side of her body. Two of her hands are held together, palm to palm, while the other six hold a sun, moon, bell, golden seal, bow, and halberd. *Dou Mu* is regarded as holding a very senior position in the Taoist hierarchy, and she is assumed to be in charge of the *Sixty Year Cycle Gods*. She is also credited with the ability to save people from many types of evil and trouble. Her birthday is celebrated on the 9th day of the 9th lunar month. There are famous Temples to *Dou Mu* at Tai Mountain in Shandong, at the White Cloud Monastery in Beijing, Qian Mountain in Liaoning, and Weibao Mountain in Yunnan.

Sun Bu'er 孫不二

Sun Bu'er is among the most famous of *Wang Chongyang's* students — the *Seven Perfected Beings*. Originally married to fellow student *Ma Danyang*, *Sun* and *Ma* opted to live only as brother and sister in order to facilitate their Taoist training. *Bu'er* roughly translates as 'no other' and *Sun's* fierce determination is evidenced throughout her life. At one point she burned her face with hot oil because she felt that her beauty was an impediment to her progress! She eventually became a powerful Immortal, and has long been worshipped for her achievements as well as her intense devotion.

Sun Bu'er

Taoist Worship

Sun Simiao: See Medicine King

Tai Bai Jinxing 太白金星

Taiyi Jiuku Tiancun

Tai Bai Jinxing is considered to be the deified planet Venus. Generally speaking, the deities associated with particular planets or stars are among the most ancient of Taoist deities (and among the most purely Taoist), and *Tai Bai Jin-xing* is no exception. He is considered to bestow upon his favorites a high level of fame, riches, and honors.

Taiyi Jiuku Tianzun (Heavenly Worthy Tai Yi The Savior from Suffering) 太一救苦天尊

Taiyi is one of Taoism's most important Gods, reporting directly to the *Great Jade Emperor* and is one of the highest rulers in the 10-stage Taoist hell. Upon death, all human souls must appear before *Taiyi* and be sentenced. *Taiyi* is frequently depicted riding on a nine-headed lion. He generally carries a vase in his left hand and a sword in his right. The vase is filled with holy cleansing water, while the sword is used to subdue demons and punish the wicked. Taoists believe that they can improve their fate if they repeatedly call *Taiyi's* name. An emanation of *Taiyi* presides in hell (see *King of Ghosts*). *Taiyi's* birthday is the 11th day of the 11th lunar month.

Tao Hongjing 陶弘景

Tao Hongjing (456-536) was a Mao Mountain Taoist who became famous for succesfully promoting a formal structure for the Taoist pantheon. *Tao's* Taoist knowledge and mystic prophecies were so well regarded that when *Tao* refused an Emperor's summons to the court, the Emperor instead came to *Tao's* mountain retreat. *Tao*, a lineal descendant of *Wei Huacun* and *Ge Hong,* is still revered by Taoists as an Immortal. He is especially revered near Mao Mountain.

Thirty-Six Celestial Generals 三十六天將

Tao Honjing

These *Celestial Generals* reside in the 'handle' of the big dipper, and are available to assist people who are faced with natural disasters.

45

The Three Purities

Three Officials 三官

First documented by the son of *Zhang Daoling* (the original Celestial Master), the Three Officials are:

1) *The Upper Part of the Year First-Rank Heavenly Official,* also called the *Shang Yuan Emperor* or the *Ziwei Emperor,* commonly known as the *Heavenly Official.*
2) *The Middle Part of the Year Second-Rank Earthly Official,* also called the *Zhong Yuan Emperor* or the *Qing Ling Emperor,* commonly known as the *Earthly Official.*
3) *The Lower Part of the Year Third-Rank Water Official,* also called the *Xia Yuan Emperor* or the *Yang Gu Emperor,* commonly known as the *Water Official.*

Their respective responsibilities are:

Heavenly Official: Fame, wealth, and good luck;
Earthly Official: Absolution of sins; and,
Water Official: Avoidance of disasters.

The Three Officials, also called the *San Yuan Emperors* (the Emperors of the Three Parts of the Year), are very common deities in Taoist temples.

Three Purities 三清

The *Three Purities* are the highest deities in all of Taoism. While the *Great Jade Emperor* rules the Heavenly hierarchy, the *Three Purities* are so lofty they transcend the entire hierarchy. In the middle is the absolute highest image of religious Taoism, the *Heavenly Worthy of Primordial Origin,* or the *Jade Purity.* To his right (as you face them) is the *Heavenly*

Thunder God

Worthy of the Numinous Treasure, or the High Purity, and to his left is the Heavenly Worthy of the Tao and its Virtues, or the Great Purity. Some people believe in the Three Purities as Gods representing and controlling the various stages of energy in the cosmos (tao gestating, mediating, and indwelling), while some people prefer to focus on the Three Purities as purely representative of the three energies (*jing, qi,* and *shen*) cultivated by Taoist meditations.

Thunder God 蕾神

There is no greater evidence of the power of nature than thunder. Taoists believe that thunder results from the beating of heavenly drums, and that the *Thunder God* uses thunder to strike evil and to uphold justice. He is sometimes depicted as a half man – half dragon, with a green human face. Sometimes he is depicted, however, as just a man riding a dragon. Some Taoists believe he uses his belly as a drum, while some Taoists believe his retinue carries drums. He is also occasionally depicted as having the beak, wings, and claws of a bird of prey.

Tuo Luo 陀羅

Tuo Luo is a female deity who is the representative of the deified stars of the Northern Dipper.

Wang Chongyang: See Five Northern Patriarchs

Wang the Spirit Protector 王靈官

Wang the Spirit Protector

At the front gate of almost every Taoist temple is an oversized statue of a fierce warrior, in full amour, with a scowling red face, three eyes, and holding a whip. That not so friendly Taoist deity is *Wang the Spirit Protector. Wang* was once a powerful spirit who had no name. In his local village people built a temple to honor him. The Nameless Spirit was evil, and forced the villagers to sacrifice human children at his altar. One day the Taoist Immortal *Sa Shoujian* saw the blood and carnage at the temple and burnt it to the ground. The Nameless Spirit was enraged, and took his case to the celestial authorities. They decided that if the Nameless Spirit could catch *Sa Shoujian* in one evil act, they would punish him for indiscriminately destroying the Nameless Spirit's temple. He then followed *Sa* for twelve years, and never once saw him commit an immoral act. The Nameless Spirit was so astonished by *Sa's* holiness that he became *Sa's* disciple. He was rewarded with the post of Taoist Temple Protector, for which he uses his three eyes (to be always vigilant), his armor, and his whip. His red face and fierce demeanor are vestiges of his evil past. *Sa* gave the name *Wang the Good* to the new Taoist Protection deity. The heavenly authorities recognized his conversion as well, and bestowed upon him the title of *Wang Lingguan* (*Wang the Spirit Protector*).

Wei Boyang

Wang Wenqing 王文卿

Wang Wenqing (1093-1153) was a Northern Song Dynasty Taoist who was credited with establishing a traditon called Divine Heaven Taoism (*Shenxiao Pai*). *Wang* eventually received a wide variety of imperial titles during his mortal lifetime. Taoists believe that *Wang* was a master of Thunder Magic, and that he was the teacher of *Sa Shoujian*.

Wang Xuanpu: See **Five Northern Patriarchs**

Wei Boyang 魏伯陽

Wei Boyang, a 2nd Century A.D. Taoist, wrote the earliest known alchemical treatise: *On the Uniting of Correspondences*. He is widely respected by Taoists for researching and expounding upon both internal and external alchemical practices. Taoists believe that *Wei* became an Immortal (and experienced mortal death) upon purposefully ingesting an external elixir of his own decoction.

Wei Huacun 魏華存

Wei Huacun was a 4th Century Taoist mystic who lived near Taoism's sacred Mao Mountain in Jiangsu Province. *Wei* was an ordained Taoist and a powerful shaman and mystic. Most importantly, she was also a great and innovative meditator. She is credited with devising the meditations described in the famous *Gold Pavilion Classic,* and with transmitting those meditations via a dream to a direct lineal descendant some decades after her own mortal death. This meditation system became one of the main foundations for Mao Mountain's Highest Clarity

Wenchang

Xu Xun

(*Shangqing*) Taoist tradition and is described in the *Gold Pavilion Classic*. Taoists at Mao Mountain continue to worship *Wei Huacun*.

Wenchang 文昌

Wenchang is the *God of Literature and Culture,* and is the patron saint of scholars, students, and bureaucrats. He is usually depicted as a stern mandarin in formal dress. His function is to sit in judgment upon mortal men and to write his verdict in the *Cinnamon Record* (a constantly updated ledger of people and their fates as ordained by heaven and modified by human actions). *Wenchang* has also been worshipped for over two millennia as a constellation of six stars near the Northern Dipper. Taoists believe that *Wenchang* has manifested himself on earth in human form at least seventeen times in various guises. *Zhang the Immortal*, or *Zhang Xian*, is often considered to be an emanation of *Wenchang*. The cult of *Wenchang* was once one of China's largest, and still exists throughout the Chinese world.

Wen Qiong: See **Four Divine Marshals**

Xue Shi: See **Five Southern Patriarchs**

Xu Xun 許遜

Xu Xun (239-374) was an Eastern Jin Dynasty official from Henan Province who later became an Orthodox Unity Taoist. Famous for his ability to control floods and forces of nature, *Xu Xun* went on to establish a separate but related tradition, founding the prominent *Jing Ming* lineage of Orthodox Unity Taoism. The *Jing Ming* lineage was closely aligned with the Celestial Masters (and remains so to this day). Taoists believe *Xu Xun* to have become an Immortal upon his mortal death at age 135!

Yellow Emperor 黃帝

The *Yellow Emperor* is one of China's great proto-historical Emperors, who Taoists believe ruled around 3000 B.C.! He is credited with many inventions (including the creation of mankind itself), and is thought by Taoists to be one of the founders of Taoism. *Yellow Emperor* is thought to have possessed great magical powers, and when over 100 years old to have attained immortality. He is credited with having written the

Yellow Emperor

first medical treatise, the *Inner Classic of the Yellow Emperor*, and is often thought to be the *Central Emperor* from the *Emperors of the Five Directions*.

Yue Fei: See **Four Divine Marshals**

Zhang Boduan: See **Five Southern Patriarchs**

Zhang Daoling 張道陵

Zhang Daoling

Zhang Daoling, also entitled *Celestial Master Zhang,* was a very powerful Taoist mystic who founded institutionalized Taoism in 142 A.D. In that year he founded the Five Pecks of Rice tradition, dedicated to a somewhat socialist society worshipping the Taoist gods through spirit-writing, mediumship, and other occult practices. The Five Pecks of Rice tradition eventually grew into one of Orthodox Unity Taoism's most popular variants, Celestial Master Taoism, which is still active across China. *Zhang Daoling's* Taoist abilities have caused Taoists to venerate him for almost two millennia!

Zhang Guolao: See **Eight Immortals**

Zhang the Immortal 張仙

Zhang the Immortal is responsible for providing male offspring to couples lacking heirs. He is often depicted with his son, who carries a male infant to bestow upon the faithful. Taoists generally consider him to be an old man who fulfills his duty by shooting arrows towards the heavens, and he is often thought to be an emanation of *Wenchang*.

Zhang Sanfeng 張三丰

Zhang Sanfeng

Zhang Sanfeng was a historical Ming Dynasty (1368 – 1644) Taoist hermit, who was regarded in his day as having great Taoist achievement. He is credited with the creation of *taiji quan*, and with the authorship of several books on Taoist cultivation. *Zhang* received titles from several Ming Emperors, and went on to found a Taoist tradition centered at Wudang Mountain (See Chapter 5.4 – *Taoist Pilgrimage*). He is still respected and remembered by internal martial artists around the world.

Zhao Gongming: See **Four Divine Marshals**

Taoist Worship

Zhong Kui 鐘馗

Zhong Kui

Zhong Kui is a very common and popular deity believed to drive away ghosts and evil fortunes while bringing good luck and success. He is typically depicted as a physically large warrior with a wild beard. He carries a sword, which he uses in performing his duties. He often has ghosts following him as servants, and is usually surrounded by bats (a symbol of good fortune). There are countless stories of *Zhong Kui's* adventures in taming evil, and Chinese people traditionally hang pictures of *Zhong Kui* in their doorways on the 5th day of the 5th lunar month and on lunar New Year's Eve.

Zhou Cang, General 周倉

An assistant to *Guan Gong*, *General Zhou Cang* is generally not seen independent of *Guan Gong* and *General Guan Ping*.

It is important to remember this is not an exclusive list of Taoist deities. It is far, far short of that. There are too many Taoist deities to list them all. Moreover, Taoists' belief in and about these deities is quite varied, and this book only includes a sampling of the most standard beliefs. As you become more Taoist and gain more Taoist experience, not only will you learn a great deal more about these and other deities, but you will also naturally develop your own views and opinions regarding them. Allow your natural feelings to emerge, and see for yourself which deities may resonate with you and which may not.

2.3 Suggested Altar Deities

Many people may read the deity descriptions in the preceding chapter and still be unsure as to which deities may be appropriate for their altars. That would not be a surprising reaction, given the large number of Taoist deities from which one may choose. Depending on your personal circumstances and interests, however, you may well have a natural fit with specific deities. The following suggested guidelines will hopefully present you with a few useful suggestions to consider:

Medicine, Healing, Acupuncture, Energy Work:
Consider Guan Yin, the Medicines King, Lü Dongbin, Hua Tuo, Li Tieguai

Meditation and Alchemy:
Consider Lady Wei Huacun, Lü Dongbin, Ge Hong, Wang Chongyang, Queen Mother of the West, Chen Tuan, Wei Boyang, Han Zhongli, Five Southern Patriarchs (any), Five Northern Patriarchs (any)

Music:
Consider Han Xiangzi

Philosophy:
Consider Laozi, Han Xiangzi

Physical Impairment:
Consider Li Tieguai

Police Work:
Consider Guan Gong, Wenchang

Prison, Personal Reform:
Consider Cao Guojiu

Protection:
Consider Zhang Daoling, Lü Dongbin, Sao Shoujian, Wang the Spirit Protector, Zhong Kui

Psychic Prowess, Magic, Exorcism:
Consider Zhang Daoling, the Mysterious Lady of the 9th Heaven, the Three Mao Brothers, Zhang Guolao, Lü Dongbin, Jiang Taigong

Abused or Unhappy Wives:
Consider Chang E

Artistry, Creative Expression:
Consider Wenchang, Han Xiangzi, He Xiangu, Lan Caihe

Asceticism:
Consider Wang Chongyang, Qiu Chuji, He Xiangu, Sun Bu'er, Liu Haichan

Bicycles, Motorcycles, Anything with Wheels:
Consider Li Nezha

Childbirth and Children's Concerns:
Consider Guan Gong, Zhang the Immortal, Zhang Guolao, Songzi Niang Niang, The Princess of the Azure Clouds, Goddess of Midwifery, The Lady of Good Eyesight

Compassion:
Consider Guan Yin, Ci Hang, Taiyi Jiuku

Construction, Woodworking, Carpentry, Masonry, Trades, Etc.:
Consider Lu Ban

Cooking, Baking:
Consider the Kitchen God

Death and the Souls of the Deceased:
Consider Tai Yi, the Three Officials, Ci Hang, the Eastern Mountain Emperor, the Fengdu Emperor, the King of Ghosts

Taoist Worship

Dogs, Hunting:
Consider Erlang

Dragon Tiger Mountain:
Consider Zhang Daoling

Financial Affairs:
Consider the God of Wealth, Guan Gong, Wenchang

Fire Prevention:
Consider the Fire God, the Thunder God, Dragon Kings

Heng Mountain (Hunan):
Consider Southern Mountain Emperor Si Tian, Lü Dongbin, Fire God

Heng Mountain (Shanxi):
Consider Northern Mountain Emperor An Tian, Zhang Guolao, Mao Ying

Hua Mountain:
Consider Western Mountain Emperor Jin Tian, Chen Tuan, Hua Tuo

Mao Mountain:
Consider Wei Huacun, the Three Mao Brothers, Ge Hong, Tao Hongjing

Martial Arts, The Military:
Consider Guan Gong, the Dark Emperor of the North, Zhang Sanfeng, Han Zhongli

Matchmakers:
Consider the Mysterious Lady of the 9th Heaven

Qigong:
Consider Hua Tuo, Zhang Sanfeng

Qingcheng Mountain:
Consider Zhang Daoling, Zhang Sanfeng, Du Guangting

Ritual:
Consider Du Guangting, Kou Qianzhi, Tao Hongjing, Lu Xiujing

Sailing, Anything Involving Water:
Consider Mazu, Dragon Kings, Han Zhongli

Song Mountain:
Consider Central Mountain Emperor Zhong Tian, Kou Qianzhi, Sima Chengzhen

Tai Mountain:
Consider Eastern Mountain Emperor Tian Qi, the Princess of the Azure Clouds, Taiyi Jiuku

Tailoring, Sewing:
Consider Shi Tai

Taoism (General):
Consider the Three Purities, the Jade Emperor, Laozi, Lü Dongbin

Wudang Mountain:
Consider the Dark Emperor of the North, Zhang Sanfeng

These are only suggestions (albeit ones with religious and/or historical rationale), and do not represent the only possible appropriate choices. Remember, it will be best if you select a total of either one or three deities. You should feel free to select a number of deities from the same category, or to mix and match as you see fit. Most importantly, follow your own intuition!

2.4 Altar Location

The first step in constructing an authentic Taoist altar is to select an auspicious (*ji xiang*) space. Traditionally, the location and placement of Taoist temples and altars was the province of Taoist *feng shui* specialists who would perform complicated cosmological calculations in making their decisions (See Chapter 3.8 – *Feng Shui*). There are nonetheless a variety of general rules and principles that we can follow in choosing our altar locations.

In terms of general placement, you should adhere to the follow suggestions:

- It is best to locate your altar along a north wall, so that it faces south, as Taoism has long considered south to be the most auspicious and religious direction.
- If you do not have or cannot use a suitable north wall, try the following walls in order: west, east, or south (unless you have a specific reason to do otherwise).
- Try to avoid placing your altar against a wall shared by a bathroom or a garage, as the energies from these areas will prove to be inappropriate for altar use.
- You should also avoid placing your altar at the foot of your bed, or on the opposite side of a wall at the foot of your bed. To do so would mean that your feet are pointing at the altar while you sleep, which would be a sign of disrespect towards your altar and any resident deities.
- Try to select an area that is flush against a wall and not angled, as an angled altar will not be harmoniously integrated into the general energy flow of the room housing your altar.
- Altars in your bedroom will continue to exert influence on you while you sleep. Some people will appreciate this interaction, while for some people it could prove to be too intense. You be the judge, although bedroom altars can also represent spe-

Ji Xiang

Wealth	Fame	Marriage
Family	Health	Offspring
Wisdom	Career	Friends

Eight Trigrams Map

cial problems in terms of ongoing care (see Chapter 2.12 – *Care of Your Altar*).

These are only general guidelines, however, and will not help you to select a specific room in which to place your altar. After all, almost every room has a north wall! One of the most important considerations in choosing a room for your altar is your own instinct and intuition. Your altar should be in a place that you find personally welcoming, and a place that you feel will be spiritually inviting. Some rooms in your house will probably possess a more instinctively appropriate feel for specific altars. For instance, an altar to the *Kitchen God* could obviously be placed in the kitchen. If you hope to bring about a change in your romantic life, you might want to place an altar in your bedroom. You might find that your home office is the most appropriate place for an altar that you hope will bring you an improvement in your financial or professional life.

You may also use an Eight Trigrams Map to analyze potential altar locations within your house. First you should draw a simple aerial map of your home and overlay it upon the Eight Trigrams Map as follows:

Align the maps so that your front door falls in one of the three areas in the lowest row. If your home has an irregular shape (such as an 'L' shape or if it is missing a corner), simply draw a dotted line to fill in the missing area. The Eight Trigrams Map works equally well for all levels of your house.

Now ask yourself about your main goals in creating your altar. Are you creating one because you would like assistance or guidance in a specific area? Are you attempting to draw a certain type of energy into your life? If so, choose a room in your home that corresponds to the appropriate area of the Eight Trigrams Map. For example, if your main goal in creating a Taoist altar is to pray for the welfare of your deceased ancestors, then select the room in your home that corresponds to the 'Family' section of the Eight Trigrams Map. Follow the general guidelines presented above, and you should have determined an excellent altar location. As your goals change over time, you may decide that it is best to move your altar to a new location within your house. If that is the case, follow the instructions described in Chapter 2.5 – *Purify Your Space*, Chapter 2.6 – *Build a Taoist Altar*, and Chapter 2.7 – *'Opening' Your Altar* as if you were creating a brand new altar.

2.5 Purify Your Space

Once you have selected a specific space, you must ensure that the energy is sufficiently pure (*jing*). To be safe, everyone should perform an energetic cleansing on his or her space before proceeding. If you are pregnant, menstruating, or have any sort of an open flesh wound, you should wait for another time to perform this activity, as Taoism holds that blood serves to interact with lower energetic forms, which is contrary to your present goals.

Jing

Before you proceed, you will need to gather some of the supplies that you will require when you assemble your altar. Specifically, you will need incense, a candle, pure spring water, three beautiful flowers, a plate, and your bell or hand chimes. (See Chapter 2.6 – *Build a Taoist Altar*.)

First remove everything (if possible) from your intended altar space. This includes furniture and wall hangings. With a new sponge or cleaning rag and a prepared mixture of orange oil-based cleaning solution (commonly available at health food stores), wash your space. You should wash the floor, the walls, and everything else you can reach. If you can wash the ceiling, do so. You should personally perform this task, with the assistance only of those whom you believe will utilize the finished altar. As you wash, maintain a prayerful attitude and the willful intent to remove any negative, impure, or unneeded energy from this area. As you finish washing the intended altar area, proceed to wash the items that you have removed from the area. When you have finished, flush the remaining cleaning solution down the toilet and throw away the sponge or rag (being careful to remove it from your house as soon as you are finished).

Now that you are finished physically cleaning your intended altar space, you should proceed to clean yourself. Take a shower or bath and put on clean clothes. You may want to scent yourself with sandalwood soap or essential oil, but try not to use any other scented bathroom products such as soap, deodorant, or perfume. Do not wear any jewelry or metal (including underwire bras or wire-rim glasses), as contact with metal may interfere your own energetic sensitivity. You should remain barefoot, as that will also serve to increase your energetic sensitivity. The only people present should be those who will actively utilize your completed altar. Other energetic presences can only interfere with your activities. There should be no background noise or distractions, and you should open the windows and doors if possible. The free flow of air will allow any inappropriate energy to escape. Only if you feel healthy and centered in every sense should you proceed, as only then will your actions have the desired impact.

Take a few moments to attune yourself to the energy of your intended altar room as it is. Starting at the room's front door, walk counterclockwise in a complete circle around the perimeter of the room, with your right arm extended at the level of your heart and your palm facing the wall. Allow your hand and all of your senses to 'listen' to the energy as you circle the entire perimeter.

Now that you have established a connection (and don't worry if you didn't 'hear' anything, 'listening' was sufficient!), light your candle and place it on a plate surrounded by the three de-stemmed flower heads. Place the plate either in the center of the room, or in front of your intended altar space, whichever feels more appropriate. Let this offering remain where it is, and let the candle burn, throughout your activities. This is an offering to the energy of the room, and to the improvement of that energy. You should make this offering with a sufficiently reverential and prayerful attitude. Then light some of your incense. Chinese sandalwood incense is acceptable, but for altar space purification you may also use a tree resin incense called Dragon's Blood, which is very energetically purifying. While holding it in your left hand (with your right hand wrapped around your left hand) offer the incense in each of the five directions, including center. Repeat this offering by forming a 'sword mudra' with your right hand (first two fingers extended while the other two fingers and the thumb form a partial fist) and dipping your two extended fingers into your spring water. Purify the five directions by shaking your wet extended fingers in a given direction. While doing this maintain the same reverential and prayerful attitude, and imagine that the incense smoke and spring water are driving any unnecessary or inappropriate energy from your space and making it an appropriate receptacle for holy and healing Taoist energy.

After your incense offering, again walk the perimeter of the room in a counterclockwise fashion starting at the front door. With your right arm again extended loosely at heart level, feel for any energy irregularities or imbalances near the walls. If you feel anything strange, pause and clap your hands, starting close to the floor and gradually raising your clapping to over your head. The clapping will help to disperse static or inappropriate energy, as long as you can maintain an appropriate attitude. The pace and strength of your clapping is up to your own intuition. Then proceed with your walk. You should definitely perform the clapping at every corner (energy tends to stagnate or collect in corners). After you have completed your circle you must wash you hands in clean running water! This will ensure that you carry no residue from the energy you are trying to disperse.

Now hold your bell or hand chimes at heart level as you again walk the counterclockwise perimeter of the room starting at the front door. Walk slowly and continuously ring your bell or hand chimes near the walls so that the sound never completely fades. Pay attention to the energy of the room as you walk, but pay particular attention to the sound of the bell or hand chimes. Envision a clear ring of pure energy and sound being created as you walk. You will notice variations in sound or tone in places where the energy is still not sufficiently clean or elevated. In such places, stop walking and ring the bell or hand chimes with particular intent to purify that area. Once you are satisfied you can continue walking for as many revolutions as you think is necessary. When you have completed your last circle, but while still ringing the bell or hand chimes, trace the Chinese character 'chang.' This character means 'eternal,' 'long,' or 'continuous,' and will empower the energetic clearing effects of the bell to last long after you have stopping ringing.

Chang

Now comes a very tricky aspect of space clearing, one that may not seem natural or intuitive to everyone. But it is a necessary and effective step. Your space should now be purified, and you should use your will to create a 'shield' to protect it and to keep it clean. With your back against a corner of the wall with the front door, raise your right arm over your head on your inhalation, keeping your palm parallel to the wall. On your exhalation, sweep you arm down in a wide arc to your side. As you do this, envision a protective white or golden light shooting from your fingertips and extending along the entire wall. Affirm with your intent that this shield will allow beneficial Taoist deities and energies into your space, and will block all others. Walk counterclockwise until you get to the next corner, turn ninety degrees, and repeat the process. Repeat another two times until you have erected your protective shield along all four walls. Stand at one end of the room and envision the shield extending like a carpet beneath your feet until it covers the entire floor. Then do the same for the ceiling. Go the middle of the room and seal your shield by asking your inner self to reinforce this shield every night before you sleep. You will find this will actually occur, even if you are not aware of the activity.

Congratulations, you have performed your first Taoist ritual! Allow your candle to burn to completion, and you will have created a pure and holy space in which you can now construct your own Taoist altar!

2.6 Build a Taoist Altar

As you might expect by now, Taoists don't always agree on the exact specifics of altars or altar creation. Again, there are regional and lineal differences, with some personal preference thrown in the mix as well. Without becoming involved in too many doctrinal or methodological disputes, this book will help you to build a beautiful, functional, authentic, generally accepted Taoist altar.

Before actually constructing an altar you should be familiar with the Taoist pantheon. Consider each of the deities described in Chapter 2.2 – *Pantheon*. Do you feel a special connection with one or several of these deities? Look at their images, read their stories, meditate on them if it feels right to do so. Take as much time as you may need to gain an intuitive feeling for these deities. No Taoist altar is dedicated to all the deities, and neither should yours be. As your intuition comes into focus select either one or three deities. Two deities would seem unbalanced to a Taoist. No altars are ever dedicated to four deities, as the number four in Chinese is a homophone for 'death.' An altar could be dedicated to more than four deities, but I don't recommend such a complex arrangement for a beginning altar.

Selecting Your Altar Materials

After you decide to whom you would like to dedicate your altar, you will need to prepare at least the following basic materials:

A dedicated table or similar flat surface;

A statue or image of your selected deity or deities;

A statue stand;

An incense burner and incense;

Two candleholders and candles;

A bell or pair of hand chimes;

Two offering cups or bowls;

One small hardwood twig;

Two small vases to be periodically filled with fresh flowers.

Your Altar Table

Your altar table should be made from a natural substance. Many temples use stone or a combination of wood and stone. Stone, however, seems unpractical for most personal, household shrines. A wooden table, however should not be difficult. Unnatural surfaces, like formica or plastic, should be avoided if possible. Not only might such substances emit minute amounts of noxious fumes, but they might also interfere with the flow of energy around your altar.

Your altar will be nicer if you use a dedicated table, but not everyone will be able to do so. Perhaps your space is sufficiently small so that a separate table for your altar is not practical. You may then use a portion of a table that is being used for other purposes. If you do this, however, you must be careful that the dual uses of this table do not conflict. For instance, it seems somewhat contradictory to use the same table for the application of cosmetics and for your altar. An even greater contradiction would be to store personal items like drugs, birth control pills, or condoms in a drawer underneath your altar. Be very conscious of how you match your multiple uses for this table. Moreover, even if you combine appropriate dual uses, make sure to keep the space for your altar a dedicated area. There should be no overlap. You should never toss coins, keys, or a hairbrush on your altar. That space is reserved for your Taoist deities and energies.

If your table is wooden, it should be a natural color. If at all possible, use a table that has been prepared with a natural stain or a simple oil finish. Your table or space requirements will vary with the size of your materials. There is no minimum or maximum size limit. If you think your altar is beautiful with a gigantic table, it probably is. Yet small tables can be just as effective as large ones.

For those who want to use a traditional Taoist altar table, the options are almost endless! Styles and colors vary greatly, from the plain to the ornate. Do a bit of research, pick a favorite style, and you should be able to find a suitable altar table.

Your Deity Statue or Image

The most important part of your altar will be the statue (*shen xiang*) or image of your selected deity or deities. It will be the visual and energetic focal point of your efforts.

The single most important factor in selecting a statue or image will be your own reaction to it. By now you should have

Shen Xiang

selected a particular deity or deities because you feel an important connection to that figure or figures. In selecting a specific representation of that deity or deities, you should be guided by an even stronger sense of connection or love. If you do not inherently enjoy a given representation, do not use it. Look for another representation, or, if all else fails, review your selection of the deity in question.

If you have sufficient space and opportunity, you should attempt to incorporate a statue of your favorite deity/deities into your altar. A statue is a three-dimensional representation, and should bring a deeper presence to your altar than would a two-dimensional representation.

Statues of Taoist deities are traditionally made of wood, metal, stone, or ceramic. Any natural substance would be fine. If you are a great clay sculptor and you want to create an altar image, you should feel free to do so. Avoid plastic, synthetic, or otherwise unnatural statuary. As a beginner, I would also avoid overly modern representations of deities.

Size is also not an important consideration when choosing a statue. A large statue does not necessarily work any better than a small one. The size of the statue has no bearing upon the amount of energy that can be invoked through that statue! In fact, some of the most wonderful (and most expensive!) Taoist statuary I have ever seen has been very small.

For those with limited space or budgets, you might want to consider a two-dimensional image of your selected Taoist deity or deities. Although not as preferable as a three-dimensional representation, a plaque, photograph, drawing, or painting can work just as well. Simply find an image you enjoy (not an overly modern representation!), keep it free from dirt and fingerprints, and place it in a simple and natural wooden frame.

It is important to remember that one never 'buys' a Taoist statue or representation. You cannot, after all, 'buy' a deity! Taoists say they 'invite' a statue or representation. This term actually better reflects the reality of building an altar – we are 'inviting' particular deities into our homes and into our lives.

Your Statue Stand

Taoists would never place a representation of a deity directly onto an altar table. A deity must always be raised off the 'floor,' and is usually placed onto a type of stand.

For statuary, stands are usually made of wood. The stand can include a roof and walls to resemble a small temple (some-

Personal Taoist Altar

times called a 'spirit house'), or it can be simple and minimalist. The important point is just to raise the statue in a traditional manner. The wood used in a statue stand is sometimes stained and sometimes lacquered. The height of the stand is best left to individual preference. The size of the stand's footprint is also a matter of personal taste, although the footprint should be sufficiently large to provide a spacious area upon which to rest your statue.

For those who will use a two-dimensional representation of a deity or deities, it is no less important to raise your image off the 'floor' of the altar table. If you believe that it looks strange to set a framed image of a deity upon a statue stand, I would then recommend folding a length of red silk and placing that underneath your framed representation. The frame's natural standing mechanism will still work, but you will have succeeded in raising the deity in a manner that will look quite traditional (and should be fairly inexpensive as well!).

Your Incense Burner and Your Incense

You will need an incense burner (*xianglu*) and some incense. Your incense burner can be of any style, although it should at a minimum not conflict with traditional Chinese aesthetics.

To start with, an incense burner can be made from metal or ceramic. Wood is not used, as it is too easily flammable.

Taoist Worship

Incense Burners

Stone is also rarely used indoors. The decision between metal and ceramic is a totally personal one. No matter which one is chosen, the design and coloration should be appropriate. Your incense burner should not include images of Western wizards or dragons or the like, but should tend towards either simple or traditional Chinese shapes. A ceramic incense burner should have a neutral color or a sedate design. Chinese pottery is famously beautiful, and your incense burner should freely utilize traditional Chinese pottery patterns.

It is important to note that incense burners improve with age and use. Each time you make an offering in an incense burner, you leave behind a tiny resonance of that humble piety. In China, antique incense burners are thus highly prized (and accordingly expensive!). You would not want to use an incense burner that has previously been used in the service of other, non-Taoist religious traditions. Conversely, an incense burner that has been long used for Taoist rituals and offerings may add a significant positive energy to your own practice.

Once you have an incense burner, you will need incense. Incense is a much more complicated issue that most people realize.

While it does not matter which form of incense you use (cones, sticks, or powders), the type or scent of the incense is important. You should use a type that is not incongruous with a Chinese altar. Flavored incense (such as cherry, vanilla, or musk) and directed incense (such as relaxation incense or relationship incense) should be avoided. Among the countless traditional types of Chinese incense, sandalwood is perhaps the most famous and among the most commonly used. When in doubt, sandalwood is always a good choice.

Xianglu

Your altar and the surrounding area will become your dedicated space for prayer, meditation, *qigong*, deep breathing, or communing with deities. It is the absolutely last place on earth you would want to introduce any even remotely toxic or otherwise adverse substance. This goes doubly for incense, which is not only your primary offering to your favorite Taoist deities, but also becomes widely dispersed into the very air you are breathing, and into which you will attempt to invoke the positive, healing energies of the deities. Incense should be made from completely organic ingredients, like wood ash, herbs, flowers, or essential oils. Most common incense, especially very inexpensive varieties, is made from a variety of impure substances. Watch out for incense that derives its scent from unnatural oil added to an already formed piece of incense. The scent should come from the natural ingredients and not from any inorganic additive.

Lazhu

There are some Taoists who believe that incense must be local in order to have an energetic effect upon a space. If you want to experiment with this theory, try a local incense. For example, if you live in the Western U.S., try white sage or sweetgrass (or a delightful combination of the two). No matter where you live, you should be able to find a locally grown incense. Just make sure that it is natural and organic, and that you enjoy its odor.

If you want to be absolutely certain of the purity of your incense, you should consider adopting the old fashioned method of burning a pure resin or a freshly ground powder on a miniature charcoal disc. This method is less convenient than using pre-formed sticks or cones, but it does allow you to be absolutely certain that nothing has been added to your pure incense. You simply place a charcoal disc in your incense burner and light it. It will quickly turn red with heat, and you can then add your own powder or gum incense with a teaspoon. I have never known anyone to use this method repeatedly and not to soon favor it over all other methods! You might want to at least consider using this method on special occasions or whenever you feel that extra quality or purity is needed.

Your Candleholders and Your Candles

You will need one pair of candles (*lazhu*), and one pair of candleholders. Your candleholders should be either simple or in a traditional Chinese style. Almost all candleholders are metal. Some (including many traditional Chinese styles) use a metal prong to secure the candle. The metal prong is inserted into the bottom of the candle and holds the candle upright. I prefer candleholders that instead use a 'cup' or a large base 'plate' to hold the candle. The prong system has two drawbacks: the candle is free to drip on your altar table, and breakage when the candle burns low could lead to an accidental fire. The 'cup' or 'plate' system provides a more stable base for the candle as well as a receptacle for any dripping wax. This is especially important if you believe you will ever leave your candle unattended (not recommended by Moms or modern Western fire prevention experts, but called for in some Taoist rituals).

Your candles, like your incense, are extremely important. Most modern candles are made from a petroleum-derived substance. If you light a common candle you will see a small trail of black smoke rising from the tip of the flame. That black smoke is petroleum! When oil wells occasionally catch fire, they undergo the same process and it is declared to be an ecological disaster. We should not allow even tiny ecological disasters to occur near our altars and sacred spaces. The U.S. Environmental Protection Agency recently announced that the pollution from a burning candles can exceed EPA standards for outdoor air quality!

You may also notice that if you burn common candles over time your altar and its surrounding area will become coated with a sticky, black petroleum residue. This residue is very hard to remove, and does not make for a particularly inviting space into which we can easily invoke deities and their energies!

In ancient times candles were hand-made without the use of petroleum, and were non-toxic. Today the easiest way to achieve that result is to use beeswax candles. Beeswax is a natural product, with no toxic residues. Beeswax candles are generally more expensive than regular candles, but they have a variety of important benefits. Not only are they non-toxic, but they burn for much longer periods of time (your cost per burning hour may be equivalent to, or even lower than, that of regular candles). They are practically dripless, which not only contributes to long burn times but also reduces mess and improves aesthetics. Finally they emit a delightful and completely natural honeyed scent (and do so even when not being used).

When purchasing beeswax candles, you have the option between honeycomb, solid rolled, or hand-dipped, all of which come in filtered or unfiltered varieties.

The honeycomb variety is the least expensive. It is made by rolling sheets of honeycombed beeswax into a pillar. The air

Beeswax Candles and Candleholders

pockets in honeycomb, however, serve to shorten burn times significantly.

A solid rolled beeswax candle is made by rolling sheets of solid beeswax into pillars. While these candles are much more solid than the honeycomb variety, there is still minute separation between the rolled layers. The burn times for these candles are extremely long.

The absolute best (and most expensive) variety is the hand dipped or molded beeswax candle. These candles are made the traditional way, by continually dipping a wick into molten beeswax, or by pouring the beeswax into a preformed mold. The result is a completely solid candle with absolute maximum burn time.

Filtering is really a matter of preference. A filtered candle will have an even, pale, sometimes whitish appearance, and will emit a delicious but very delicate scent. An unfiltered candle will have a rich, sometimes uneven, yellowish appearance, and will emit a stronger, earthier scent.

Bell

Your Bell or Hand Chimes

Every altar requires a bell. For a personal altar, hand chimes will also suffice. The bell/chimes will be made of metal, and should be either simple or in a traditional Chinese style. Bell/chime sounds are a matter of personal preference, but you should aim for a clear, clean, crisp sound that is stable as it lingers. The longer the sound lingers, the better the quality of your bell or chimes.

The traditional Taoist bell is a high-lipped metal bowl that sits on a cushion. In order to ring the bell a Taoist strikes the bowl along the rim with a leather-clad (sometimes a rubber sleeve is used!), hand-held clapper. Traditional hand chimes (which are very popular throughout SW China) are concave metal disks with a hole through the center. A silken string is often used to tie the disks together (leaving at least 6-8 inches if string between the disks). The chimes are rung by grasping the string immediately behind the disks and knocking the rims of the two disks together. They are often ornamented with dragons or even Tibetan religious symbols.

Hand Chimes

Your Offering Cups or Bowls

You will need to make offerings at your altar, and you will thus need dedicated cups or bowls for this purpose. These items should not be used for any activity other than making offerings at your altar. Your cups/bowls can be made of metal, wood, or ceramic, depending upon your own instinct. Again, however, the offering containers should be simple and natural, or traditionally Chinese in style. Unless you think you will need something larger, I would recommend one container that could hold a medium orange, perhaps 4'-6' in diameter. The height of your offering cup or bowl should not exceed an inch or two over the height of your statue stand. The other container will be used to hold a small amount of ritually cleansing water.

Your Hardwood Twig

This twig will be used to cleanse your altar area with the water from your offering bowl (as described below). Select a twig that is sufficiently long so as to enable you to dip it into the altar water, and sufficiently thick so as to be able to withstand repeated shaking and usage. You may replace your older twig with a new one at any time.

If you carefully follow the above guidelines, each of the Five Phases (See Chapter 4.3 – *Five Phases*) should be represented on your altar – Earth (incense and ash), Metal (incense burner), Water (water-filled offering bowl), Wood (altar table), and Fire (candle and incense flame). This will help to bring to your altar and your practice a sense of Taoist balance and harmony. If you find that your materials somehow do not include each of the Five Phases, you should reconsider one or more of your selections.

Assembling Your Altar

Now that you have collected your necessary materials, it is time to actually construct your Taoist altar! Arrange your furniture (including your altar table) in your room as you see fit, according to the suggestions in Chapter 2.4 – *Altar Location*. Now place your statue stand (or Spirit House or red silk) in the center of your altar table or space, about 2/3 towards the rear edge. Place your statue (or framed image) on top of your stand (or red silk). Take your two candleholders and place each of them on one side of the statue stand (or red silk). You should decide for yourself how much space to leave between the candleholders and the statue stand (or red silk), keeping in mind that burning candles should be kept a safe distance from all other objects. You may also slightly alter the distance of the candleholders from the rear edge, so that they are either slightly in front of or slightly behind the statue stand (or red silk). Once you have decided upon a location, place a candle in each candleholder. Your flowers or vases should be placed just outside the candleholders. Again, exact placement is a matter of personal preference.

Centered slightly in front of your statue stand (or red silk) should be your offering cups or bowls. You may adjust the exact distance between the cup or bowl and the representation of the deity. It is important that the cups or bowls be close to the deity but still not overly obscure the sightlines to or from the representation of the deity.

Centered slightly in front of your offering cups or bowls should be your incense burner (the position of the offering cups/bowls and the incense burner can be reversed if desired). Again, sightlines should not be overly obstructed, but this is less of a problem as you move farther away from the representation of the deity. A completely empty incense burner should not be used, so fill your incense burner to within one inch of its rim with salt. You may use any type of salt, but I prefer natural sea salt. Some people prefer kosher salt or any type of religiously consecrated salt. With use, the salt will mix with your incense ash, and the mixture will absorb energy from your offerings. As this mixture accumulates, do not throw it away. Taoists have a long history of using the ash from an old burner to give life to a second, new burner. This will make a wonderful housewarming gift for anyone creating a Taoist altar, anyone who is need of spiritual strength or direction, or anyone who simply enjoys the beauty of incense. There are also various advanced ritual uses for this mixture. If you have the opportunity to use ash from an existing Taoist incense burner in the establishment of your own altar, you should definitely do so.

Your bell or hand chimes can be placed anywhere on your altar, but must be accessible to you during your ritual activities. You will use the sound of your bell or hand chimes to clear the energy around your altar, to focus yourself, and to carry your own energy and prayers to heavenly realms.

For those of you who have selected three Taoist deities instead of one, the rules for creating your altar are distinctly similar. The only differences in this process are:

    Horizontally align your representations about 2/3 towards the rear edge of your altar table;

- Place the two candleholders to the outside of the first and third representations;
- You will need four identical offering cups or bowls. You should place one in front of each deity (for offerings), and one in front of the center deity (for ritually cleansing water);
- Place your incense burner in front of the offering cups or bowls in front of the middle deity;

Other than this, the instructions are the same as detailed above.

If you would like to keep a photo or a memento of a deceased family member on your altar (a very traditionally Taoist desire!), you should do so on the west end of your altar (west is the direction of death). This means, assuming your altar is against a northern wall, these objects will be on your left as you face your altar. If your altar is primarily dedicated to the spirits of deceased ancestors, you may want to locate it against a eastern wall.

For those who would like to keep items relating to divination (See Chapter 3.4 – *Divination*) on your altar, you should do so on the east end of your altar. That means, again assuming that your altar is against a northern wall, these objects will be on your right as you face your altar. If your altar is primarily dedicated to divinatory activities, you may want to locate it against an western wall.

2.7 'Opening' Your Altar

Now your Taoist altar is complete and is ready for you to start using it in your Taoist practice. Most Taoist temples and advanced Taoists create far more complex altars, often utilizing a wider variety of offerings, selected ritual objects, and divination tools. But your altar, although basic, is not necessarily inferior to these more complex varieties. In fact, your new Taoist altar will become as potent a tool in your personal Taoist practice as you are prepared to make it.

We should note that when traditional Taoist altars are constructed, they typically undergo an energizing or 'opening' (*kaiguang*) ritual performed by a ritual specialist called a 'Gao Gong.' The Gao Gong first determines the most appropriate date and time to officially open the altar (an altar is officially opened when it is consecrated with the 'opening' ritual and not when it is physically constructed), and then infuses the new al-

Kaiguang

tar with the appropriate deity energy at the assigned time. Only after the Gao Gong has performed such a ritual do Taoists begin to use the altar.

Most people, however, will be unable to have a Gao Gong research the timing of their efforts, or come to their homes and consecrate their altars. This might be a small blessing, as Gao Gongs are commonly regarded as among the most difficult and complex of all Taoist personalities! Does the absence of a Gao Gong, however, mean that your altar won't work, or that it is inappropriate for Taoist use? Absolutely not!

Ancestor End

If you would like to determine an appropriate day upon which to start using your own altar, you have several options. It is very safe to use the Lunar New Year for this sort of ritual activity. The Lunar New Year is a new start both for human beings and for Taoist deities. It is always acceptable to start a new relationship with a new deity on the first day of a new year! If you would prefer not to wait for the Lunar New Year, you can also ask a Lunar Astrologer to calculate your propitious days and times. You can find relatively inexpensive Lunar Astrologers through most major New Age publications. Finally, if you would like immediate satisfaction (as most of us do!), you can simply select the first or fifteenth of any lunar month, which will correspond with each new and full moon. If you use this simple method, I would recommend that you assemble and 'open' your altar during between the hours 11:00 PM – 1:00 AM. Taoists believe this period represents the daily highpoint of *yin* energy, and is thus the most appropriate time for meditation and associated activities (ignore the fact that the second hour of that period is technically the second or the sixteenth day of the lunar month!).

While it is infinitely preferable to have a ritual specialist 'open' your altar, there is also a long-standing tradition of altar creation by China's peasantry. Large temples may be able to afford a Gao Gong's consecration fees and expenses, but peasants building village shrines cannot. Instead, these Taoists and Taoist Practitioners use the sincerity of their devotions to consecrate their altars. Which is precisely what you should do, according to the following suggestions:

If you are 'opening' your altar immediately after purifying your space and assembling the required materials, your space should be physically and energetically clean. If you decided to delay your 'opening' until a more appropriate time (like the first or fifteenth day of a lunar month), you should start by making sure that your space is still sufficiently clean. If it is not, take any necessary measures to sufficiently improve the conditions. No matter how much or how little time has passed since your purified your space, you should again take a shower or a bath immediately before attempting to 'open' your altar. Some of the same prohibitions still apply:

> Wear clean clothes;
>
> Avoid using scented bathroom products, although you may scent yourself with sandalwood soap or essential oil;
>
> Do not wear any jewelry or metal (including underwire bras or wire-rim glasses), as contact with metal may interfere your own energetic sensitivity;
>
> Remain barefoot, as that will also serve to increase your energetic sensitivity.
>
> There should be no background noise or distractions;
>
> Open the windows and doors if possible;
>
> Only if you feel healthy and centered in every sense should you proceed, as only then will your actions have the desired impact.

One major difference between this 'opening' ritual and the previous purifying ritual is that you should enlist the assistance of everyone who will use the completed altar, and even all those people who will live within the same house as the altar or who will regularly interact with it. This of course extends only to those people who can be relied upon to respect your altar and your religious activities. Anyone who cannot be so relied upon should be excluded from these activities, and should not be present in the area during the 'opening' ritual.

Now you should ready to 'open' your altar. Assume your favorite meditative or prayerful position (See Chapter 2.8 – *How to Worship*) and focus your energy until you feel calm and centered. Light your candles, fill one offering cup/bowl with fresh spring water, and place a clean, organic orange in the other. Place fresh flowers in the flower vases at appropriate places on the altar.

Divination End

Light three sticks or pieces of incense, taking care to never blow on them, as human breath is not sufficiently pure for a religious offering. You should instead wave the incense in order to extinguish its open flame. If you are using powder or gum incense, you must burn incense on three charcoal blocks. Hold the incense in your left hand, right hand wrapped around left, in front of your 'third eye,' the space between your eyebrows. Focus your energy and intent, and when you feel ready use your left hand only to place your incense into your incense burner. You should now perform three prostrations before your altar. Stand before your altar and again hold your hands in front of your 'third eye,' with your open right hand wrapped around your closed left hand. As you lower your hands to the area between your sternum and your waist, begin to bow before your altar. As your hands fall to your sides, drop to your knees and touch your forehead to the ground. Simultaneously with your bow, or immediately after your bow, ring your bell or hand chimes with the express intent of preparing the energy of your altar for the energy of your selected deity or deities. Repeat this entire process two more times.

Stand before your altar and use your hands to 'catch' smoke from your incense and rub that smoke on your face and head. This will imbue your own energy field with the energy of the incense offering, and will help you to connect with your chosen deity. Repeat this two more times. Take the hardwood twig and wave it through the incense smoke three times for the same reasons. Dip it into the water, and shake it in the five directions around your altar (don't forget the center!). This serves to cleanse your self and your altar with fire/*yang* energy and with water/*yin* energy. Your altar should feel balanced. If it does not, repeat these activities before proceeding.

You should now write down in black or gold ink on red paper your prayers to your selected deity. Your prayers should invite the deity into your altar and into your life. Tell the deity why you have requested this, and explain the offerings you have left for the deity. Since this is really the province of a high ritual specialist, no one can tell you exactly how to ask the deities to do this. But if you are sincere in expressing your devotion, and if your energy comes from your heart, you should do fine and your requests should be honored. I would suggest writing a prayer (actually creating a talisman, See Chapter 3.5 – *Talismans*) along the following lines (subject to your own intuition):

> To [Name Of Your Chosen Deity]
>
> [List the major attributes of this Deity]
>
> I/we humbly request that you acknowledge the Taoist altar I/we have created in your honor, and I/we further request that you lend your honored presence and authority to this altar. My/our goal in creating this altar, and in humbly asking for your assistance, is to [increase my/our Taoist knowledge and to elevate my/our Taoist practice]. I/we willingly left you an insufficient offering of [incense, spring water, fresh flowers, candlelight, and fresh fruit], and I/we pray that you will accept this humble offering, and that you will continue to preside over and protect this altar. Please excuse any mistakes I/we may have made with this altar or this petition.
>
> [Your Dated Signature]

Everyone present should sign and date the talisman. You should then place the talisman in the incense burner with your left hand and ignite it. Use your own prayers to direct the smoke and energy from the talisman to the appropriate deity.

When you are finished praying you must bow again three times, using the same form as described above, ringing your bell or hand chimes with each bow. If you have three deities you must make these offerings and create a separate talisman in front of each one. After a period of time (no less than three days) you can remove your offerings, which should now be charged with Taoist energy from the altar. While you can eat the fruit personally or leave it for animals, birds, etc., you should leave any remaining water on your altar, where it will continue to absorb cleansing energy. You should allow the candles and incense to continue to burn until they are finished. If you must extinguish the candles, do so with a candle snuffer and not by blowing on them!

Your altar is now officially open for business! On the one hand, you deserve great congratulations, but on the other hand, your Taoist work is just beginning!

2.8 How to Worship

Before anyone starts to perform Taoist devotions they should read the rest of this book. You may learn many things that you will want to incorporate into your Taoist practice, or that will increase the effectiveness of your worship.

Assuming you have welcomed, opened, and celebrated your new altar as described in the last chapter, you are now ready to learn how to interact with your altar on a regular basis. Now that your altar has been 'opened,' every time you interact with it you should start by following this *basic ritual*:

Light your candles, taking care to use your left hand and to first light the right one and then the left one (as you face them). Then take your bell or hand chimes from your altar and place them within easy reach. Assume a relaxed but meditative position. You should attempt to sit Taoist-style, on a cushioned, rear-elevated platform (called a 'wedge') with your legs crossed in a lotus position with each ankle resting on the opposite inner thigh or knee. If you prefer, you may also sit Japanese-style (on a low bench with your lower legs tucked underneath you), or without the bench at all (if your legs and hips are quite flexible), or you may stand in a *qigong* stance. No matter which method you choose, it is important to make sure that no joint is locked, and that your spine remains straight from the base of the skull to tailbone. If you can achieve these two goals while remaining still and breathing deeply, tension will leave your body and your energy will start to flow. Close your eyes and focus on your breath until you feel calm and centered. Until

Altar Central Bay

Ketou

you are calm and centered, you will not be able to perform any Taoist ritual effectively.

Once you are prepared, kneel (*ketou*) in front of your altar and take three sticks (or pieces) of incense into your left hand. You may now use a single piece if you are worried about creating too much smoke in an enclosed area. If you are using powder or gum incense, you may now use a single charcoal disc. Light the incense with one of your lit candles, taking care to never blow on it, as human breath is not sufficiently pure for a religious offering. You should instead wave the incense in order to extinguish its open flame. Hold the incense, right hand wrapped around left, in front of your 'third eye,' the space between your eyebrows. As you lower your hands to the area between your sternum and your waist, bow before your altar. Simultaneously with your bow, or immediately after your bow, ring your bell or hand chimes with the express intent of preparing the energy of your altar for the energy of your selected deity or deities. Repeat this process two more times. With your left hand only place the incense into the incense burner.

Stand and take the hardwood twig and wave it through the incense smoke three times. Dip it into the water, and shake it in the five directions around your altar (don't forget the center!). This serves to cleanse your self and your altar with fire/*yang* energy and with water/*yin* energy. Your altar should feel balanced. If it does not, repeat these activities before proceeding.

After performing this **basic ritual**, you are now prepared to meditate or to use your altar in any fashion. You should now feel free to undertake specific meditations or visualizations, to practice *qigong*, to pray or otherwise communicate with your selected deity, or to give thanks. When you are finished with such activity, bow again three times, following the method described above. Allow your incense to fully burn, and manually extinguish your left candle and then your right candle with a candle snuffer (again taking care never to blow on them!).

Every morning and every evening, preferably at sunrise and at sunset, you should perform your **basic ritual**, followed by prayer or meditation. Incense and water must be offered on each occasion, although fruit and flower offerings can be made on a periodic basis, or on specific holidays. This is an ongoing daily event at every Taoist temple, and you should make it a permanent part of your own routine. The energy of your altar will sharpen with use, and will decrease with neglect. The only certainty is that over time you will develop the altar (and the Taoist practice) that you earn and deserve.

Times to Avoid Your Altar

There are some times during normal people's lives that they should avoid their altars, or at least not actively use their altars.

When Under the Influence of Alcohol or Chemical Substances

If you are under the influence of alcohol or drugs, even if it's a very small influence, you should not interact with your altar in any way. Your altar's purpose is to help you internally raise your spiritual energy, and you cannot achieve this when you are already manipulating your energy in such gross, external manners.

Whenever physically, mentally, or emotionally 'unclean'

You should cleanse yourself prior to using your altar. This could mean taking a shower, calming down after an argument, or simply giving yourself time to shed the concerns of your workday. Until you feel that you are ready, you should resist using your altar.

For Females – During Menses

Females should avoid performing any ritual at their altars during menses. This is not because menses is somehow negative or evil. It is natural, and should be accepted until such time as you can control your menses (a goal of advanced female Taoists' internal work). But your energy during this time is incompatible with the energy of Taoist ritual. Taoists believe that a woman should energetically rest during this time. Taoists also consider blood to be a powerful exorcistic influence capable of drawing interaction with lower energetic spirits and forms, and such an element is not to be introduced into an altar area without careful forethought. This is a very traditional prohibition (having been adopted by Taoism from earlier folk religious traditions), and should be respected.

Anyone with an Open Flesh Wound

For many of the same reasons listed above, anyone with an open flesh wound should avoid using their altars.

For Females – After Pregnancy

For twenty-four days after giving birth, a woman should not utilize her altar. During this time period a woman's energy is considered to be too unstable from the recent trauma of childbirth to be suitable for altar use.

After Engaging In Sexual Relations

Not all Taoists are celibate. But all Taoists refrain from major ritual activity unless they have abstained from sexual relations for at least one week. Use your own judgment as to what constitutes major ritual activity. Small offerings are probably OK, but if you are hoping to seriously invoke the energy of a specific deity (as in an 'opening' ritual), or if you wish to sincerely celebrate a specific deity's festival day, you may want to observe this seven-day prohibition. Under any circumstances, you must shower between sexual relations of any kind and interaction with your altar.

Other Prohibitions

Taoists traditionally do not engage in major ritual activity while wearing the color white (the color of death), or when wearing wool or leather (which carry energetic traces from the animal 'donors'). Taoists (even Orthodox Unity Taoists) also refrain from eating any animal products for one week prior to engaging in major ritual activity. Again, use your own judgment as to what constitutes major ritual activity. Small offerings are probably OK, but if you are hoping to seriously invoke the energy of a specific deity (as in an 'opening' ritual), or if you wish to sincerely celebrate a specific deity's festival day, you may want to observe this prohibition.

2.9 Religious Calendar

The Taoist calendar (*lishu*) is filled with an almost constant stream of religious holidays. Many Taoists disagree on a number of specific dates throughout the calendar. Most of the disagreements, however, involve a mere day or two here and there. There are some important holidays that are simply celebrated at two distinctly different times throughout the year, following two separate traditions. The following is a list of holidays based upon generally accepted dates. Several Taoists from both China and SE Asia have independently reviewed this list and have accepted it. So while some Taoists may take exception to some specific dates, this list does include generally accepted notions regarding the Taoist calendar.

These dates are first listed according to the lunar calendar, which Taoism traditionally follows. This calendar does not change, and remains the same from year to year. Due to the differences between the lunar and solar calendrical systems, Taoist lunar holidays translate to different solar dates in any given year. The lunar calendar is translated as follows into solar (Gregorian) calendars for the years 2005 – 2007:

Lishu

Celestial Master Cave — Qingcheng Mountain — Sichuan Province

TAOIST WORSHIP

First Moon

- 1st
  - New Moon (Altar 'Opening' and Cleaning)
  - Yuanshi Tianzun's Birthday (Jade Purity)
- 3rd
  - Hao Taigu's Birthday (Seven Perfected Beings)
  - Yao Wang's Birthday (Sun Simiao, Medicine King)
- 4th
  - All Deities Descend to the Mortal World
- 5th
  - Cai Shen's Birthday (God of Wealth)
  - Sun Bu'er's Birthday (Seven Perfected Beings)
- 8th
  - Zhu Rong's Birthday (Fire God)
- 9th
  - Yuhuang Dadi's Birthday (Great Jade Emperor)
- 15th
  - Full Moon (Altar 'Opening' and Cleaning)
  - Lantern Festival
  - Shangyuan Tianguan's Birthday (Heavenly Official)
  - Wang Xuanpu's Ascension (Five Northern Patriarchs)
- 19th
  - Qiu Chuji's Birthday (Seven Perfected Beings)

Second Moon

- 1st
  - New Moon (Altar 'Opening' and Cleaning)
- 2nd
  - Tudi Gong Festival (Land/Earth God)
- 3rd
  - Wenchang Dijun's Birthday (God of Culture and Literature)
- 6th
  - Donghua Dijun's Birthday (Eastern Emperor)
  - Liu Changsheng's Ascension (Seven Perfected Beings)
- 13th
  - Ge Xianweng's Birthday (Ge Hong)
- 15th
  - Full Moon (Altar 'Opening' and Cleaning)
  - International Taoism Day
  - Taishang Laojun's Birthday (Laozi — Great Purity)
- 19th
  - Guan Yin's Birthday (Goddess of Mercy)
- 29th
  - Mazu's Ascension (Goddess of the South China Sea)

Third Moon

- 1st
  - New Moon (Altar 'Opening' and Cleaning)
  - Tan Changzhen's Birthday (Seven Perfected Beings)
- 3rd
  - Qingming Festival (Cleaning of Gravesites)
  - Xiwang Mu's Birthday (Queen Mother of the West)
  - Yin's Annual Nadir
  - Zhenwu Dadi's Birthday (Dark Emperor of the North)
- 15th
  - Full Moon (Altar 'Opening' and Cleaning)
  - Zhang Tianshi's Birthday (Celestial Master Zhang)
  - Zhao Gongming's Birthday (Four Divine Marshals)
- 16th
  - Wang Yuyang's Birthday (Seven Perfected Beings)
- 18th
  - Zhongyue Dadi's Birthday (Song Mountain Great Emperor)
- 23rd
  - Mazu's Birthday (Goddess of the South China Sea)
- 28th
  - Dongyue Dadi's Birthday (Eastern Mountain Great Emperor)

Fourth Moon

- 1st
  - New Moon (Altar 'Opening' and Cleaning)
  - Tan Changzhen's Ascension (Seven Perfected Beings)
- 10th
  - He Xiangu's Birthday (Eight Immortals)
- 14th
  - Lü Dongbin's Birthday (Eight Immortals)
- 15th
  - Full Moon (Altar 'Opening' and Cleaning)
  - Han Zhongli's Birthday (Eight Immortals)
- 17th
  - Goddess of Midwifery's Birthday
- 18th
  - Beiji Ziwei Dadi's Birthday (Great Emperor of Purple Tenuity & the Northern Pole)
  - Bi Xia's Birthday (Princess of the Azure Clouds)
  - Hua Tuo's Birthday (Immortal Physician and *Qigong* Master)
- 20th
  - Yan Guang's Birthday (Lady of Good Eyesight)
- 23rd
  - Wang Yuyang's Ascension (Seven Perfected Beings)
- 28th
  - Yao Wang's Birthday (Sun Simiao, Medicine King)

Fifth Moon

1st . **Nanji Changsheng Dadi's Birthday** (Southern Pole Long Life Great Emperor)

. **New Moon** (Altar 'Opening' and Cleaning)

5th . **Ascendancy of Yang**

. **Duan Wu Jie** (Dragon Boat Festival)

. **Zhang Tianshi's Festival** (Celestial Master Zhang)

. **Zhong Kui Festival** (Exorcistic Protector)

11th . **Cheng Huang's Birthday** (City Deity)

13th . **Guan Gong's Birthday** (Immortal General Representing Virtue)

15th . **Full Moon** (Altar 'Opening' and Cleaning)

. **Lingbao Tianzun's Birthday** (High Purity)

18th . **Han Zhongli's Ascension** (Eight Immortals)

20th . **Ma Danyang's Birthday** (Seven Perfected Beings)

Sixth Moon

1st . **New Moon** (Altar 'Opening' and Cleaning)

13th . **Lu Ban's Birthday** (Immortal of Woodworking and Carpentry)

. **Wang Lingguan's Birthday** (Taoist Temple Protector)

15th . **Full Moon** (Altar 'Opening' and Cleaning)

. **Liu Haichan's Ascension** (Five Northern Patriarchs)

. **Wang Xuanpu's Birthday** (Five Northern Patriarchs)

19th . **Guan Yin's Enlightenment** (Goddess of Mercy)

20th . **Beidou's Birthday** (Nine Kings of the Northern Dipper)

23th . **Huo Shen's Birthday** (Fire God)

. **Wang Lingguan's Birthday** (Taoist Temple Protector)

24th . **Lei Shen's Birthday** (Thunder God)

25th . **Lan Caihe's Birthday** (Eight Immortals)

26th . **Erlang's Birthday** (Fighter of Floods and Demons)

Seventh Moon

1st . **New Moon** (Altar 'Opening' and Cleaning)

7th . **Festival of the Seven Sisters** (Great Jade Emperor's Daughters, Celebration of Mediums and Shamans)

10th . **Li Tieguai's Birthday** (Eight Immortals)

15th . **Full Moon** (Altar 'Opening' and Cleaning)

. **Zhongyuan Diguan's Birthday** (Earthly Official)

18th . **Xiwang Mu's Birthday** (Queen Mother of the West)

19th . **All 60 Jiazi Deities' Birthdays** (Annual Protectors of the 60-Year Cycle)

20th . **Liu Changsheng's Birthday** (Seven Perfected Beings)

30th . **Dizhang Wang's Birthday** (King of the Underworld)

Eighth Moon

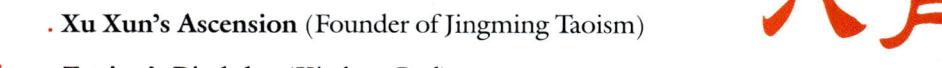

1st . **New Moon** (Altar 'Opening' and Cleaning)

. **Xu Xun's Ascension** (Founder of Jingming Taoism)

3rd . **Zaojun's Birthday** (Kitchen God)

10th . **Beiyue Dadi's Birthday** (Northern Heng Mountain Great Emperor)

11th . **Ge Xuan's Ascension** (Immortal Uncle of Ge Hong)

15th . **Chang E Festival** (Moon Goddesss)

. **Full Moon** (Altar 'Opening' and Cleaning)

27th . **Confucius' Birthday** (Venerated by Taoists)

Ninth Moon

1st - 9th . **Beidou Descends to Earth** (Nine Kings of the Northern Dipper)

1st . **Nandou Descends to Earth** (Six Star Lords of the Southern Dipper)

Ninth Moon

- 9th
  - Bei Dou's Birthday (Nine Kings of the Northern Dipper)
  - Doumu Yuanjun's Birthday (Star Mother Goddess)
  - Fengdu Emperor's Birthday (Judge of Hell)
  - Guan Gong's Ascension (Immortal General Representing Virtue)
  - Immortal Ge's Birthday (Ge Hong)
  - Jiutian Xuannu Niangniang's Festival (Mysterious Lady of the 9th Heaven)
  - Li Nezha's Birthday (Boy Immortal)
  - Wang Chongyang's Birthday (Wang Chongyang - Five Northern Patriarchs)
  - Xuanwu Dadi's Ascension (Dark Great Emperor of the North)
  - Yang's Annual Nadir
  - Zhang Sanfeng's Birthday (Creator of *Taiji quan*)
- 15th
  - Full Moon (Altar 'Opening' and Cleaning)
- 17th
  - Cai Shen's Birthday (God of Wealth)
- 19th
  - Guan Yin's Ascension (Goddess of Mercy)

Tenth Moon

- 1st
  - New Moon (Altar 'Opening' and Cleaning)
- 3rd
  - Mao Ying's Birthday (Eldest of Three Mao Brothers)
  - San Mao Zhenjun's Festival (Three Mao Brothers)
- 10th
  - Zhang Guolao's Birthday (Eight Immortals)
- 14th
  - Fuxi's Festival (Patron of Divination)
- 15th
  - Full Moon (Altar 'Opening' and Cleaning)
  - Xiayuan Shuiguan's Birthday (Water Official)
- 18th
  - Mao Ying's Ascension (Eldest of Three Mao Brothers)
- 19th
  - Qiu Chuji's Ascension (Seven Perfected Beings)

Eleventh Moon

- 1st. **New Moon** (Altar 'Opening' and Cleaning)
- 6th. **Xiyue Dadi's Birthday** (Hua Mountain Great Emperor)
- 11th. **Taiyi Jiuku Tianzun's Festival** (Great Savior From Suffering)
- 15th. **Full Moon** (Altar 'Opening' and Cleaning)
- 19th. **Riguang Tianzi's Birthday** (Deity of Sunlight)
- 23rd. **Nandou Ascends to Heaven** (Six Star Lords of the Southern Dipper)

Twelfth Moon

- 1st. **New Moon** (Altar 'Opening' and Cleaning)
- 9th. **Han Xiangzi's Birthday** (Eight Immortals)
- 14th. **Liu Haichan's Birthday** (Five Northern Patriarchs)
- 15th. **Full Moon** (Altar 'Opening' and Cleaning)
- 16th. **Nanyue Dadi's Birthday** (Southern Heng Mountain Great Emperor)
- 22nd. **Hao Taigu's Ascension** (Seven Perfected Beings)
  - **Ma Danyang's Ascension** (Seven Perfected Beings)
  - **Wang Chongyang's Birthday** (Five Northern Patriarchs)
- 24th. **Kitchen God Reports to Great Jade Emperor**
- 25th. **Great Jade Emperor Inspects Mortal World**

Wang Lingguan Shrine
Eight Immortals Temple
Shaanxi Province

TAOIST WORSHIP

January 2005

- 3rd . Nandou Ascends to Heaven (Six Star Lords of the Southern Dipper)
   . Zhang Guolao's Birthday (Eight Immortals)
- 10th . New Moon (Altar 'Opening' and Cleaning)
- 18th . Han Xiangzi's Birthday (Eight Immortals)
- 23rd . Liu Haichan's Birthday (Five Northern Patriarchs)
- 24th . Full Moon (Altar 'Opening' and Cleaning)
- 25th . Nanyue Dadi's Birthday (Southern Heng Mountain Great Emperor)
- 31st . Hao Taigu's Ascension (Seven Perfected Beings)
   . Ma Danyang's Ascension (Seven Perfected Beings)
   . Wang Chongyang's Birthday (Five Northern Patriarchs)

February 2005

- 2nd . Kitchen God Reports to the Great Jade Emperor
- 3rd . Great Jade Emperor Inspects the Mortal World
- 7th . Sun Bu'er's Ascension (Seven Perfected Beings)
- 9th . New Moon (Altar 'Opening' and Cleaning)
   . Yuanshi Tianzun's Birthday (Jade Purity)
- 11th . Hao Taigu's Birthday (Seven Perfected Beings)
   . Yao Wang's Birthday (Sun Simiao — Medicine King)
- 12th . All Deities Descend to the Mortal World
- 13th . Cai Shen's Birthday (God of Wealth)
   . Sun Bu'er's Birthday (Seven Perfected Beings)
- 16th . Zhu Rong's Birthday (Fire God)
- 17th . Yuhuang Dadi's Birthday (Great Jade Emperor)
- 23rd . Full Moon (Altar 'Opening' and Cleaning)
   . Lantern Festival
   . Shangyuan Tianguan's Birthday (Heavenly Official)
   . Wang Xuanpu's Ascension (Five Northern Patriarchs)
- 27th . Qiu Chuji's Birthday (Seven Perfected Beings)

March 2005

- 10th . **New Moon** (Altar 'Opening' and Cleaning)
- 11th . **Tudi Gong Festival** (Land/Earth God)
- 12th . **Wenchang Dijun's Birthday** (God of Culture and Literature)
- 15th . **Dong Hua Dijun's Birthday** (Eastern Great Emperor)
  . **Liu Changsheng's Ascension** (Seven Perfected Beings)
- 22nd . **Ge Xianweng's Birthday** (Ge Hong)
- 24th . **Full Moon** (Altar 'Opening' and Cleaning)
  . **International Taoism Day**
  . **Taishang Laojun's Birthday** (Laozi – Great Purity)
- 28th . **Guan Yin's Birthday** (Goddess of Mercy)

April 2005

- 7th . **Mazu's Ascension** (Goddess of the South China Sea)
- 9th . **New Moon** (Altar 'Opening' and Cleaning)
  . **Tan Chengzhen's Birthday** (Seven Perfected Beings)
- 11th . **Qingming Festival** (Cleaning of Gravesites)
  . **Xiwang Mu's Birthday** (Queen Mother of the West)
  . **Yin's Annual Nadir**
  . **Zhenwu Dadi's Birthday** (Dark Emperor of the North)
- 23rd . **Full Moon** (Altar 'Opening' and Cleaning)
  . **Zhang Tianshi's Birthday** (Celestial Master Zhang)
  . **Zhao Gongming's Birthday** (Four Divine Marshals)
- 24th . **Wang Yuyang's Birthday** (Seven Perfected Beings)
- 26th . **Zhongyue Dadi's Birthday** (Song Mountain Great Emperor)

TAOIST WORSHIP

May 2005

- 1st   . Mazu's Birthday (Goddess of the South China Sea)
- 6th   . Dongyue Dadi's Birthday (Eastern Mountain Great Emperor)
- 8th   . New Moon (Altar 'Opening' and Cleaning)
        . Tan Changzhen's Ascension (Seven Perfected Beings)
- 17th . He Xiangu's Birthday (Eight Immortals)
- 21st . Lü Dongbin's Birthday (Eight Immortals)
- 22nd . Full Moon (Altar 'Opening' and Cleaning)
        . Han Zhongli's Birthday (Eight Immortals)
- 24th . Goddess of Midwifery's Birthday
- 25th . Beiji Ziwei Dadi's Birthday (Great Emperor of Purple Tenuity & the Northern Pole)
        . Bi Xia's Birthday (Princess of the Azure Clouds)
        . Hua Tuo's Birthday (Immortal Physician and *Qigong* Master)
- 27th . Yan Guang's Birthday (Lady of Good Eyesight)
- 30th . Wang Yuyang's Ascension (Seven Perfected Beings)

Ceremony for the Deceased
White Cloud Monastery
Shanghai

June 2005

- 4th · **Yao Wang's** (Sun Simiao – Medicine King)
- 7th · **Nanji Changsheng Dadi's Birthday** (Southern Pole Long Life Great Emperor)
  · **New Moon** (Altar 'Opening' and Cleaning)
- 11th · **Annual Ascendancy of Yang**
  · **Cheng Huang's Birthday** (City Deity)
  · **Duan Wu Jie** (Dragon Boat Festival)
  · **Zhang Daoling Festival** (Celestial Master Zhang)
  · **Zhong Kui Festival** (Exorcistic Protector)
- 19th · **Guan Gong's Birthday** (Immortal General Representing Virtue)
- 21st · **Full Moon** (Altar 'Opening' and Cleaning)
  · **Lingbao Tianzun's Birthday** (Three Purities)
- 24th · **Han Zhongli's Ascension** (Eight Immortals)
- 26th · **Ma Danyang's Birthday** (Seven Perfected Beings)
- 28th · **Lü Dongbin's Ascension** (Eight Immortals)

July 2005

- 6th · **New Moon** (Altar 'Opening' and Cleaning)
- 18th · **Lu Ban's Birthday** (Immortal of Woodworking and Carpentry)
  · **Wang Lingguan's Birthday** (Taoist Temple Protector)
- 20th · **Full Moon** (Altar 'Opening' and Cleaning)
  · **Liu Haichan's Ascension** (Five Northern Patriarchs)
  · **Wang Xuanpu's Birthday** (Five Northern Patriarchs)
- 24th · **Guan Yin's Enlightenment** (Goddess of Mercy)
- 25th · **Beidou's Birthday** (Nine Kings of the Northern Dipper)
- 28th · **Huo Shen's Birthday** (Fire God)
  · **Wang Lingguan's Birthday** (Taoist Temple Protector)
- 29th · **Lei Shen's Birthday** (Thunder God)
- 30th · **Lan Caihe's Birthday** (Eight Immortals)
- 31st · **Erlang's Birthday** (Fighter of Floods and Demons)

TAOIST WORSHIP

August 2005

- 5th . **New Moon** (Altar 'Opening' and Cleaning)
- 11th . **Festival of the Seven Sisters** (Great Jade Emperor's Daughters – Celebration of Mediums and Shamans)
- 14th . **Li Tieguai's Birthday** (Eight Immortals)
- 19th . **Full Moon** (Altar 'Opening' and Cleaning)
  . **Zhongyuan Diguan's Birthday** (Earthly Official)
- 22nd . **Xi Wangmu's Birthday** (Queen Mother of the West)
- 23rd . **All Jiazi Deities' Birthdays** (Annual Protectors of the Sixty-Year Cycle)
- 24th . **Liu Changsheng's Birthday** (Seven Perfected Beings)

September 2005

- 3rd . **Dizhang Wang's Birthday** (King of the Underworld)
- 4th . **New Moon** (Altar 'Opening' and Cleaning)
  . **Xu Xun's Ascension** (Founder of Jingming Taoism)
- 6th . **Zaojun's Birthday** (Kitchen God)
- 13th . **Beiyue Dadi's Birthday** (Northern Heng Mountain Great Emperor)
- 14th . **Ge Xuan's Ascension** (Immortal Uncle of Ge Hong)
- 18th . **Chang E Festival** (Moon Goddess)
  . **Full Moon** (Altar 'Opening' and Cleaning)
- 30th . **Confucius' Birthday** (Venerated by Taoists)

Front Gate
Dragon Tiger Mountain
Jiangxi Province

89

October 2005

- **1**st. **Erlang's Birthday** (Fighter of Floods and Demons)
- **3**rd. **Beidou Descends to Earth** (Seven Star Gods of the Northern Dipper)
  - **Nandou Descends to Earth** (Six Star Lords of the Southern Dipper)
  - **New Moon** (Altar 'Opening' and Cleaning)
- **11**th. **Beidou's Birthday** (Nine Kings of the Northern Dipper)
  - **Doumu Yuanjun's Birthday** (Star Mother Goddess)
  - **Fengdu Emperor's Birthday** (Judge of Hell)
  - **Guan Gong's Ascencion** (Immortal General Representing Virtue)
  - **Immortal Ge's Birthday** (Ge Hong)
  - **Jiutian Xuannu Niangniang Festival** (Mysterious Lady of the 9th Heaven)
  - **Li Nezha's Birthday** (Boy Immortal)
  - **Wang Chongyang's Birthday** (Five Northern Patriarchs)
  - **Yang's Annual Nadir**
  - **Zhang Sanfeng's Birthday** (Creator of *Taiji quan*)
  - **Zhenwu Dadi's Ascension** (Dark Emperor of the North)
- **17**th. **Full Moon** (Altar 'Opening' and Cleaning)
- **19**th. **Cai Shen's Birthday** (God of Wealth)
- **21**st. **Guan Yin's Ascension** (Goddess of Mercy)
- **25**th. **Sazu Zhenren's Birthday** (Sa Shoujian)

Elaborate Front Gate
Qingcheng Mountain
Sichuan Province

TAOIST WORSHIP

November 2005

- 2nd . **New Moon** (Altar 'Opening' and Cleaning)
- 4th . **Mao Ying's Birthday** (Three Mao Brothers)
       . **San Mao Zhenjun Festival** (Three Mao Brothers)
- 11th . **Zhang Guolao's Birthday** (Eight Immortals)
- 15th . **Fuxi Festival** (Patron of Divination)
- 16th . **Full Moon** (Altar 'Opening' and Cleaning)
       . **Xiayuan Shuiguan's Birthday** (Water Official)
- 19th . **Mao Ying's Ascension** (Three Mao Brothers)
- 20th . **Qiu Chuji's Ascension to Heaven** (Seven Perfected Beings)

December 2005

- 1st . **New Moon** (Altar 'Opening' and Cleaning)
- 6th . **Xiyue Dadi's Birthday** (Hua Mountain Great Emperor)
- 11th . **Taiyi Jiuku Tianzun Festival** (Great Savior From Suffering)
- 15th . **Full Moon** (Altar 'Opening' and Cleaning)
- 19th . **Riguang Taizi's Birthday** (Deity of Sunlight)
- 23rd . **Nandou Ascends to Heaven** (Six Star Lords of the Southern Dipper)
       . **Zhang Guolao's Birthday** (Eight Immortals)
- 31st . **New Moon** (Altar 'Opening' and Cleaning)

Yue Fei
(Four Divine Marshals)

Zhao Gongming
(Four Divine Marshals)

January 2006

- 8th — Han Xiangzi's Birthday (Eight Immortals)
- 13th — Liu Haichan's Birthday (Five Northern Patriarchs)
- 14th — Full Moon (Altar 'Opening' and Cleaning)
- 15th — Nanyue Dadi's Birthday (Southern Heng Mountain Great Emperor)
- 21st — Hao Taigu's Ascension (Seven Perfected Beings)
  - Ma Danyang's Ascension (Seven Perfected Beings)
  - Wang Chongyang's Birthday (Five Northern Patriarchs)
- 23rd — Kitchen God Reports to the Great Jade Emperor
- 24th — Great Jade Emperor Inspects the Mortal World
- 28th — Sun Bu'er's Ascension (Seven Perfected Beings)
- 29th — New Moon (Altar 'Opening' and Cleaning)
  - Yuanshi Tianzun's Birthday (Jade Purity)
- 31st — Hao Taigu's Birthday (Seven Perfected Beings)

February 2006

- 1st — All Deities Descend to the Mortal World
- 2nd — Cai Shen's Birthday (God of Wealth)
  - Sun Bu'er's Birthday (Seven Perfected Beings)
- 5th — Zhu Rong's Birthday (Fire God)
- 6th — Yuhuang Dadi's Birthday (Great Jade Emperor)
- 12th — Full Moon (Altar 'Opening' and Cleaning)
  - Lantern Festival
  - Shangyuan Tian Guan's Birthday (Heavenly Official)
  - Wang Xuanpu's Ascension (Five Northern Patriarchs)
- 16th — Qiu Chuji's Birthday (Seven Perfected Beings)

March 2006

- 3rd
  - **Tudi Gong Festival** (Land/Earth God)
  - **Wenchang Dijun's Birthday** (God of Culture and Literature)
- 5th
  - **Dong Hua Dijun's Birthday** (Eastern Emperor)
  - **Liu Changsheng's Ascension** (Seven Perfected Beings)
- 12th
  - **Ge Xianweng's Birthday** (Ge Hong)
- 14th
  - **Full Moon** (Altar 'Opening' and Cleaning)
  - **International Taoism Day**
  - **Taishang Laojun's Birthday** (Laozi Great Purity)
- 18th
  - **Guan Yin's Birthday** (Goddess of Mercy)
- 28th
  - **Mazu's Ascension** (Goddess of the South China Sea)
- 29th
  - **New Moon** (Altar 'Opening' and Cleaning)
  - **Tan Chengzhen's Birthday** (Seven Perfected Beings)
- 31st
  - **Qingming Festival** (Cleaning of Gravesites)
  - **Xiwang Mu's Birthday** (Queen Mother of the West)
  - **Yin's Annual Nadir**
  - **Zhenwu Dadi's Birthday** (Dark Emperor of the North)

April 2006

- 12th
  - **Full Moon** (Altar 'Opening' and Cleaning)
  - **Zhang Tianshi's** (Celestial Master Zhang)
  - **Zhao Gongming's Birthday** (Four Divine Marshals)
- 13th
  - **Wang Yuyang's Birthday** (Seven Perfected Beings)
- 15th
  - **Zhongyue Dadi's Birthday** (Song Mountain Great Emperor)
- 20th
  - **Mazu's Birthday** (Goddess of the South China Sea)
- 25th
  - **Dongyue Dadi's Birthday** (Eastern Mountain Great Emperor)
- 28th
  - **New Moon** (Altar 'Opening' and Cleaning)
  - **Tan Changzhen's Ascension** (Seven Perfected Beings)

May 2006 　日　五月

- **5**ᵗʰ　. **He Xiangu's Birthday** (Eight Immortals)
- **11**ᵗʰ　. **Lü Dongbin's Birthday** (Eight Immortals)
- **12**ᵗʰ　. **Full Moon** (Altar 'Opening' and Cleaning)
  - . **Han Zhongli's Birthday** (Eight Immortals)
- **14**ᵗʰ　. **Goddess of Midwifery's Birthday**
- **15**ᵗʰ　. **Beiji Ziwei Dadi's Birthday** (Great Emperor of Purple Tenuity & the Northern Pole)
  - . **Bi Xia's Birthday** (Princess of the Azure Clouds)
  - . **Hua Tuo's Birthday** (Immortal Physician and *Qigong* Master)
- **17**ᵗʰ　. **Yan Guang's Birthday** (Lady of Good Eyesight)
- **20**ᵗʰ　. **Wang Yuyang's Ascension** (Seven Perfected Beings)
- **25**ᵗʰ　. **Yao Wang's** (Sun Simiao - Medicine King)
- **27**ᵗʰ　. **Nanji Changsheng Dadi's Birthday** (Southern Pole Long Life Great Emperor)
  - . **New Moon** (Altar 'Opening' and Cleaning)
- **31**ˢᵗ　. **Annual Ascendancy of Yang**
  - . **Duan Wu Jie** (Dragon Boat Festival)
  - . **Zhang Daoling Festival** (Celestial Master Zhang)
  - . **Zhong Kui Festival** (Exorcistic Protector)

June 2006 　六月

- **6**ᵗʰ　. **Cheng Huang's Birthday** (City Deity)
- **8**ᵗʰ　. **Guan Gong's Birthday** (Immortal General Representing Virtue)
- **10**ᵗʰ　. **Full Moon** (Altar 'Opening' and Cleaning)
  - . **Lingbao Tianzun's Birthday** (Three Purities)
- **13**ᵗʰ　. **Han Zhongli's Ascension** (Eight Immortals)
- **15**ᵗʰ　. **Ma Danyang's Birthday** (Seven Perfected Beings)
- **17**ᵗʰ　. **Lü Dongbin's Ascension** (Eight Immortals)

TAOIST WORSHIP

July 2006

8th	.	**Lu Ban's Birthday** (Immortal of Woodworking and Carpentry)
	.	**Wang Lingguan's Birthday** (Taoist Temple Protector)
10th	.	**Full Moon** (Altar 'Opening' and Cleaning)
	.	**Liu Haichan's Ascension** (Five Northern Patriarchs)
	.	**Wang Xuanpu's Birthday** (Five Northern Patriarchs)
14th	.	**Guan Yin's Enlightenment** (Goddess of Mercy)
15th	.	**Beidou's Birthday** (Nine Kings of the Northern Dipper)
18th	.	**Huo Shen's Birthday** (Fire God)
	.	**Wang Lingguan's Birthday** (Taoist Temple Protector)
19th	.	**Lei Shen's Birthday** (Thunder God)
20th	.	**Lan Caihe's Birthday** (Eight Immortals)
21st	.	**Erlang's Birthday** (Fighter of Floods and Demons)
25th	.	**New Moon** (Altar 'Opening' and Cleaning)
31st	.	**Festival of the Seven Sisters** (Great Jade Emperor's Daughters –Celebration of Mediums and Shamans)

August 2006

3rd	.	**Li Tieguai's Birthday** (Eight Immortals)
8th	.	**Full Moon** (Altar 'Opening' and Cleaning)
	.	**Zhongyuan Diguan's Birthday** (Earthly Official)
11th	.	**Xi Wangmu's Birthday** (Queen Mother of the West)
12th	.	**All 60 Jiazi Deities' Birthdays** (Annual Protectors of the Sixty-Year Cycle)
13th	.	**Liu Changsheng's Birthday** (Seven Perfected Beings)
23rd	.	**Dizhang Wang's Birthday** (King of the Underworld)

95

THE TAOIST MANUAL

September 2006

22nd . **New Moon** (Altar 'Opening' and Cleaning)
       . **Xu Xun's Ascension** (Founder of Jingming Taoism)
24th . **Zaojun's Birthday** (Kitchen God)

October 2006

1st   . **Beiyue Dadi's Birthday** (Northern Heng Mountain Great Emperor)

2nd   . **Ge Xuan's Ascension** (Immortal Uncle of Ge Hong)

6th   . **Chang E Festival** (Moon Goddess)
      . **Full Moon** (Altar 'Opening' and Cleaning)

18th . **Confucius' Birthday** (Venerated by Taoists)

19th . **Erlang's Birthday** (Fighter of Demons and Floods)

22nd . **Beidou to Earth** (Nine Kings of the Northern Dipper)
      . **Nandou Descends to Earth** (Six Star Lords of the Southern Dipper)
      . **New Moon** (Altar 'Opening' and Cleaning)

30th . **Beidou's Birthday** (Nine Kings of the Northern Dipper)
      . **Doumu Yuanjun's Birthday** (Star Mother Goddess)
      . **Fengdu Emperor's Birthday** (Judge of Hell)
      . **Guan Gong Ascencion** (Immortal General Representing Virtue)
      . **Immortal Ge's Birthday** (Ge Hong)
      . **Jiutian Xuannu Niangniang Festival** (Mysterious Lady of the 9th Heaven)
      . **Li Nezha's Birthday** (Boy Immortal)
      . **Wang Chongyang's Birthday** (Five Northern Patriarchs)

TAOIST WORSHIP

November 2006

- 5th   . **Full Moon** (Altar 'Opening' and Cleaning)
- 7th   . **Cai Shen's Birthday** (God of Wealth)
         . **Guan Yin's Ascension** (Goddess of Mercy)
- 13th   . **Sa Zu Zhenren's Birthday** (Sa Shoujian)
- 21st   . **New Moon** (Altar 'Opening' and Cleaning)
- 23rd   . **Mao Ying's Birthday** (Three Mao Brothers)
         . **San Mao Zhenjun Festival** (Three Mao Brothers)
- 30th   . **Zhang Guolao's Birthday** (Eight Immortals)

December 2006

- 4th   . **Fuxi Festival** (Patron of Divination)
- 5th   . **Full Moon** (Altar 'Opening' and Cleaning)
         . **Xiayuan Shuiguan's Birthday** (Water Official)
- 8th   . **Mao Ying's Ascension** (Three Mao Brothers)
- 9th   . **Qiu Chuji's Ascension to Heaven** (Seven Perfected Beings)
- 20th   . **New Moon** (Altar 'Opening' and Cleaning)
- 25th   . **Xiyue Dadi's Birthday** (Hua Mountain Great Emperor)
- 30th   . **Taiyi Jiuku Tianzun Festival** (Great Savior From Suffering)

Ma Sheng
(Four Divine Marshals)

Wen Qiong
(Four Divine Marshals)

January 2007

- 3rd . **Full Moon** (Altar 'Opening' and Cleaning)
- 7th . **Riguang Tianzi's Birthday** (Deity of Sunlight)
- 11th . **Nandou Ascends to Heaven** (Six Star Lords of the Southern Dipper)
  - . **Zhang Guolao's Birthday** (Eight Immortals)
- 19th . **New Moon** (Altar 'Opening' and Cleaning)
- 27th . **Han Xiangzi's Birthday** (Eight Immortals)

February 2007

- 1st . **Liu Haichan's Birthday** (Five Northern Patriarchs)
- 2nd . **Full Moon** (Altar 'Opening' and Cleaning)
- 3rd . **Nanyue Dadi's Birthday** (Southern Heng Mountain Emperor)
- 9th . **Hao Taigu's Ascension** (Seven Perfected Beings)
  - . **Ma Danyang's Ascension** (Seven Perfected Beings)
  - . **Wang Chongyang's Birthday** (Five Northern Patriarchs)
- 11th . **Kitchen God Reports to the Jade Emperor**
- 12th . **Great Jade Emperor Inspects the Mortal World**
- 16th . **Sun Bu'er's Ascension** (Seven Perfected Beings)
- 18th . **New Moon** (Altar 'Opening' and Cleaning)
  - . **Yuanshi Tianzun's Birthday** (Jade Purity)
- 20th . **Hao Taigu's Birthday** (Seven Perfected Beings)
  - . **Yao Wang's Birthday** (Sun Simiao, Medicine King)
- 21st . **All Deities Descend to the Mortal World**
- 22nd . **Cai Shen's Birthday** (God of Wealth)
  - . **Sun Bu'er's Birthday** (Seven Perfected Beings)
- 25th . **Zhu Rong's Birthday** (Fire God)

TAOIST WORSHIP

March 2007

- 4th
  - . **Full Moon** (Altar 'Opening' and Cleaning)
  - . **Lantern Festival**
  - . **Shangyuan Tianguan's Birthday** (Heavenly Official)
  - . **Wang Xuanpu's Ascension** (Five Northern Patriarchs)
- 8th
  - . **Qiu Chuji's Birthday** (Seven Perfected Beings)
- 19th
  - . **New Moon** (Altar 'Opening' and Cleaning)
- 20th
  - . **Tudi Gong Festival** (Earth/Land God)
- 21st
  - . **Wenchang Dijun's Birthday** (God of Culture and Literature)
- 24th
  - . **Donghua Dijun's Birthday** (Eastern Emperor)
  - . **Liu Changsheng's Ascension** (Seven Perfected Beings)
- 31st
  - . **Ge Xianweng's Birthday** (Ge Hong)

April 2007

- 2nd
  - . **Full Moon** (Altar 'Opening' and Cleaning)
  - . **International Taoism Day**
  - . **Taishang Laojun's Birthday** (Laozi – Great Purity)
- 6th
  - . **Guan Yin's Birthday** (Goddess of Mercy)
- 16th
  - . **Mazu's Ascension** (Goddess of the South China Sea)
- 17th
  - . **New Moon** (Altar 'Opening' and Cleaning)
  - . **Tan Chengzhen's Birthday** (Seven Perfected Beings)
- 19th
  - . **Qingming Festival** (Cleaning of Gravesites)
  - . **Xiwang Mu's Birthday** (Queen Mother of the West)
  - . **Yin's Annual Nadir**
  - . **Zhenwu Dadi's Birthday** (Dark Emperor of the North)

May 2007

- 1st
  - . **Full Moon** (Altar 'Opening' and Cleaning)
  - . **Zhang Tianshi's Birthday** (Celestial Master Zhang)
  - . **Zhao Gongming's Birthday** (Four Divine Marshals)
- 2nd
  - . **Wang Yuyang's Birthday** (Seven Perfected Beings)

日　　　　　　　　　　　　　　　　　　　　　　　　　　　　　　　　　五月

- 4th . **Zhongyue Dadi's Birthday** (Song Mountain Emperor)
- 9th . **Mazu's Birthday** (Goddess of the South China Sea)
- 14th . **Dongyue Dadi's Birthday** (Eastern Mountain Emperor)
- 17th . **New Moon** (Altar 'Opening' and Cleaning)
  . **Tan Chengzhen's Ascension** (Seven Perfected Beings)
- 26th . **He Xiangu's Birthday** (Eight Immortals)
- 30th . **Lü Dongbin's Birthday** (Eight Immortals)
- 31st . **Full Moon** (Altar 'Opening' and Cleaning)
  . **Han Zhongli's Birthday** (Eight Immortals)

June 2007

- 2nd . **Goddess of Midwifery's Birthday**
- 3rd . **Beiji Ziwei Dadi's Birthday** (Great Emperor of Purple Tenuity & the Northern Pole)
  . **Bi Xia's Birthday** (Princess of the Azure Clouds)
  . **Hua Tuo's Birthday** (Immortal Physician and Qigong Master)
- 5th . **Yan Guang's Birthday** (Lady of Good Eyesight)
- 8th . **Wang Yuyang's Ascension** (Seven Perfected Beings)
- 13th . **Yao Wang's Birthday** (Sun Simiao, Medicine King)
- 15th . **Nanji Changsheng Dadi's Birthday** (Southern Pole Long Life Great Emperor)
  . **New Moon** (Altar 'Opening' and Cleaning)
- 19th . **Ascendancy of Yang**
  . **Duan Wu Jie** (Dragon Boat Festival)
  . **Zhang Tianshi's Festival** (Celestial Master Zhang)
  . **Zhong Kui Festival** (Exorcistic Protector)
- 25th . **Cheng Huang's Birthday** (City Deity)
- 27th . **Guan Gong's Birthday** (Immortal General Representing Virtue)
- 29th . **Full Moon** (Altar 'Opening' and Cleaning)

July 2007

- 2nd · **Han Zhongli's Ascension** (Eight Immortals)
- 4th · **Ma Danyang's Birthday** (Seven Perfected Beings)
- 6th · **Lü Dongbin's Ascension** (Eight Immortals)
- 14th · **New Moon** (Altar 'Opening' and Cleaning)
- 26th · **Lu Ban's Birthday** (Immortal of Woodworking and Carpentry)
  · **Wang Lingguan's Birthday** (Taoist Temple Protector)
- 28th · **Full Moon** (Altar 'Opening' and Cleaning)
  · **Liu Haichan's Ascension** (Five Northern Patriarchs)
  · **Wang Xuanpu's Birthday** (Five Northern Patriarchs)

August 2007

- 1st · **Guan Yin's Enlightenment** (Goddess of Mercy)
- 2nd · **Beidou's Birthday** (Nine Kings of the Northern Dipper)
- 5th · **Huo Shen's Birthday** (Fire God)
  · **Wang Lingguan's Birthday** (Taoist Temple Protector)
- 6th · **Lei Shen's Birthday** (Thunder God)
- 7th · **Lan Caihe's Birthday** (Eight Immortals)
- 8th · **Erlang's Birthday** (Fighter of Floods and Demons)
- 13th · **New Moon** (Altar 'Opening' and Cleaning)
- 19th · **Festival of the Seven Sisters** (Jade Emperor's Daughters, Celebration of Mediums and Shamans)
- 22 · **Li Tieguai's Birthday** (Eight Immortals)
- 27th · **Full Moon** (Altar 'Opening' and Cleaning)
  · **Zhongyuan Diguan's Birthday** (Earthly Official)
- 30th · **Xiwang Mu's Birthday** (Queen Mother of the West)
- 31st · **All 60 Jiazi Deities' Birthdays** (Annual Protectors of the 60-Year Cycle)

日　　　　　**September 2007**　　　　　　　　　　九月

- 1st . **Liu Changsheng's Birthday** (Seven Perfected Beings)
- 10th . **Dizhang Wang's Birthday** (King of the Underworld)
- 11th . **New Moon** (Altar 'Opening' and Cleaning)
  - . **Xu Xun's Ascension** (Founder of Jingming Taoism)
- 13th . **Zaojun's Birthday** (Kitchen God)
- 20th . **Beiyue Dadi's Birthday** (Northern Heng Mountain Great Emperor)
- 21st . **Ge Xuan's Ascension** (Immortal Uncle of Ge Hong)
- 25th . **Chang E Festival** (Moon Goddess)
  - . **Full Moon** (Altar 'Opening' and Cleaning)

October 2007　　　　　　　　　　十月

- 7th . **Confucius' Birthday** (Venerated by Taoists)
- 8th . **Erlang's Birthday** (Fighter of Floods and Demons)
- 11th . **Beidou Descends to Earth**
  - . **Nandou Descends to Earth**
  - . **New Moon** (Altar 'Opening' and Cleaning)
  - . **Wang Chongyang Festival** (Five Northern Patriarchs)
- 19th . **Beidou's Birthday** (Nine Kings of the Northern Dipper)
  - . **Doumu Yuanjun's Birthday** (Star Mother Goddess)
  - . **Fengdu Emperor's Birthday** (Judge of Hell)
  - . **Guan Gong's Ascension** (Immortal General Representing Virtue)
  - . **Immortal Ge's Birthday** (Ge Hong)
  - . **Jiutian Xuannu Niangniang's Festival** (Mysterious Lady of the 9th Heaven)
  - . **Li Nezha's Birthday** (Boy Immortal)
  - . **Wang Chongyang's Birthday** (Five Northern Patriarchs)
  - . **Xuanwu Dadi's Ascension** (Dark Emperor of the North)
  - . **Yang's Annual Nadir**
  - . **Zhang Sanfeng's Birthday** (Creator of Taiji Quan)
- 25th . **Full Moon** (Altar 'Opening' and Cleaning)
- 27th . **Cai Shen's Birthday** (God of Wealth)
- 29th . **Guan Yin's Ascension** (Goddess of Mercy)

TAOIST WORSHIP

November 2007

- 2nd . Sazu Zhenren's Birthday (Sa Shoujian)
- 10th . New Moon (Altar 'Opening' and Cleaning)
- 12th . San Mao Zhenjun's Festival (Three Mao Brothers)
  . Mao Ying's Birthday (Eldest of Three Mao Brothers)
- 19th . Zhang Guolao's Birthday (Eight Immortals)
- 23rd . Fuxi's Festival (Patron of Divination)
- 24th . Xiayuan Shuiguan's Birthday (Water Official)
  . Full Moon (Altar 'Opening' and Cleaning)
- 27th . Mao Ying's Ascension (Eldest of Three Mao Brothers)
- 28th . Qiu Chuji's Ascension (Seven Perfected Beings)

December 2007

十二月

- 10th . New Moon (Altar 'Opening' and Cleaning)
- 15th . Xiyue Dadi's Birthday (Hua Mountain Great Emperor)
- 20th . Taiyi Jiuku Tianzun's Festival (Great Savior From Suffering)
- 24th . Full Moon (Altar 'Opening' and Cleaning)
- 28th . Riguang Tianzi's Birthday (Deity of Sunlight)

East Peak Staircase — Hua Mountain — Shaanxi Province

2.10 Taoist Prayer

Prayer (along with meditation) is the absolute fundamental bedrock of Taoist practice. Most Taoists pray on a regular basis. Taoist prayer, however, can be a complicated business. It can take years of training before one is prepared for, or can properly execute, advanced Taoist prayer.

One doesn't, however, have to engage in such complicated prayer. Most Westerners have some exposure to prayer, whether from previous experience in typical Western houses of worship, or from bedside prayer rituals performed as children. In this instance, 'go with what you know.' Have faith in your newly built, self-consecrated altar and pray with reverence, sincerity, and regularity. Remember, the more often you open this particular line of communication, the stronger it will become.

Basic Prayers Suggestions

There are some basic meditation instructions regarding which everyone should be aware. These guidelines can be applied to practically all meditations within the Taoist tradition.

Try to pray at your altar whenever possible. Repeated and regular use will increase the power of your altar and provide you with significant benefits in terms of your practice.

Always undertake your basic ritual prior to prayer. This ritual prepares both you and your altar space for the impending prayers. Think of it as being similar to physical stretching before exercise.

If you are prohibited from using your altar, skip your prayers (except in times of emergency). These prohibitions, whether or not we understand them or agree with them, are a traditional part of Taoist practice.

Taoist Practitioners in China often pray in conjunction with requests of the deities; while this is OK, you should also pray as a means of giving thanks, centering, etc. The ultimate focus of your altar and your practice is not what Taoism or its deities can do for you, but is to provide you with a gateway through which you may be able to elevate your own spiritual energy.

If you are meditating in a seated or kneeling position, assume a 'yin-yang' hand position as follows: with your left hand in a relaxed position, touch the tip of your thumb to the tip of your ring finger. With your right hand in a relaxed position, touch the tip of your right thumb to the inner third knuckle of your left ring finger, while simultaneously touching the tip of your right ring finger to the outer third knuckle of your left ring finger. The resulting position is considered to symbolize the *'yin-yang'* symbol. Rest your hands in this position in front of your navel area.

Although it is not necessary to know specific Taoist prayers, or to be fluent in Taoist ritual protocol or mannerisms, in order to effectively pray at your altar, the following is a brief example of a translated Taoist prayer. Its sole purpose is to provide a clear example of the type of prayers frequently used by Taoists, and perhaps to give you ideas on how to develop your own style or corpus.

According to Michael Saso's **Taoist Master Chuang**:

> "...the nine stars of the northern heaven must be especially invoked in order to win power over the Six Jia spirits. That is to say, each of the Six Jia spirits is a general leading an army of spiritual soldiers. All are ready to leap forth at the summons of the Taoist...".

Thus the Taoist recites the following prayer to the Tian Xin Star (one of the nine stars of the northern heaven):

Out of the chaos came the first gestation.
Floating above, pure and clean.
Yang, like a diamond, moved and created.
Yuan Xiang Li Zhen! (The Trigram Ch'ien)
The four seasons were put in order,
The myriad creatures brought forth by
transformation!

Six dragons await your majesties!
Used to transport precious gems!
Beautiful, resplendent, awesome, dreadful!
Generals leading a multitude of the realized immortals
In front of and behind the Six Jia spirits,
A hundred million fighting troops!
I do here and now command you,
Together assemble, in purity and quiet.

This prayer is not recited free-form, but rather in the exact order in which it was written. Taoists believe that otherwise it will not have the desired invocative impact.

Many Taoists begin and end each day with a structured recitation of such prayers, called *gongke*. As an example, the Complete Perfection Taoists at Beijing's White Cloud Monastery recite prayers each morning and evening according to a complicated outline.

Gongke

Morning prayers may include:

The Clear and Pure Rhythm, the Hanging Rhythm, the Outline Rhythm, the Divine Incantation for Purifying the Mind, the Divine Incantation for Purifying the Mouth, the Divine Incantation for Purifying the Body, the Incantation for Pacifying the Earth Spirits, the Divine Incantation for Purifying Heaven and Earth, the Joss Stick Prayer Incantation, the Divine Incantation of Golden Light, the Mysterious and Profound Incantation, the Book of the Supreme Venerable Sovereign's Teachings on Eternal Purity and Tranquility, The Supreme Sublime Book of the Numinous Treasure of Pervasive Mystery for Ascending to Mystery, Eliminating Calamities and Protecting Lives, the Perfect Book of the Supreme Heavenly Lord of the Numinous Treasure's Teachings on Averting Misfortunes and Adversities, the Lofty Jade Emperor's Sublime Book of the Mind Seal, the Precious Declarations of Jade Clarity, the Precious Declarations of the Highest Clarity, the Precious Declarations of Supreme Clarity, the Precious Declarations of the Jade Emperor, the Precious Declarations of the Heavenly Emperor, the Precious Declarations of the Stellar Ruler, the Precious Declarations of the Earth God, the Precious Declarations of the South Pole, the Precious Declarations of the Five Northern Patriarchs, the Precious Declarations of the Five Southern Patriarchs, the Precious Declarations of the Seven Perfect Ones, the Precious Declarations on Universal Salvation, the Written Prayers to the Sages, the Written Confessions, and the Small Odes for Morning Recitation (also, the Incantations of the Numinous Officials, the Incantations of the Earth Spirits, the Great Conversion, and the Three Conversions).

Evening prayers may include:

The Hanging Rhythm, Offering Joss Sticks to the Heavenly Lord of Supreme Oneness and Benevolence, the Outline Rhythm, the Mysterious and Profound Incantation, the Precious Declarations of the Elder Lady of the Big Dipper, the Precious Declarations of the Three Heavenly Officials, the Precious Declarations of Mysterious Northern Heaven, the Precious Declarations of Patriarch Lü, the Precious Declarations of Patriarch Qiu, the Precious Declarations of Patriarch Sa, the Precious Declarations of the Numinous Officials, the Precious Declarations on Saving the Suffering, the Precious Declarations on Showing Gratitude, the Incantations of the Earth Spirits, the Three Conversions, the Incantation for Offering Sacrifices, and the Incantation for Ending Fasts.

You can see that these Taoists are responsible for learning a good many texts. Moreover, the most famous Taoist texts in the West (such as the *Dao De Jing* and the *Zhuangzi*) are not part of this common prayer outline! You may want to develop your own set of prayers that, respectfully presented time and time again by exact rote, can become your own 'Book of Common Prayer.' You now have an idea of the form and intent of Taoist prayer, and you can also learn to direct your prayers to the deity or deities that you have incorporated into your altar.

It is also important to note that Taoist prayer typically utilizes both mudra (secret and energetically powerful hand gestures) and mantra (secret and energetically powerful sounds or chants). They are used to control and direct energy and spirits for prayerful purposes. Many Taoist prayers also contain what we would typically call spells and incantations, to be used for various interactions with spirits and deities (such as invocation or purification). These things, however, are generally restricted to Taoist initiates, and are typically communicated by a Master or Teacher directly to a disciple or student. It is potentially quite dangerous for someone who is not an initiate and who does not have the benefit of an experienced Taoist's instruction to attempt to engage in these activities. This is one of the areas that may be revealed to you as you further progress along your Taoist path.

2.11 Taoist Meditation

Meditation (along with prayer) is the absolute fundamental bedrock of Taoist practice. Most Taoists meditate on a regular basis. Meditation (*dazuo*) serves to align your energy with that of the Taoist deities, and serves to alter your consciousness so that it is in tune with Taoist sensibilities. Your question should not be *if* you should meditate, but how often, for how long, and under which specific conditions.

Meditation Basics

There are some basic meditation instructions of which everyone should be aware. These guidelines apply to all meditations within the Taoist system, and to many meditations from other systems as well.

First find an appropriate place to meditate. All of you should already have one perfect place: before your new altar! If you are going to meditate inside your house, in front of your altar is the absolute best place to do so. But that is not the only place you can meditate. You may want to meditate outside some days. Meditation under the stars, by a stream, or near an old tree will also provide you a nice experience. The important point

Dazuo

is that your selected place should be quiet and peaceful. There is no such thing as Taoist meditation in front of the television!

Any lighting should be natural and not electric. Sunlight, moonlight, starlight, and candlelight are all perfect for meditation. Avoid excessive use of, and proximity to, electricity during meditation. Electromagnetic impulses can impact the subtle workings of meditative energy.

Make an incense offering. Before I meditate I like to make such an offering, regardless of whether I am inside at my altar or outside in nature. If you are at your altar, you can follow the **basic ritual** described in Chapter 2.6 – *How to Worship*. If you are outside, you can make a similar offering to the five directions (including the center!).

Assume a position as described in Chapter 2.6 – How to Worship. It is again preferable that you sit Taoist-style, on a cushioned, rear-elevated platform (called a 'wedge') with your legs crossed in a lotus position with each ankle resting on the opposite inner thigh or knee. You may, however, still elect to use any position you like, as long as none of your joints are locked, and your spine is straight from the base of the skull to the tailbone. Breathing should always be as deep and natural as possible.

Meditation is best practiced on an empty stomach, but not so empty that your hunger disrupts you! Your digestive process makes energetic demands upon your physical body that are contradictory to the energetic demands of meditation. You should wait at least one, but probably two, hours after eating before attempting to meditate. I prefer to avoid this entire issue by meditating before eating. In this case, however, one should also wait an hour or so after meditating before eating. This will allow your energetic system to slowly return to its normal state before starting its next activity.

Some Taoists prefer to keep their eyes closed during meditation, while some prefer to keep them open just a bit, so that they can see the tips of their noses. For some people the images seen by the eyes are distracting, while for others the lack of images may prompt the mind to distraction. Whatever feels more comfortable is more appropriate.

If you are meditating in a seated or kneeling position, assume a 'yin-yang' hand position as follows: with your left hand in a relaxed position, touch the tip of your thumb to the tip of your ring finger. With your right hand in a relaxed position, press the tip of your right thumb to the inner third knuckle of your left ring finger, while simultaneously touching the tip of your right ring finger to the outer third knuckle of your left ring finger. The resulting position is considered to symbolize the *'yin-yang'* symbol. Rest your hands in this position in front of your navel area.

Now focus inward. Let external stimuli, like assorted sounds, pass by as if they are unable to penetrate your sacred space. Let internal stimuli, like assorted thoughts that may suddenly appear in your mind, melt away and be carried off by the river of energy that passes through you. Keep your focus inward. It helps most people to focus on their breath when external or internal stimuli become too strong. Your breath should be long, slow, even, and deep. At no point should the breath stop, nor should it be rushed.

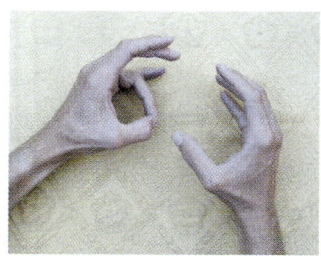

Finally, Taoist tradition holds that the hours between 11 PM — 1 AM are the most appropriate for meditation and related activities. If you are one of the lucky ones who can accommodate this schedule, give it a try. Taoists believe this period of time represents the daily cyclical highpoint of *yin* energy, and the natural universal energy accessible during this period should provide a boost to your meditative efforts.

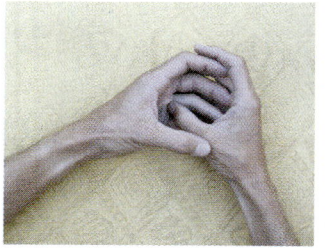

Practice these meditation basics until you become comfortable with them. Whether you are standing, sitting, or kneeling, you will learn a great deal about your energy and your breath from this exercise. You may also notice that particular parts of your body start to ache after a few minutes of meditation. That is probably because your meditation practice is pointing out areas of tension to you. A shoulder pain, for instance, may occur because there is tension in your back muscles. If your posture is correct, you should take this as a helpful message. Is there too much tension in your life? Use your mind to help melt the tension away. Is your spine in good health? Perhaps you need to start a stretching routine, begin learning an internal martial art, or see a professional bodyworker. As you practice more and more, these messages will become your instructions for obtaining further progress. When the messages start to decrease, you will have achieved a significant sensitivity to the energy of your own body, and will be prepared to move forward to the next step. This first step in your meditative process may take several months, and should not be rushed. Patience is a Taoist virtue, and should be thoroughly exercised here!

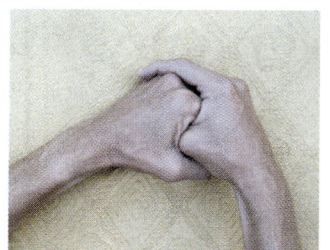

Once you possess a serious understanding of meditation basics, you are ready to begin practicing a basic and simple, yet important, Taoist meditation.

Lower Cinnabar Field Breathing

This practice is the root of all Taoist meditative work. Many of Taoism's more complicated meditations are based on this simple exercise. Assume your favorite meditation position at your favorite meditation spot. Let your hands assume the '*yin-yang*' position described earlier in this chapter. Breathe in and out through your nose in long, slow, even, deep breaths. Instead of just being observant of breath and energy, however, lead your energy with each inhalation from your nose straight down the front of your body to a place Taoists call the Lower Cinnabar Field (the '*xia dan tian*'). It is located an inch or two below your navel, and is recessed an inch or two into the body. Taoists feel the Lower Cinnabar Field in slightly different places, and if you are calm, still, and relaxed your own energy will lead you to yours. If you feel it would assist you, you may place your open palms on top of your Lower Cinnabar Field (one hand on top of the other) or in front of your Lower Cinnabar Field (with fingertips touching).

After a while of practice, you will start to feel a warm buzzing or tingling sensation running down your midsection from your nose area to your Lower Cinnabar Field. This is a positive development, as you are now sufficiently sensitive to feel the energy within your body. This sensation will also help to provide you with a more defined focus as you continue to breathe. Stay relaxed, without locks in the body or undue curves in the spine, and use your sensitivity to follow this energy as it moves downwards. As you do this, the sensations will grow.

It should take an average of *at least* three months of daily practice prior to receiving these sensations. But every body is different, and everyone possesses a different fate. Do not be concerned if you require more or less time. Taoism is not a race that is won by the swift. It is a marathon that rewards the unshakably dedicated.

After you are receiving strong, regular sensations each time your meditate, you should continue with this practice for a couple of additional months before moving forward. See how much you can learn about yourself during this period. Such knowledge will be tremendously valuable to you as you progress along your Taoist path.

Xia Dantian

The Microcosmic Orbit

Once you have completed the process for learning the Lower Cinnabar Field Breathing, you are probably ready to learn the Microcosmic Orbit meditation. The Microcosmic Orbit is really a continuation of the Lower Cinnabar Field Meditation. Once you are able to bring the energy down to your Lower Cinnabar Field, continue using your intent and your breath to bring your energy down further to the base of your trunk. From there bring the energy up around the tailbone and up the spine, over the top of the head and down to the upper palette. That completes your orbit. Make sure the tip of your tongue continually touches your upper palette, as this will connect your orbit and allow your energy to keep flowing.

Do not rush your progress with this meditation! Do not jump ahead of your energy, or of your sensitivity to your energy. Such impatience will not bring benefits to you, and may cause harm. Instead, work on moving the energy slowly, in discrete stages. Eventually you will complete the orbit with a strong and stable meditation foundation.

If you want to proceed further with Taoist meditation, you will need personal guidance from a qualified instructor. Please do not disregard this warning! No inexperienced meditator should attempt to discover for himself the inner energetic workings of Taoist meditation. If you practice incorrectly, you can damage your energetic system, and thus make Taoist spiritual progress more difficult, if not impossible.

You must also have great patience when learning Taoist meditation. Taoists study with meditation teachers for many decades in order to learn important meditation systems and practices. You will not become a Master overnight, nor should you wish to do so. Just take your time and progress at your own speed.

I will share one more advanced Taoist meditation that, because it focuses more on mysticism and less on internal energetic workings, can be practiced safely by those beginners who desire to learn it.

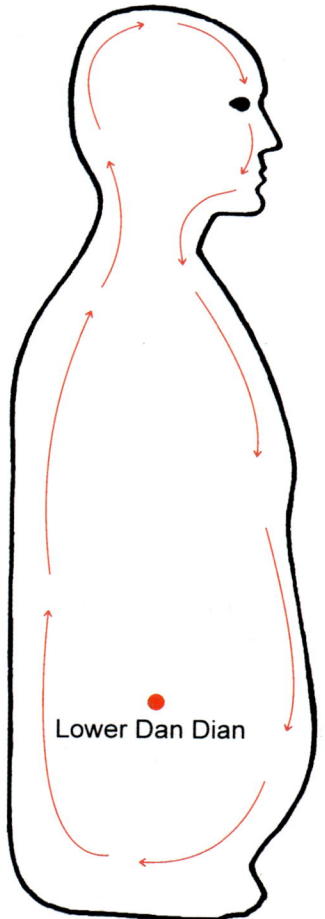

Lower Dan Dian

Healing the Five Organs

This series of seasonal meditations has been dramatically simplified and adapted from ***The Gold Pavilion Classic*** as translated by Michael Saso, and as originated by the great 4th Century Taoist Immortal from Mao Mountain, *Wei Hua Cun*. As with other meditations, it is best to incorporate the **basic ritual** into your preparation process for these meditations.

Spring Meditation

Assume your favorite meditation position at your favorite spot. Perform Lower Cinnabar Field Breathing until you feel calm and centered. With the eyes closed, envision a field of bright green (like grass or moss) in front of you. Breathe this color into your body through the nostrils. Imagine that the bright green circulates down to your toes, and then up around the tailbone, up the spine, over the top of the head, and down to the mouth. The bright green energy revives you, and eliminates cares, worries, or anxieties. Exhale this green through the mouth, and examine it to see if it remains a bright green or if it has become sullied. Repeat the meditation until the color remains bright. At that point inhale the color again and store it in the liver (on the right side of the body just below the rib cage). While doing this press the tip of the thumb on the left hand to the middle joint of the index finger on the left hand. This mudra helps to store the bright green energy in the liver and to recall it whenever such healing is needed.

Summer Meditation

Assume your favorite meditation position at your favorite spot. Perform Lower Cinnabar Field Breathing until you feel calm and centered. With the eyes closed, envision a field of bright pink or red (as a sign of love or affection) in front of you. Breathe this color into your body through the nostrils. Imagine that the bright pink/red circulates down to your toes, and then up around the tailbone, up the spine, over the top of the head, and down to the mouth. The bright pink/red energy helps to cleanse the body of feelings of anger, frustration, or vengeance. Exhale this bright pink/red through the mouth, and examine it to see if it remains a bright pink/red or if it has become sullied. Repeat the meditation until the color remains bright. Then inhale the color again and store it in the heart. While doing this press the tip of the thumb on the left hand to the tip of the middle finger on the left hand. This mudra helps to store the bright pink/red energy in the heart and to recall it whenever you would like to arouse or restore a sense of benevolence.

The Taoist Manual

Fall Meditation

Assume your favorite meditation position at your favorite spot. Perform Lower Cinnabar Field Breathing until you feel calm and centered. With the eyes closed, envision the bright white rays from the brilliant afternoon sun enveloping you. Breathe this bright white energy into your body through the nostrils. Imagine that the bright white energy circulates down to your toes, and then up around the tailbone, up the spine, over the top of the head, and down to the mouth. The bright white energy helps to purify the lungs and rid the entire body of negative or excess sensuality, greed, corruption, or related selfish desires and impure motives. Exhale this white energy through the mouth, and examine it to see if it remains a bright white or if it has become sullied. Repeat the meditation until the color remains bright. Then breathe the color in again and store it in the lungs. While doing this press the tip of the thumb on the left hand to the middle joint of the ring finger on the left hand. This mudra helps to store the bright white energy in the lungs and to recall it whenever one wishes to purify the mind, will, or senses.

Winter Meditation

Assume your favorite meditation position at your favorite spot. Perform Lower Cinnabar Field Breathing until you feel calm and centered. With the eyes closed, envision a field of bright purple (like an orchid or morning glory) in front of you. Breathe this color into your body through the nostrils. Imagine that the bright purple circulates down to your toes, and then up around the tailbone, up the spine, over the top of the head, and down to the mouth. The bright purple energy brings health to the kidneys, creativity to the mind, and deep peace during meditation. Exhale this purple through the mouth, and examine it to see if it remains a bright purple or if it has become sullied. Repeat the meditation until the color remains bright. Then breathe the color in again and store it in the kidneys. While doing this press the tip of the thumb on the left hand to the base of the middle finger on the left hand. This mudra helps to store the purple energy in the kidneys and to recall it whenever one wishes to achieve a state of meditative peace.

TAOIST WORSHIP

Between Seasons Meditation

To be performed at the change from any one season to the next. Assume your favorite meditation position at your favorite spot. Perform Lower Cinnabar Field Breathing until you feel calm and centered. With the eyes closed, envision a field of bright golden yellow in front of you. Breathe this color into your body through the nostrils. Imagine that the bright golden yellow circulates down to your toes, and then up around the tailbone, up the spine, over the top of the head, and down to the mouth. The bright golden yellow energy transforms negative feelings of the body, judgments of the heart, and worries of the spirit into positive healing powers. Exhale this golden yellow through the mouth, and examine it to see if it remains a bright golden yellow or if it has become sullied. Repeat the meditation until the color remains bright. Then breathe the color in again and store it in the spleen. While doing this press the tip of the thumb on the left hand to the middle joint of the middle finger on the left hand. This mudra helps to store the bright golden yellow energy in the spleen and to recall it whenever one desires a positive influence.

When Taoists perform this set of meditations, they follow an infinitely more elaborate set of instructions. Not only are the five organs aligned with the five directions in a very complex mandala, but each of the organs is also home to a resident deity. The deity is called forth and seen in great detail, whereupon it is changed into a sacred symbol and finally into a specific color. Finally even that is washed away so that the meditator can exist in pure emptiness, and can proceed alone to his or her encounter with the tao! But such a complicated process takes many years of intensive training. The beginning Taoist performs a great service for him or herself by learning the meditations as described above.

I would also add that the meditations presented in this chapter, while important to Taoist practice, are by no means the sole available Taoist meditations. There are too many Taoist meditations to count. As your Taoist experience grows, you will undoubtedly learn a good many more. I would again note that Taoist meditations often utilize both mudra and mantra to control and direct energy and spirits for meditative or alchemical purposes. Many Taoist meditations also call for the use of what we would typically call spells and incantations, to be used for various interactions with spirits and deities (such as invocation or purification). Many advanced Taoist meditations will require a practitioner to regulate or even cease the flow of semen (for men) and menstrual blood (for women). It is potentially quite dangerous for someone who is not an initiate and who does not have the benefit of an experienced Taoist's instruction to attempt to engage in these activities. This is one of the areas that may be revealed to you as you further progress along your Taoist path.

2.12 Care of Your Altar

Now you have a Taoist altar, and you know how to put it to basic regular use. As you use your altar, through prayer, meditation, and ritual, its energy will evolve along with your spiritual practice. One of your most important responsibilities will thus be to keep your altar in good working condition.

There are many things you should keep away from your altar. You have gone to great lengths to fill your altar with Taoist energy, and to fill it with the particular energy of your chosen deity or deities. You should respect that energy and those deities. Assume that they are *always* present, and that they are *always* aware of what goes on around your altar.

For this reason a Taoist would physically touch the statue or framed image on his altar as infrequently as possible. A Taoist would neither curse nor use inappropriate language near his altar. Nor should you bring any negative energy near your altar. If you are to engage in an argument, you should do so in some other area. Drug use, as a crude external manipulation of energy, is antithetical to the purpose of your altar, which is to promote natural, internal, energetic improvements.

Sexual relations are sometimes a difficult matter as far as your altar is concerned. Ideally, no Taoist would expose an altar to nudity or sexual relations. Such activity is considered highly inappropriate near a Taoist altar. But many people will not have unlimited space in their homes, and may be forced to locate their altars in their bedrooms. Moreover, some people enjoy sleeping next to an altar (this may help to impart meaningful dreams). How can one live in such close proximity to an altar and still keep profanity to a minimum? Many people tie a blindfold around the eyes of a representation of a deity too shield it from profanity. Some Taoists also place a cloth over the entire representation. I prefer the second method, as I find it to be more respectful, and to involve less physical contact. Either way, the cloth used should be a red silk (unless you have a special reason for thinking that your particular deity would be better served by some other solution). The absolute best solution, however, is still to simply eliminate any offensive or profane behavior from your altar area.

Another difficult issue is often that of other people. Your altar should be a daily part of your life, and should not be readily disassembled and reassembled. In the West, not everyone will have the open-mindedness and experience to appreciate the spiritual direction you have taken, nor the progress you have made in your spiritual life. Taoism has no requirement that all of your friends and family must be Taoists or Taoism Practitioners, but you should attempt to keep your altar space free of disrespectful non-believers.

There are also a number of things you should actively do in order to keep your altar in top condition. Cleanliness will not only be a sign of your respect for your altar, but it will also keep positive energy flowing through it. You will have to decide for yourself how to balance your desire to clean your altar with your desire to minimize physical contact with the representation of your deity. Try to restrict altar cleanings to days that fall on the first or fifteenth of any lunar month, although an emergency (something spilled or dropped) should be dealt with as soon as possible. Remember to make a small offering of thanks (as described in Chapter 2.6 — *How to Worship*) both before and after cleaning your altar.

You should use your altar daily, but don't forget to adhere to the Taoist calendar or to make periodic offerings. These things will help to keep your altar as a positive, beneficial influence in your spiritual life, and will gradually increase the spiritual power available to you through your altar.

If You Need To Remove Your Altar Energy

Traditionally, a new Taoist would work within a community (a home, a temple, a village, or lineage) where he or she could access the knowledge and assistance of more experienced Taoists. Rarely would a new or hopeful Taoist build and operate his or her own altar. The best way to learn about Taoism is to study with an experienced Taoist teacher (See Chapter 5.2 – *Selecting a Teacher*). In the West, however, most people do not have this type of opportunity.

Despite all of our efforts, Taoism remains a wonderfully complex tradition that utilizes and believes in a variety of subtle energies. As a relatively inexperienced person who is nonetheless choosing to work with these energies, you should at least be aware of the possibility that you could incur results from your altar work that you did not intend or do not enjoy. Although it is extremely unlikely, there is always a risk when invoking deities or working with unknown energies, and that risk is compounded when inexperienced people are forced to operate without the benefit of experienced guidance.

What kind of problems could you possibly encounter? In some cases, your altar could simply accumulate an energy that leaves you uncomfortable. This could happen as the result of any one of countless reasons. In more extreme (and extremely rare) cases, you may accidentally invoke an unintended energy as you attempt to invoke a separate energy. In any case, you will know if your altar energy is inappropriate. If you think it is, it is.

Once you have determined that you would like to clean your altar energy, you should do so according to the following process:

Take a Spiritually Cleansing Bath

Before you can cleanse your altar, you need to make sure that your own energy is sufficiently clean. First take a regular shower or bath in order to be physically clean. Then clean your bathtub. Once clean, fill halfway with lukewarm water and add a mixture of one cup apple cider vinegar and one teaspoon sea salt to the water. Enter the tub completely naked and immediately immerse your entire body. Soak for at least five minutes with a minimum of three full body immersions. While you are soaking, pray to the deity or deities of your altar to remove any negative influence or energy that you may feel. Try not to let your mind wander from your prayers. Do not use any soap, as you should be physically clean prior to taking this bath. After your bath, you may cover your body or your hair, but do not towel dry. Allow yourself to air day. You should rest and continue to pray for at least 30-60 minutes after your bath.

Cleanse Your Altar Area

You are now physically and energetically clean enough to attempt to cleanse your altar. Make sure that you are alone in your altar area, without the presence of any pets. You should first make a small offering of thanks (as described in Chapter

2.6 – *How to Worship*) and then physically clean your altar area. This includes the altar itself, any adjoining walls, and the floor. Although this is best done on the 1st or 15th of a lunar month, you are the best judge of the immediacy of your desire to remove inappropriate altar energy.

After you have made an altar offering and physically cleaned your altar space, prepare a mixture of one-ounce creosote oil cleaner (not creosote wood preservative), one-quarter cup of household ammonia, one-teaspoon sea salt, and four gallons of hot water (you may freely adjust the amounts to fit the size of your area, although you should keep the same overall ratio). Having opened any windows in your altar room, use a new mop head to apply this solution to the walls and to the floor. Let the solution air dry.

Perform an Incense Cleansing

While you are still alone in your altar area, and with the windows still open, light some Dragon's Blood resin incense. Your normal incense is fine for most occasions, but if you are attempting to remove an inappropriate energy from your altar space, Dragon's Blood is perhaps the best incense you can use. It is quite obnoxious to most malefic energy forms, while being quite attractive to most positive energetic forms. While praying to your selected altar deity or deities to help purify your altar space, literally offer your incense to the five directions (including center). Bow towards each direction as you make this offering. Do this slowly, and with the intention that the smoke from the incense, along with the aid of the appropriate Taoist deities, will remove any inappropriate energy from your altar and replace with a more comfortable or beneficial energy. Afterwards make an offering at your altar (as described in Chapter 2.6 – *How to Worship*).

After you have taken these steps, you should have removed any problematic energy from your altar area. You should not, however, perform these activities unless you feel that it is absolutely necessary to do so. Most people will never have such a need!

After you have removed any inappropriate or undesired energy from your altar area, your altar will be empty or naked. To perform these activities is equivalent to reformatting your computer's hard drive – everything is deleted without discernment! If you want to continue to use your newly cleansed altar, you must then proceed to 'reopen' your altar according to the procedures outlined in Chapter 2.7 – *'Opening' Your Altar*.

Misterious Lady of the 9th Heaven Temple — Heng Mountain — Shanghai City

3
Fundamental Taoist Activities

3.1 Fundamental Taoist Activities

Religious devotions are indeed an absolute constant across Taoist traditions, but they are by no means the only activity common to all Taoists. There are a number of traditional activities that interest all Taoists. Individual emphases vary according to region, lineage, and personal preference, but almost every Taoist would be familiar with each of these fundamental activities (*genben huodong*).

It is important not to confuse activities commonly beloved and practiced by Taoists for activities that define Taoism. Many people in the West seem to mistakenly believe that their participation in any one of the activities discussed in this chapter makes them Taoists. Many non-Taoists, however, also engage in these activities. These activities are firmly rooted in general traditional Chinese culture. So while Taoists often practice *taiji quan* or *feng shui*, for example, to merely engage in these activities does not make one a Taoist. Even a canonical expert is not necessarily a Taoist (although he or she would still be widely respected by Taoists). Only by following the traditional and ritual dictates of Taoism can one become a Taoist (See Chapter 1.3 – *What is a Taoist*). Anyone interested in Taoism will want to investigate the following activities according to their personality and interests.

Genben Huodong

Zhengtong Daozang

To provide a detailed analysis of any one of these activities would require a book unto itself. Indeed, a Taoist may undertake 100 years of intensive, daily training and only master one or two of these activities. In order to be a master of all, one would need the length of years of a true Immortal, combined with unnatural talent and single-minded focus. But before one can become a masterful Immortal, one has to start by developing, at the very least, a general awareness and basic understanding of all these activities. Once you have achieved that goal, then you can decide for yourself which Taoist activities speak most deeply to your inner self.

3.2 The Canon

The Taoist Canon (the *Daozang*) is the extensive collection of historical writings that comprise the basis of Taoist doctrine and practice. Many people mistakenly assume that the writings of Laozi and Zhuangzi are the sole source of Taoist doctrine. Those two authors actually represent only a miniscule proportion of the traditional Canon!

Fundamental Taoist Activities

The Taoist Canon

The Canon has existed in some form since at least the 4th Century, and early versions are reported to have contained many thousands of volumes. By the 10th Century, however, the Canon was no longer extant, and in 1010 the Emperor ordered a new version to be compiled. By 1118 the Canon had assumed its general modern form, with roughly 5,500 volumes. The current standard version of the Canon was completed in the Ming Dynasty, in 1444-1445 during the reign of the Ming Emperor Zhengtong. It is thus frequently referred to as the 'Zhengtong Daozang.' This version of the Canon was preserved in relative anonymity until 1926, when it was finally lithographed. Thus Western scholars were mostly unaware of the Canon's existence until the 1930's. Modern scholars have high hopes that ancient versions of the Canon are still to be discovered, and that they will provide great insight into Taoism's historical development.

The Canon is divided into three main 'caverns,' each one of which starts with a text mystically revealed by a particularly important Taoist deity. The texts within the Canon not only deal with myriad types of Taoist doctrine and practice, but also contain much information on medicine, botany, astrology, and astronomy. Taoists believe that a good many of the texts were the result of mystical revelations from various deities. It should also be noted that various Taoist lineages use slightly different versions of the Canon, to better reflect their lineal peculiarities.

A Taoist can spend a lifetime studying the Canon. All Taoists study the Canon, but few become true Canonical experts.

Such scholarship requires great intelligence and scholarship, and many decades of dedicated and intensive study. People of such accomplishment are rare, and are widely respected throughout Taoist communities.

Only small parts of the Canon have been translated into Western languages, and very little of the Canon has received serious academic or scholarly attention. Most of the volumes are accessible only to those who can read Classical Chinese. This is not likely to change in the near future. A team of ten professional translators working full-time solely on translating works within the Canon could not finish more than a small percentage of its texts during long and productive careers!

Studying Taoist Works

What should an aspiring Taoist who cannot read Classical Chinese do? If you cannot study the Canon, you should at least emulate the spirit of the great Taoist scholars. You should never be satisfied with your knowledge regarding Taoism. Always know with certainty that your knowledge is insufficient. Read the Taoist books that have been translated into a language you can understand. The number of translated Canonical works will undoubtedly grow over time. Discuss Taoist issues and practices with teachers, scholars, and Taoists. Your own spiritual life is also your best laboratory. You can always delve into your own store of Taoist knowledge to gain a greater understanding. The Canon should represent your quest for this understanding, and your commitment to gaining it.

3.3 Philosophy 哲學

We have already discussed the unfortunate misconception held by many people that Taoism is purely a philosophy (*zhexue*). But while Taoism is indeed a complex religious tradition, we also cannot deny the extremely important role of philosophy in Taoism. Dating all the way back to Laozi, Taoism is a tradition of deep-thinkers. There is much imagery of 'simple-mindedness' surrounding Taoism, but it is only the deep application of Taoist philosophy that provides this appearance. So while Taoism includes much more than just philosophy, it is equally true that all Taoist activities, without exception, occur in front of an omnipresent backdrop of Taoist philosophy.

Fundamental Taoist Activities

Accordingly, all Taoists are philosophers. They read major works of Taoist philosophy over and over, throughout their lives. Part of their purpose is to understand and incorporate into their subconscious minds a Taoist philosophic outlook. Such an outlook is a crucial component of the 'emptiness' required for many Taoist meditations and devotions. It also helps to strengthen one's internal energy, and aids in the Taoist quest for long life. We should note, however, that initiated Taoists are usually taught to interpret many Taoist philosophic works in a unique and sometimes secret manner so as to provide them with great meditative, religious, and ritual insights. Our standard Western interpretations sometimes correspond to these Taoist interpretations, and sometimes they do not.

Major Taoist philosophers and philosophic works (and those that are not strictly Taoist, but are still relevant to Taoism) are summarized below (and available translations listed whenever possible):

Laozi 老子

Taoist legend places Laozi (*Old Master*) as a 6th Century B.C. contemporary of Confucius. While we know with some degree of certainty that Confucius was a historical person, there are academic doubts about Laozi's historical authenticity. What is known is that a book called *The Classic Book of Integrity and the Way* or the *Dao De Jing* was formulated sometime during the 4th Century B.C., and these writings are attributed to a person named Laozi.

This book is a highly poetic rendition of ancient collected oral sayings. The central concept of Laozi's work is *Tao* or *the Way*. Tao is the all-pervading, self-existent, eternal cosmic unity. It is the source from which all things spring, and it the place to where all things must inevitably return. It is unborn and without beginning or end.

Another major concept in Laozi's work is *te*, or the personalized nature of the universal tao. The sum total of your being, your personal slice of the tao, represents your *te*. Taoists seek the tao through the cultivation of *te*. Someone who is able to do this becomes a Sage, an idealized man or ruler. He achieves this through non-action (spontaneity, pure motivation, and non-interference), and a return to the natural state inherent to the cosmic principle from which we all have come. A main focus of the book is thus the creation of a Taoist government or ruler.

Virtue
De

Ancient Seal Script

Taoists worship Laozi as a literal deity, and not merely as the author of a great philosophical treatise. This reverence has lead to the formation of a literary tradition of commentaries on the *Dao De Jing*. Some commentaries, like those of Wang Bi or Heshang Gong, are well-known, but the most obviously Taoist early commentary is the Xiang'er.

Available Translations:

Ames, Roger, *Dao De Jing: A Philosophical Translation* (Ballantine Books)

Bokenkamp, Stephen, *Early Taoist Scriptures* (University of California Press)

Henricks, Robert G., *Lao-Tzu Te-Tao Ching: A New Translation Based on the Recently Discovered Ma-wang-dui Texts* (Ballantine Books)

Mair, Victor, *Tao Te Ching: The Classic Book of Integrity and the Way* (Bantam)

Red Pine (Porter, Bill), *Lau-Tzu's Taoteching* (Mercury House)

Zhuangzi 莊子

Zhuangzi (355? – 275?) was a verifiable historic person who wrote the philosophic book that bears his name. His book was largely a response to the widespread philosophical debates of the Warring States Period (475-221 B.C). While Laozi discusses society and government, Zhuangzi prefers to ignore those themes in favor of personal transcendence. Zhuangzi's method was to skewer any analytic thought process through the use of tales, stories, and jokes. He instead preferred to operate according to nature and intuition. Through total reliance upon nature and intuition to the exclusion of intellect, one can achieve a transforming liberation of the soul. As part of this process, one must avoid absolute judgments and allow for complete equality and diversity in all things.

The *Zhuangzi* is regarded as one of the two most important Taoist philosophic works (along with the *Classic of Integrity and the Way*), but it is also regarded as being among the most beautiful examples of Classical Chinese writing in existence.

Available Translations:

Mair, Victor, *Wandering on the Way: Early Taoist Parables and Tales of Chuang Tzu* (Bantam)

Watson, Burton, *The Complete Works of Chuang Tzu* (Columbia University Press)

Xunzi 荀子

Xunzi (3rd Century B.C.) is not regarded as a mainstream Taoist philosopher, and is generally associated with Confucianism. Yet Xunzi's strangely beautiful conception of heaven as an impersonal, mechanical nature surely owes a debt of gratitude to both Laozi and Zhuangzi. This important philosopher is still worth examination.

Available Translations:

Watson, Burton. *Hsun Tzu: Basic Writings* (Columbia University Press)

Hanfeizi 韓非子

Hanfeizi (d. 233 B.C.) was a student of Xunzi. He was a Prince in the state of Han, and mostly concerned his writings with statecraft. He was primarily a Legalist, but also clearly based his beliefs upon the earlier Laozi and Zhuangzi. The legalistic aspects of Hanfeizi's statecraft attempted to create the state of non-activity addressed by both of those authors.

Available Translations:

Watson, Burton, *Han Fei Tzu* (Columbia University Press)

Huainanzi 淮南子

The *Huainanzi* is a 2nd Century B.C. collection of writings. This book is noted for its description of the origin of the cosmos, which is regarded as being more lucid than most other descriptions. The book also contains important descriptions of *yin yang* and five phase theories (See Chapter 4.2 – *Yin & Yang* and Chapter 4.3 – *Five Phases*, respectively). Of the books' original 53 chapters, only the 21 that directly concern Taoism have survived.

Available Translations:

Major, John S., *Heaven and Earth in Early Han Thought: Chapters Three, Four, and Five of the Huainanzi* (Suny Press)

Hua Hu Ching 化胡經

This book has been the cause of great dispute for many centuries. The title literally means, *The Classic on the Conversion of Barbarians*, and describes Laozi's influence after leaving

China for the 'west.' The book claims that Buddha was a disciple of Laozi. Early Taoists used this belief to counter the growing influence of Buddhism in China, while Buddhists responded by changing the date of Buddha's birth by several centuries, so as to make such a claim impossible. Whether or not the book's claims are authentic, the book is well worth reading.

Available Translations:

Walker, Brian. *Hua Hu Ching: The Unknown Teachings of Lao Tzu* (Harper)

Laozi's Treatise of the Exalted One on Response and Retribution 太上感應篇

This Southern Sung Dynasty (1127 – 1279) work by the Taoist Li Ying Chang established the framework for the development of Complete Perfection Taoism. It includes a healthy synthesis of Taoism, Buddhism, and Confucianism. The book claims that ethical action is the source of good karma or fate.

Available Translations:

Carus, Paul. *Laozi's Treatise to Treatise of the Exalted One on Response and Retribution* (Open Court)

Liezi 列子

Liezi is thought by Taoists to be a 4th Century B.C. contemporary of Zhuangzi. There is considerable doubt as to the historical authenticity of Liezi. Nonetheless, *The True Book of the Expanding Emptiness* is often just called the *Liezi*.

The *Liezi* is similar to the *Zhuangzi* in that it contains a more dismissive attitude towards society. Whereas Laozi advocates an attitude of societal involvement, Liezi believes that nature and life are more mechanical and that man should have a more internal focus rather than attempting to fight fate. Like Zhuangzi, he is fond of making his point through reinterpretation of folk tales and myths.

Available Translations:

Graham, A.C., *The Book of a Lieh-Tzu: A Classic of the Tao* (Morningside Bookshop)

Wong, Eva, *Lieh Tzu: A Taoist Guide to Practical Living* (Shambhala)

Classic
Jing (Ching)

Ancient Seal Script

Zhanbu

All of these works are available in translation, and some in multiple translations. Things have become so silly over the last decade that several 'translators' of ancient Chinese philosophic works cannot even read Classical Chinese, and base their translations on the previously translations of other authors. Avoid these false translators if at all possible.

Most importantly, in order to reach a reasonable understanding of Taoist thought, one should continually read and re-read these works, and seek to apply the lessons therein to one's daily life and Taoist practice. Your meditation, prayer, and ritual will be greatly enhanced by your ability to integrate them into an omnipresent Taoist philosophic outlook.

3.4 Divination

Many Taoists engage in divination (*zhanbu*), although at different times and for different reasons. A Taoist might simply say that a careful study of the past movements of *yin* and *yang* will lead to inescapable conclusions regarding their future movements. But perhaps it's not all that simple. At any rate, aspiring Taoists should be familiar with all of these methods.

Astrology 星占學

Astrology also plays an important role in Taoist divination. While most Westerners are familiar with the twelve Chinese zodiac signs, the traditional Taoist system actually goes much farther. The twelve-year system actually rotates according to Five Phases (See Chapter 4.3 — *Five Phases*), producing a sixty-year cycle. Taoists believe that each year in this cycle is different, and that a person born in any given year will carry the characteristics of that year. Moreover, a particular deity governs each year. The deity governing the year in which you were born may be thought of as your 'patron saint.' It is also interesting to note that many Taoists believe that each household or city requires a special ritual cleansing every sixty years, after this cycle has been completed. Needless to say, Taoist astrology can be quite complex, and requires a good deal of patient study before one becomes truly proficient.

I Ching 易經

The Taoist divination method most commonly known throughout the West is the consultation with the *I Ching*, or

The Book of Changes. The *I Ching* is one of the world's oldest extant books. It originated in the Shang Dynasty (16th Century B.C. – 11th Century B.C.). The book outlines a system of describing the interplay between the forces of *yin* and *yang*. It does so through the use of trigrams, or sets of three lines, with broken lines representing *yin* and solid lines representing *yang*. There are eight possible combinations, each of which has distinct symbolism and related associations:

Qian	☰	Heaven		Earth	☷	Kun	
Li	☲	Fire		Water	☵	Kan	
Sun	☴	Wind		Lake	☱	Dui	
Zhen	☳	Thunder		Mountain	☶	Gen	

Book of Changes
I Ching

Ancient Seal Script

Since trigrams are read one on top of another (producing a hexagram), there are a total of sixty-four potential outcomes. The diviner seeks to randomly obtain a result (by drawing yarrow sticks or tossing coins) in response to a question. The results are then interpreted (along with psychic intuition) and an answer is given.

The overwhelming message of the *I Ching* is a Taoist one: move with the rhythm of *yin* and *yang*, and do not contradict those forces. That is the key to success in every endeavor. Taoists, however, typically access the wisdom of the *I Ching* in a slightly different manner than described above. Instead of the diviner obtaining a hexagram result through some human method, a Taoist deity is allowed to select the appropriate hexagram.

Most Taoist temples have canisters on the eastern ends of their altars that are filled with 64 bamboo sticks (one for each hexagram). People are free to make an offering to the deity of the altar, and then to shake the canister while kneeling in supplication. After a moment or two, one stick invariably emerges from the canister and falls to the ground. The presiding Taoist then interprets that particular response in light of the questioner's concerns.

Moon Blocks 神杯

Another divination method used in Taoist temples throughout Hong Kong, Taiwan, and SE China is the tossing of moon blocks. These blocks are shaped like crescent moons, and are flat on one side and rounded on the other. In chinese they are called *shen bei*, literally 'spirit cups.' A Taoist Practitioner will make an offering at an altar and request the intended deity to fill the 'cups' with observable celestial energy. He will then toss the blocks on the floor in response to a particular question. If both blocks land on their flat side, the answer from the resident deity is 'yes.' If both blocks land on their rounded sides, the answer is 'no.' If there is a mixed result, the answer cannot be determined yet, or the question should not be asked at this time. The sound of crashing wooden blocks so resounds through some temples that one can barely hear oneself think. I have waited in line for over thirty minutes to throw moon blocks at temples in Taiwan!

Planchette 扶乩寫字盤

One means of divination that is commonly seen at Taoist temples is the planchette. The planchette is basically a small sandbox with a sharpened pointing instrument hanging above. A Taoist medium goes into a trance and channels a particular Taoist deity, who then uses the pointing instrument to write out messages in the sand. Specialist assistants stand by recording the writings, and periodically use a bar or rod to smooth the sand in preparation for further writings. After the session is complete, another type of specialist assistant reads and interprets the writing (which is frequently difficult for non-specialists to understand). Many important Taoist books have been obtained this way, as messages received from deities. It is important to note that today Taoists themselves rarely use the planchette, as Taoism generally holds the channelling of spiritual entities to be somewhat heterodox. Taoist temples nonetheless often allow planchette specialists to engage in divination on temple grounds.

Psychism

Almost all meditative traditions produce psychics, and Taoism is no exception. As Taoists delve into their own interior spaces, and as they unite their essence with the tao, they frequently derive different types of psychic abilities (such as precognition, clairaudience, clairvoyance, and astral travel). So the old Taoist sitting on a temple doorstep may well be able to engage in 'divination through meditation.' Most Taoists, however, are very reluctant to demonstrate these abilities. This is because Taoism holds that such abilities are not particularly valuable, and to concern oneself with things of low value is to demonstrate one's unpreparedness for things of higher value. So you should never ask a Taoist to reveal these abilities, but you should always be aware that he or she might possess them!

Astronomy Device
(1500 B.C.)

It is important to note that any items relating to divination that you may keep on your altar (such as books, yarrow sticks, or coins) should be kept on the eastern end of your altar. Assuming your altar faces south, these objects should be kept on the right side as you face your altar.

It is unfortunate, but the Chinese government still looks askance at divinatory activities. Many temples in China either reject all such activity in light of government pressure, or severely restrict it. This does not mean that Chinese Taoists do not engage in divination. They certainly do. But exposure to these ancient methods is rare, and is typically reserved for advanced Taoists or for those with exceptional fate. In Hong Kong, Taiwan, and other places outside China with Taoist communities, however, one can easily find Taoists willing to engage in public divination.

3.5 Talismans 符

Taoists believe that words hold great spiritual power. In ancient times, the mere possession of particular texts (and thus the words contained therein) was thought to deliver immortality to a seeker. This is one important reason why Taoists so typically use mantra in their prayers. Many mudra are in fact based upon physical representations of secret words. Taoists communicate with the deities and spirits of the Taoist universe through the use of such potent words, and they commonly do so through the use of talismans (*fu*).

Good Luck Talisman

Taoist talismans are typically written calligraphic scrolls that are prepared for the dedicated purpose of communicating with a deity or a spirit. Taoists study and create long lists of secret symbols (many based upon versions of Chinese characters) that they believe hold varying degrees of magical or energetic power. In almost all cases, a talisman must be burned after its creation. This serves to transfer the power of the talisman from the human realm to the heavenly realm. If you ever see a talisman in a book or a museum, it is almost undoubtedly not a complete work. The creator of a talisman must affix a particular symbol (or a particular series of symbols) along the bottom of a talisman in order to empower it. Once done, however, the talisman must be quickly used. To raise and focus the energy of a talisman and then not to use it would be to invite difficulty or ill-fortune upon the creator of the talisman, as too much energetic pressure has been stored. It must be released, or the perpetrator must accept the inevitable consequences.

Fundamental Taoist Activities

Talisman
Fu

Ancient Seal Script

Talismans are typically created in preparation for important ritual ceremonies, and are burned in front of an altar during those ceremonies. At a particular point in the ceremony, a Taoist will set the talisman aflame and toss it into the air. It quickly burns, and the Taoist then continues with the ceremony. Taoists believe that a deity is present at an active altar, and they follow precise guidelines in preparing an effective communication with that deity. The burning of the talisman during a ceremony at which the deity is thought to be present guarantees that the deity will receive the intended communication.

As some Taoist deities are thought to reside within the human body, talismans are sometimes burned before an altar in such a way so as to collect the ash from the burned talisman. The ash is then used is a variety of manners, including human consumption. The ash is sometimes mixed with water and drunk. This is a common form of spiritual healing, although it serves other purposes as well. Similarly, some talismans must be pasted or even tattooed onto the body at specific places.

Only initiated Taoists, however, may prepare or utilize talismans. Initiation serves to introduce a new Taoist to the Taoist heavenly realms, and to prepare the new Taoist for interactions with those realms. Without initiation, one cannot hope to use a direct means of communication with Taoist deities like that represented by talismans. Moreover, Taoists are quite protective of their secret written language. The symbols themselves carry power, and Taoists are traditionally quite reluctant to share that power with people who are not part of their tradition (and sometimes even with those who are!).

Remember that any talismans you see are most probably incomplete (and were intentionally left incomplete by their creators). You should not attempt to use complete, traditional talismans until such time as you are an initiated Taoist with a willing Taoist teacher. To do so would be to risk causing danger to yourself by attempting to communicate with or invoke deities or spirits that you do not yet understand or cannot yet manage. This can cause a serious risk to your ability to progress to the upper stages of a Taoist path. But it is also important that you recognize and understand the Taoist talismanic tradition, as it is quite an important aspect of Taoist practice. It is especially (although not exclusively) important to the Taoist lineal traditions that adhere to the five classical sets of Taoist registers.

Standing *Qigong*

3.6 Qigong 氣功

Taoist meditation generally involves the mental control and development of one's *qi* as a means to achieving health and spiritual goals (with the occasional invocation of a deity to aid in this process). *Qigong*, or literally *qi skill* or *qi practice,* is a very similar activity. *Qigong* aims to harness *qi* towards the same goals with a combination of movement, stretching, and mental intent.

Qigong goes by various names, including *Dao Yin* (Leading and Guiding the Energy), *Nei Gong* (Internal Work), *Tu Gu Na Xin* (Expelling Old Energy and Drawing In New Energy), and host of others. No matter which name we use, one thing we know is that Taoists have been engaged in these activities since the beginning of Taoism. The *Dao Yin Classic*, a book formally incorporated into the Taoist Canon (See Chapter 3.2 – The Canon), details *qigong* exercises dating back to the 6th Century. Many ancient *qigong* works are similarly included in the Taoist Canon. It is a strong probability that *qigong* gave birth to the internal martial arts mentioned in the next chapter.

There are countless types of *qigong*. Most are modeled after specific animals or patterns of nature. Some involve standing still and using the breath to move, stimulate, or regulate one's *qi*. Others involve choreographed and sometimes complex movements that combine with one's breath to move, stimulate, or regulate one's *qi*. During *qigong* practice one can often

Neigong

Wudang Mountain Taoist Displays His Skill

feel the buildup of *qi* along one's meridians, or in certain energy points. The results can be as varied as improved health, greater strength, deeper meditations, faster or more explosive martial arts, and stronger projection of healing energy.

Qigong is better practiced with a qualified instructor. It is always somewhat dangerous for someone not experienced with the human energy system to undertake such exercises. That being said, however, there is an amazing number of *qigong* practitioners in the West right now, all of whom have varying skills and backgrounds. Read Chapter 5.2 – *Selecting a Teacher* before engaging in a course of practice.

3.7 Internal Martial Arts

Ancient Taoists lived in a difficult and dangerous environment. Food was often scarce, and medical treatment invariably had to be self-administered. Moreover, living in remote places increased Taoists' exposure to dangerous animals and brigands of all sorts. So isolated Taoists had a real need to protect their health and defend their persons. The typical Taoist lifestyle, heavy on sedentary meditation and prayer, also created a need for periodic physical rejuvenation. Taoists gradually developed exercises (the internal martial arts) and grew to use these exercises primarily in ritual interactions with deities and spirits.

Most martial arts are 'external' or 'hard' martial arts, the objective of which is the physical domination of one's opponent. To oversimplify things, in external martial arts one seeks to hit one's opponent faster and harder than one's opponent is allowed to reciprocate. It is a physical struggle.

Taoists, however, developed a variety of martial arts that, like Taoism, focus on the practitioner's sense of *qi*. 'Internal' or 'soft' martial arts replace physical struggle with energetic and mental competition. Instead of trying to be physically superior to your opponent, in internal martial arts one tries to build and project more *qi* than one's opponent, and to develop a greater sensitivity to *qi* than one's opponent. This sensitivity enables one to 'listen' to the *qi* of one's opponent, which can then be used against him. These systems place a premium on *qi* development and sensitivity, and place relatively little value on physical stature or superiority. A grandfatherly old man can easily defeat a strapping young thug through the use of an internal martial art!

Because internal martial arts rely on *qi* sensitivity and projection, they are suitable for people of all ages and constitutions. The 'internal work' of such practice also has great health benefits in addition to their obvious martial benefits. Internal martial arts, however, generally require a significantly longer time to master than do the major external martial arts.

The primary internal martial arts schools are:

Taiji Quan

Taiji Quan (T'ai Chi Ch'uan)

Taiji Quan (Great Ultimate Fist) has four major schools, Yang (the general standard), Chen, Sun, and Wu. Each is named after the family that originated or propagated that particular style. To generalize, movements are generally practiced in a slow and flowing manner, with each position rolling into the next. The body must remain relaxed and unblocked, enabling the practitioner's *qi* to flow smoothly despite the rigors of controlled and sustained athletic exercise. Students spend years learning choreographed sequences of movements, until new physical principles of movement have been internalized. At that time students can then begin to study various exercises (like 'push hands') that teach the rapid application of the principles and movements in fighting situations.

Bagua Zhang 八卦掌

Bagua Zhang (Eight Trigrams Palm) is a style that demands tremendous lower body strength. Students practice by circling around a pole or a tree while transferring through eight different positions. The student's center of gravity must be kept as low as possible at all times, which combines with the continuous torque of the eight twisting positions to produce tremendous stress on the practitioner's legs. The goal is to make the practitioner extremely elusive, constantly whirling at circular or angular directions and attacking one's opponent from

Taiji Quan

odd, unsuspected, and undefended angles. *Bagua Zhang* should probably not be anyone's first martial art. It would be better to start with a different martial art until one's physical body becomes used to some of the general principles of martial arts training.

Xing Yi Quan 形意拳

Xing Yi Quan (Form and Intent Fist) is probably the most immediately martial of the internal martial arts. It is practiced at a faster pace than the other internal martial arts, and includes pounding, thrusting, and moving with bursts of energy. As opposed to *Bagua Zhang*, *Xing Yi Quan* utilizes a great deal of straight-forward and backward movement. Despite its external appearance, *Xing Yi Quan* is a highly internalized martial art, with the body learning the same energetic sensitivity as described above.

3.8 Feng Shui 風水

Feng Shui can be seen as the study of the flow of *qi* as it impacts our environment. It can literally be translated as the study of 'wind and water.' Taoists have long believed that the natural environment around us (such as topography and various geological conditions), along with the shapes and characters of our man-made structures (including homes, offices, and related buildings,) all have a profound impact upon our *qi*, and thereby on our lives. Many modern *feng shui* practitioners possess an unfortunately limited concept of *Feng Shui*, and believe that it extends only to interior decorating and design. While *feng shui* does cover these topics, it also includes:

- Cleansing and consecration of buildings, structures, and altars;
- Interpreting local geographic energies and thereby choosing sites for buildings, structures, and altars;
- Enhancements and cures (various techniques people can enact in order to overcome problematic situations);
- The orientation of buildings, structures, and altars in relation to local geography and topology;
- Directionology (the effects of moving in a particular direction);
- As well as astrology, color, diet, and medical diagnoses.

Bagua Zhang

Hanging Temple
Heng Mountain
Shanxi Province

The original Taoist mandate of *feng shui* was to select appropriate places for Taoist structures, and to assist in determining the optimal design of those structures. Optimal location and design allow a Taoist structure to maximize its religious or healing energy. A well-placed and well-designed temple will make it easier for its resident Taoists to achieve meditation goals, to engage in profound religious transformations, to have mystical visions, etc. It is thus the dictates of *feng shui* that have caused so many Taoist structures to be built in seemingly senseless or dangerous places. Taoists obviously want their temples to be located at points of intense energetic power, and to be built in ways that maximize the effectiveness of that power. But this often results in structures that are perched on dangerous peaks (as are almost all of the temples on Hua Mountain), or on unbelievably steep cliff-sides (as is the famous Hanging Temple in Shanxi Province). Taoists typically employ *feng shui* specialists to determine the exact location, size and shape of new temples. These specialists, who are often initiated Taoists, commonly spend decades immersed in the study of *feng shui* before earning the respect of mastery.

Today there are many schools of *feng shui* in the West, some of which are more traditionally Taoist and some of which are less so. All schools, however, teach methods to improve one's *feng shui* environment through decorating techniques, the placement of special or sacred objects, the use of specific colors and directions, etc. While this may be slightly removed from the original Taoist use of *feng shui*, it is still a valid, modern application of Taoism-based principles. Many Western Taoists and Taoist Practitioners are now bringing *feng shui* back to its roots by using it to improve the *qi* flowing through their altar spaces, *taiji quan* practice rooms, meditation areas, and anywhere else where they engage in Taoist and *qi*-based activities.

Some Westerners have a hard time accepting the validity of *feng shui*, or the possibility that a particular design arrangement or color scheme will dramatically impact their lives. It is undeniable, however, that *feng shui* is an ancient Taoist art. All Taoists should at least be familiar with *feng shui*, and such familiarity will, in almost all cases, be wholly sufficient to erase all skepticism.

3.9 Taoist Medicine 道教醫學

Most precepts of what we in the West know as Traditional Chinese Medicine have their origins in Taoist concepts of the body and health. A traditional Taoist would never say, 'I have a cold,' but might instead say, 'I have a wind-cold invasion.' Is this a mere language difference? Absolutely not! Taoism views everything in terms of energy flows, and human health and physiology is no exception.

Taoism sees the human body as being filled with major and minor meridians (*jingluo*), which serve to carry the *qi* energy that powers human life throughout our bodies. The meridians are to energy as blood vessels are to blood, except that there are no physical structures limiting *qi* to specific places within the body. All illness is a result of some imbalance within the human energy system. The energy in one meridian might

Jingluo

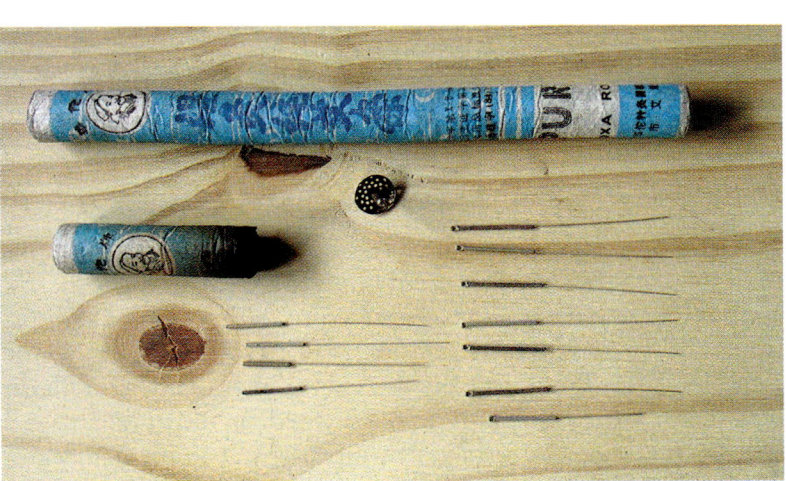
Moxa 'Cigars' and Acupuncture Needles

be too active, or the energy in another meridian might be too stagnant. Either extreme will result in illness, and only a fluid balance will result in excellent physical, emotional, mental, and spiritual health. The meditations described in Chapter 2.11 – *Taoist Meditation* are exercises wherein you learn to move and alter this same energy flowing through these same meridians.

Taoists manage this energy system so as to achieve optimal overall health through a variety of lifestyle factors, including diet (Chapter 4.5), sexual regulation (Chapter 4.4), exercise (Chapters 3.6 & 3.7), and meditation (Chapter 2.11). But Taoists also utilize some direct medical practices, such as herbalism, acupuncture, and moxibustion.

Herbalism 藥草學

For thousands of years, Taoists have classified plants, herb, foods, and even animal parts in terms of their energetic impact upon the human energy system. The consumption of these particular substances, in specific ratios and prepared in specific manners (generally and somewhat misleadingly called 'herbalism' for our purposes), is the Taoist's first line of medical defense. At the first sign of illness, a medical specialist will prescribe a specific formula of ingredients. The results can be slow to emerge, but there are rarely any negative side effects or unwanted results.

Ingredients are normally boiled in water until a somewhat thick, dark sludge remains, at which time more water is usually added and the whole mixture is reduced again. The ingredients are then removed, and the liquid is consumed. More often than not, the resulting potion tastes horrible beyond belief, and can be so absolutely bitter that one momentarily believes that any illness would be preferable! But, to quote a popular Chinese saying, "Good medicine tastes bad!"

Acupuncture 針術

For cases that are too severe to patiently await the results of decocted herbs, or when a patient is too weak to digest herbs, Taoists will resort to either acupuncture (*zhenshu*) or moxibustion (*jiufa*). Acupuncture places small needles just under the skin along specific points on the energy meridians. If a Taoist sees that a patient's energy is too excited or too stagnant in a specific meridian, he or she can directly and immediately impact that meridian with acupuncture needles. Different types of needles are used in different circumstances, and needles are manipulated in different manners (twirling left, twirling right, etc.) in order to achieve desired results.

There are some important reminders for anyone considering acupuncture:

> Acupuncture should only be attempted by people who have been formally trained in that discipline.

> There is no need to fear the 'pain' of acupuncture, as qualified practitioners are able to insert the needles with little or no discomfort at all for the patient. The sensation is significantly less than that of receiving a flu shot in your typical Western doctor's office.

> Never allow anyone to use an acupuncture needle on you unless you can see that they are either using new needles that have just been removed from the packaging, or that they are using needles that have been sterilized by autoclave. If you are a regular patient, or if you are receiving a series of treatments, the new needles used in your first session may be saved in a container that has been marked as yours, although they should still be thoroughly disinfected by autoclave between sessions. If you are not sure about the status of the needles to be used, don't be afraid to ask!

Moxibustion 灸法

Moxibustion (*jiufa*) is a heat-based herbal treatment that is performed along specific points on the energy meridians. Certain herbs (usually mugwort or a mugwort-based combination) called 'moxa' are placed on the skin, or above the skin on an inserted acupuncture needle, and ignited. The heat and herbal smoke impact the *qi* along the desired meridian.

Sometimes a glass container is quickly placed over the herbs after they have been ignited (a practice commonly called 'cupping'). The use of all available oxygen by the fire creates suction under the glass container, and the fire is quickly starved to extinction. That leaves the heat and the herbal smoke to impact an energy point that is swollen with blood and *qi*. Although no pain is involved in this process, it does leave the patient with a small red mark that disappears in a few days.

Traditional Chinese Medicine ('TCM') and Taoist medicine share a significant overlap, and most of the information provided above applies equally to TCM. It is important to note, however, that the two fields are not absolutely identical. For example, they do not agree on the location or number of all the various meridians or of all the points on these meridians. Moreover, there is some disagreement regarding the ultimate goal of the practice. While TCM primarily wants to assist people in overcoming their physical, emotional, or mental ailments, Taoist medicine also places a significant emphasis upon helping people to accomplish Taoism's spiritual goals and to attain healthy spiritual energy. That is why some Taoists throughout history have ingested pills or potions that have seemingly killed them. While TCM would consider such a result as a failure (after all, the patient has died!), Taoists believe that these treatments were successful in 'freeing' the patients of their bodies in the process of achieving important spiritual or religious goals.

Qi healing is another important aspect of Taoist medicine. As Taoists become experienced meditators, and as they learn more about the human energy system, they are often able to use their intent to impact someone else's energy system, without the use of needles or herbs. This is done with their hands, by projecting energy through the hands into a patient's meridians, or simply via meditative intent (in which case the healing can often take place across remote distances).

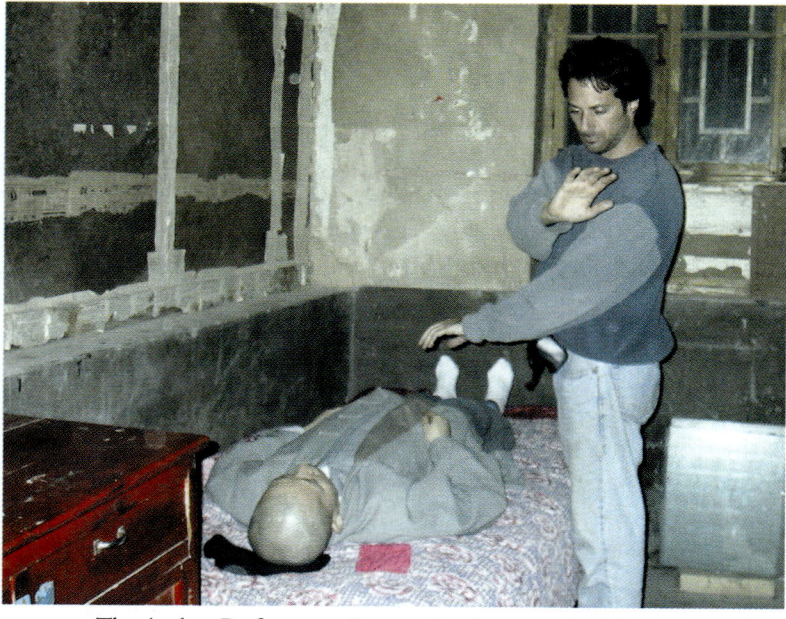

The Author Performs an Energy Healing on a Buddhist Nun at Hua Mountain's West Peak Zhen Yue Palace

Heng Mountain Emperor — Hunyuan Town Temple — Shanxi Province

Taoist Practitioners— 8 Immortals Temple — Xian, Shaanxi Province

4
Taoist Culture

4.1 Taoist Culture

Up to now we have focused on the principle activities of a Taoist, what a Taoist 'does at the office.' But a Taoist's day doesn't end when he or she leaves work. Taoism impacts all aspects of the Taoist's life. There is absolutely nothing a Taoist does that does not bear the stamp of his or her Taoist beliefs. From how Taoists think, to how they act, and how they generally engage their lives, every aspect of life is formed and driven by their religious commitment.

If you hope to create a more Taoist life for yourself, or even to become a Taoist, you should adopt an identical attitude. Your spiritual calling need not overwhelm everything else, but it should be present in everything you do.

Again, it is important to note that although each of the topics discussed in this chapter are important to Taoism and to Taoists, they are not by themselves definitively Taoist. These concepts are firmly rooted in general traditional Chinese culture, and are adopted by a number of segments of Chinese religious and cultural society. You do not need to be a Taoist in order to believe in or study *yin-yang* theory or five phase theory. But Taoists will undoubtedly take these matters to heart and use them in their lives and practices.

Daojiao Wenhua

The following topics will thus attempt to provide you with basic insight into Taoist culture (*daojiao wenhua*) – not what Taoists do, but how Taoists approach daily life.

4.2 Yin & Yang

Taoists believe that there are two fundamental polar energies in the universe, *yin* and *yang*, and that the limitless combinations of these energies create all things in our universe. This intellectual pattern is used constantly throughout Taoist thought.

These energies combine to form a cycle of constant evolution. As one energy is ascendant, one is descendant. Just as one reaches its absolute peak, it wanes as it gives birth to the ascendancy of its opposite. Thus each energy creates and defines the other. This is not, however, an antagonistic relationship. At any given moment, *yin* and *yang* combine to form an integrated and balanced whole. Neither is good nor bad, right nor wrong. Without light, how would we gauge darkness? How could we even know the meaning of dark? *Yin* and *yang* are represented together in the popular 'taiji' symbol, the symbol of the 'great

Yin Yang

Taoist Culture

Culture
Wen Hua

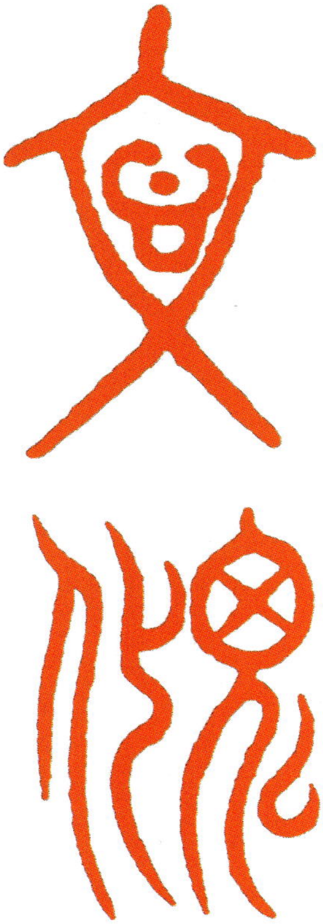

Ancient Seal Script

ultimate' (which is commonly known by an incorrect name – the '*yin-yang* symbol').

To illustrate the differences between *yin* and *yang*,

Yin is:	*Yang* is:
Feminine	Masculine
Dark	Light
Wet	Dry
Cold	Hot
Internal	External
Earth	Heaven
Down	Up
Contracting	Expanding
Soft	Hard
Night	Day
Smooth	Rough
Intuition	Intellect
Moon	Sun
Slow	Fast
Water	Fire
Lower	Higher

This concept of *yin* and *yang* is a timeless one. Taoists see the universe in a constant evolution from one to the other. The *yin* night and the *yang* day are locked in continual exchange and rebirth. So are the *yin* winter and the *yang* summer. Everything seeks its appropriate balance. Equatorial peoples live in the most *yang* of areas, so they thrive by eating a very *yin* diet heavy in fruit. Arctic peoples live in the most *yin* of areas, so they thrive by eating a very *yang* diet heavy in raw fish.

Balance between *yin* and *yang* provides health and centeredness. When *yin* and *yang* are in appropriate balance, affairs naturally progress. When *yin* and *yang* are imbalanced, problems naturally arise. A Taoist thus strives for balance unless a specific imbalance is sought for a specific reason. This theory is the basis for the *I Ching* (See Chapter 3.4 – *Divination*).

You should keep *yin*, *yang*, and their various attributes in mind at all times. Start to see things through this prism, and you will start to see how everything can be understood through a Taoist lens. Moreover, you will be developing a wonderful Taoist tool that will change your perception of the world around you.

4.3 Five Phases 五行

Five phase (*wuxing*) theory is another intellectual prism through which the entire Taoist universe is viewed. It is thus crucial for any Taoist to have an understanding of the forward and backward workings of this system.

Taoists believe that everything in the universe belongs to one of the five phases of fire, earth, metal, water, or wood. There may be multiple influences, but everything can be traced back to these five phases. The five phases also have particular relationships amongst themselves. Certain phases nurture and promote other specific phases, and certain phases conflict with and control other specific phases. By understanding these processes, a Taoist gains a deeper insight into the workings of the world around him. Knowing the nature of things and their relationships, the Taoist is thus better able to steer an appropriate course aiding and befitting his or her Taoist goals.

The Nurturing Relationships

Fire creates ash, which feeds earth. Earth contains the ores that are made into metal. Metal holds water and keeps it from dissipating. Water feeds the trees that give us wood. Wood provides the fuel that gives life to fire.

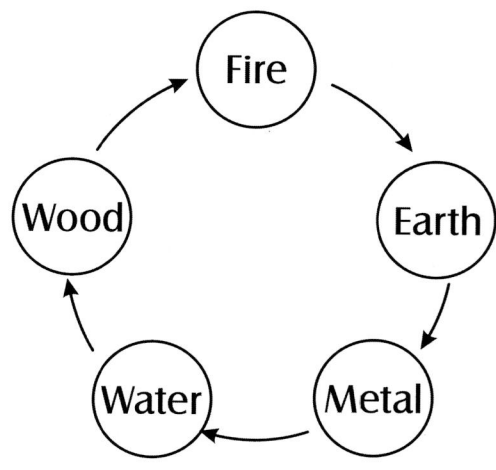

This is an endless cycle of nurturing and regeneration. Taoists will often base aspects of their training, their practices, and their relationships upon their interpretation of this cycle. An older Taoist, for example, may feel inclined to accept a particular student in part because the older Taoist was born in a wood year while the prospective student was born in fire year. Since wood feeds and nurtures fire, the teacher should 'feed' the student, and the teacher-student relationship should contain the basic necessities for success.

The Conflicting Relationships

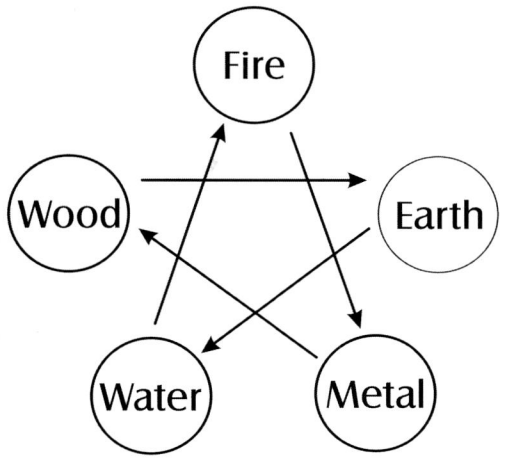

Fire melts metal. Metal chops down the trees that provide wood. The trees that provide wood extract minerals and nutrients from the earth, leaving it depleted. Earth is made into dams, which block the natural pathways of water. Water extinguishes fire.

This is an endless cycle of conflict and control. Taoists base their plans and activities just as much upon this cycle as they do upon the cycle of nurturing relationships. The same older Taoist, born in a wood year, might well reject a student born in an earth year, as he would fear that the teacher would 'deplete' the student, and that the basic relationship would not contain the seeds of success.

You should study and memorize these relationships. They will provide you with access to automatic insight into many matters. There are a great many matters, like ritual, *feng shui*, and divination, which rely heavily upon this intellectual foundation.

4.4 Sexual Relations 性交

This is a very delicate subject matter, and I have attempted to treat it with respect and delicacy. Nonetheless, this topic demands a forthright and direct discussion of the implications of sexual relations on Taoist practice. For anyone who might be offended in any way by such a discussion, please accept my sincere apologies and feel free to move directly to the next chapter.

Taoist sexual yoga has existed since at least the Han Dynasty (206 B.C. – 219 A.D.). Taoists attribute the origin of such practices to the proto-historical Yellow Emperor. Sexual yoga was seen as a valid path (or at least an important part of a valid path) towards the achievement of spiritual/physical immortality. There is a common Taoist folk saying:

The Yellow Emperor slept with 1,200 women and became an Immortal! Ordinary men have one wife and thereby destroy their lives. To have knowledge and not to have knowledge, how can these not produce different results? Knowledge of the methods will reduce the harm from sleeping with women.

There were once even a significant number of manuals dedicated to the theory and practice of sexual yoga included in the Taoist Canon. From the 4th – 7th Centuries, large communities of Taoists performed sexual yoga in public and en masse. By the Ming Dynasty (1368 – 1644), however, all such texts had been edited out of the Canon, as a result of the dominant influence of Confucianism within Chinese society.

Essence
Jing

Ancient Seal Script

Taoist sexual yoga is a complex subject, and should not be studied without the aid of a legitimate instructor. To oversimplify a complicated subject into a brief summary, practices generally aim to take an individual's internal energy (which Taoists believe resides in a person's sexual fluid) and to re-channel it back within that same person for higher, spiritual purposes. A person would thus not lose energy as a result of sexual activity (as is normal), but would instead build upon his or her existing energy. Our modern notions of love, intimacy, and emotional caring are not a prerequisite for beneficial Taoist sexual yoga. This activity is based upon the building of spiritual energy and not upon the building of romantic love. An emotional connection between partners may or may not benefit such a practice, but is definitely not required for success.

Like most ancient societies, China was not immune to gender prejudice. Women were not always given the same respect as were men. Much (but not all) of Taoism's literature on this topic includes such gender bias. The energetic development of males is often given priority over the energetic development of females. That should be taken as a sign of the times, and not as any indication that Taoist sexual yogic practices will not work for females, or that females are somehow less capable of Taoist spiritual achievement.

There are certain basic facts about the Taoist conception of sex and its relation to spiritual energy that all Taoists should know. The basic building block of your spiritual energy can be found within your sexual fluid. Males lose this energy upon climax/ejaculation, while females do not. Thus females may experience multiple orgasms while men generally cannot. Sexual relations involve an exchange and absorption of spiritual energy between partners. Such a process can be spiritually beneficial, or it can be spiritually detrimental. Men who do not practice Taoist sexual yoga should try to preserve their energy by restricting their loss of semen, especially as they become older and their natural processes for energetic rejuvenation slow.

While women do not lose their energy during sexual climax, they do lose their energy with the release of their monthly menstrual blood. Advanced Taoist energy practices lead females to stop their monthly cycle, and thus enable them to retain and utilize their energy for spiritual purposes.

Certain sexual activities are to be avoided at all times, as they provide for absorption by one or both partners of inappropriate energy. Male homosexuality is stridently rejected, as sexual acts between males invariably represent an unhealthy mixing of energies. Instead of a natural blending of complementary energies, male *yang* energy meets further male *yang* energy. Moreover, males will not only dissipate their own energy upon ejaculation, but they will fail to counter this loss with the absorption of healthy female energy. Furthering the problem, in the case of anal intercourse, the male will absorb inappropriate and unhealthy energy from his partner (no matter which gender).

Female homosexuality is somewhat less of a problem, although it still represents the mixing of female *yin* energy with further female *yin* energy. Although the goal of Taoist sexual activity is the healthy mixing of male *yang* with female *yin*, given the female retention of energy during sexual intercourse, Taoists believe female homosexuality to be more wasteful than harmful. Moreover, female homosexuality does not involve the penetration of one partner by the sexual organs of another partner, and thus does not involve the absorption of inappropriate and unhealthy energy. Taoism still rejects female homosexuality, although it does not find it as troubling as male homosexuality.

Fellatio is another sexual activity that is rejected by Taoism. Taoists view this also as a wasteful activity, one that drains a man of his energy without offering any possibility of countering that loss with the absorption of beneficial female energy.

Since Taoists believe that all sexual contact involves an energy exchange, and since Taoist practice is in large part an energetic practice, it makes sense that all people on a Taoist path would be quite circumspect regarding sexual encounters. Even if you follow an Orthodox Unity Taoist path (which does not require absolute celibacy), you should still be extremely careful when deciding with whom and how to share your valuable energy. Sexual promiscuity is not a Taoist trait!

As a word of caution, there are currently many people who claim to be teachers of authentic Taoist sexual yoga. Some of these people have become somewhat famous, and have written many popular books. These people may be teaching programs with some value, but very few of them are teaching anything that is even remotely Taoist. Be very careful in this area! One

Cinnabar Field
Dan Tian

Ancient Seal Script

particular practice that is commonly taught today that should be avoided at all costs involves the manually aided retention of semen in males during ejaculation. This is a medically dangerous practice. You should be able to control your energy with just your will and intent!

Again, this is an area into which few people should become seriously involved. You will definitely need a teacher, and the available teachers are often not reputable. If you're in doubt, skip this activity until such time as you can be certain that you have found an appropriate teacher.

4.5 Diet 日常飲食

This is a difficult area, as many Taoist beliefs differ on the topic of food. Orthodox Unity Taoists, for example, seem to eat or drink anything. They originally had a prohibition against wine, but even that restriction may or may not be observed today. Complete Perfection Taoists, on the other hand, are extremely strict in terms of their diet. A Complete Perfection Taoist strictly avoids:

Meat	Fish	Dairy
Eggs	Liquor	Tobacco
Caffeine	Garlic	Onion

These prohibitions are derived from a variety of rationales. Animal products were originally rejected solely due to their deleterious impact on *qi* patterns and energetic cultivations. The consumption of these foods fed 'worms' within the human body which were dedicated to shortening the life of their host. A restricted diet would starve these 'worms.' The later Buddhist influence on the formation of Complete Perfection Taoism reinforced the belief that meditation and internal energy work will be hampered by animal products in the diet, which will serve to reduce one's *qi* sensitivity and control.

Garlic, onion, and related pungent vegetables/herbs are rejected purely on energetic grounds. Taoists find these products to be too energetically activating, whereas a typical Taoist desires a slower, more subtle energetic presence. The activation, Taoists believe, stifles energetic sensitivity and thus hampers meditation.

Which culinary role model is more suited for your own practice? Well, to over generalize a bit, the Orthodox Unity Taoists are slightly more concerned with spirits, ritual, and magic, while the Complete Perfection Taoists are slightly more concerned with internal energy work. If you clearly fall into either of these two camps, you should follow the diet of that tradition. If you still aren't sure, you should experiment. Try each diet for several weeks. How does your diet impact your practice? Is there a noticeable difference?

You should bear in mind, however, that even Orthodox Unity Taoists will adhere to the prohibitions described above for at least one week when preparing to engage in major ritual activity. Your instinct should let you know what constitutes major religious activity, and should lead you to the right choices.

Taoists generally also follow a number of other guidelines regarding food and diet:

> ***Almost all Taoists pray before meals.*** Not only does a Taoist rightfully give thanks for his sustenance, but prayer also helps to center one's energy, and thus makes one more receptive to the benefits of the food about to be consumed. This is an excellent practice that everyone should adopt.
>
> ***Food should be fresh, clean, and organic*** to the greatest extent possible. Taoism is highly focused on your own internal energy, and your energy will be directly impacted by the fuel you provide your body.
>
> ***Never eat to fullness.*** Fullness places too great an energetic demand upon the human body, and thus detracts from the Taoist's energetic goals.
>
> ***Foods should be eaten according to their Five Phase compatibility.*** Five Phase Theory (See Chapter 4.3 – *Five Phases*) applies to foods as well as to anything else. Certain foods are appropriately eaten together, and certain foods should not be combined at one meal. While it is hard to find instruction in classical Taoist five phase cookery, it is fairly easy to study Western 'food combining,' which follows similar principles.
>
> ***Follow common-sense rules:*** eat slowly, chew your food well, and try to eat at regular times each day.

Be Vegetarian
Chi Su

Green Tea 綠茶

Traditional China's beverage of choice was undoubtedly green tea *(lü cha)*. Tea is ubiquitous in China (albeit perhaps slightly less so than in the past), and Taoists seem to drink tea throughout the day. I have yet to visit a Taoist temple without quickly being offered a cup of green tea! In fact, some of the best teas I have ever tasted have been local mountain teas from Taoist sites.

Green tea is extremely well suited to Taoist consumption. Whereas black and oolong teas are significantly caffeinated, green tea contains dramatically reduced levels of caffeine. Yet it still contains a slightly stimulating effect that is more subtle and longer lasting than that of most caffeinated drinks, and thus improves concentration and alertness without sacrificing energetic sensitivity.

Green tea is also an extremely healthy beverage. Its antioxidant properties help to prevent the formation of various cancers and cardiovascular diseases. Its high level of polyphenols (the main biological active ingredient in tea) helps to strengthen the immune system and aids digestion. Some Taoists believe it to be a key ingredient in their search for longevity.

4.6 Artistic Expression 美術

Taoists have always been great artists, and great lovers of art *(meishu)*. Artistic endeavor serves a variety of purposes in Taoist practice.

The Taoist spends a great deal of time going deep within himself, exploring the mostly internal worlds of meditation, prayer, philosophy, silence, etc. These activities are designed to provide the Taoist with a glimpse of the unknowable. Having experienced things that he or she cannot express with words, the Taoist can still resort to artistic expression.

Taoist activities can also be very ethereal. The danger is that too much focus on a different reality can cause one to lose a firm grip on this one. Artistic expression is very energetically grounding. One must pick up the pencil, pen, brush, or chisel and work with one's hands to give life to one's artistic vision. That process can help to keep a Taoist from inadvertently floating away on the clouds of Immortality.

Finally, many Taoists live amidst tremendous natural beauty. Such an environment is extremely conducive to artistic creation.

The "four treasures of a scholar's studio": brushes, inkstone, ink and paper

Taoists are still human beings, and often hear this artistic calling.

There are several traditional art forms that are generally favored by Taoists: Chinese calligraphy, landscape paintings, religious music, and poetry.

Calligraphy 書法

Calligraphy (*shufa*) is undoubtedly the most popular representative art form for Taoists. Not only is calligraphy an excellent means of artistic expression, enabling Taoists to put a tremendous amount of knowledge, skill, and insight into the act of writing, but calligraphy is also approached by Taoists as a meditative ritual. Ink is prepared, paper is secured, brushes are wetted, and a host of ritual activities are accomplished. Finally the Taoist is in such a deep meditative state that his or her inner spirit can be brought forth and poured into the writing. There are even cultivators who can project such a significant amount of *qi* into their calligraphy that their *qi* can be physically felt radiating from the ink and paper long after they have ceased writing!

For those Westerners who cannot write Chinese, you can still utilize calligraphy in the same traditional manner as a Taoist. Western calligraphy is just as great an art form as Chinese calligraphy. The meditative benefits can be the same, as are the relationships between artist, tools, message, and spirit. This Taoist activity is open to everyone!

Landscape Painting 山水畫

The favorite type of painting for Taoists has always been landscapes (*shanshui hua*). This is a somewhat natural development, as Taoists are typically found in beautiful, remote, natural areas. If you're a painter and you're a Taoist, your subject is all around you. Chinese landscape paintings typically emphasize nature at the expense of man. People are often portrayed as tiny and insignificant in comparison to the glory of nature. This message has an obvious relationship to the natural Taoist outlook.

Religious Music 道教音樂

Taoists are by nature musicians. Ritual songs (*daojiao yinyue*) are a part of everyday Taoist life, and almost every Taoist learns to play them on a traditional instrument. Although ritual accomplishment may be the primary reason for becoming a musician, most Taoists seem to also take greatest pleasure from playing traditional music during a quiet secluded moment. It is totally enchanting to suddenly come upon a Taoist playing traditional music beside a mountain pathway. I believe this sense of enchantment is the Taoist's real motivation for becoming a musician.

Should you become a musician? In reality, most Westerners are not going to ever learn to play Taoist ritual songs on traditional instruments. But musicianship still holds tremendous benefits for the beginning Taoist. Not only will playing an instrument, like other artistic endeavors, give expression to your inner self and help to keep you energetically grounded, but it will also help you to share in the Taoist enchantment of sound.

Female Taoist Plays a Lute

Taoist Culture

The music you learn to play must be energetically compatible with your Taoist goals. Angry rap, screeching rock, or other similar musical styles would not seem to be good choices. Try to select a medium that is soft and expressive. As your Taoist practice progresses, so will your ability to include music in that practice.

Poetry 詩

Poetry (*shi*) has long been one of the major staples in Taoist artistic fare. Many Taoist religious texts are written in poetic format. This not only helps to make the texts more easily memorized, but also provides a highly appropriate literary environment for the message contained in those texts.

Listen to Laozi from a purely poetic standpoint:

Taoist Painting a Landscape

The Way of heaven
 Does not war
  Yet is good at conquering,
 Does not speak
  Yet is good at answering,
 Is not summoned
  Yet comes of itself,
 Is relaxed
  Yet good at making plans.

Tao Te Ching, Chapter 38
(Victor Mair)

This simple 'call and response' meter is enchanting, and helps to convey the intended message.

Additionally, Taoism has long been a favorite of the Chinese literati. The sparseness of poetry has always been thought of as an excellent match for the internalized and fluid nature of Taoist thought. As such, it has provided Taoists with sufficient room to express their deeply mystical or internal visions.

Carved Calligraphy
Eight Immortals Temple
Shaanxi Province

From the famous T'ang Dynasty poet and Mao Mountain Taoist, Haung-fu Ran:

> *You saunter to the sylphine grotto*
>   *— to seek out the Realized Magistrates;*
> *To offer libations at a gemmy mat*
>   *— perform the rites on a stone altar.*
> *Suddenly a semblance*
>   *— disturbing the clouds!*
> *Deep in blurred shadow*
>   *— and summer is chilled.*

"Sending Lu Qianfu Off to Mao Mountain"
(Edward Schafer)

Again, very few words are necessary to convey the inner spiritual vision of the Taoist poet.

It is nice for Westerners to follow these traditional Taoist art forms. I believe such practices will provide aspiring Taoists with an added appreciation for earlier Taoist works. It is not necessary, however, for a Taoist Practitioner or a Student of Taoism to express themselves in these traditional forms. Without a basic knowledge of Chinese, you cannot express yourself with Chinese calligraphy. It is much more important for any aspiring Taoist to find any preferred avenue of artistic expression. You will be giving voice to something deep within you, and you will keep yourself energetically grounded. You will also be cultivating a more Taoist presence, as long as your subject material and medium do not contradict Taoism's basic outlook and goals.

4.7 Iconography 聖像學

Taoism is replete with symbolic meaning. Taoist art, poetry, texts, liturgy, and architecture are all meant to communicate via an incredibly rich symbolic language (*shengxiangxue*). This language was divided into two dialects – a standard iconography that was intended for everyone, and a specialized symbolic language that was intended only for Taoist initiates who had received training and oral instructions from a qualified Taoist teacher. In traditional China, this standard symbolic language was so deeply ingrained within general Chinese culture that almost everyone (including non-Taoists) would immediately understand the intended meaning of basic Taoist iconography. For modern Westerners interested in Taoism, however, this crucial cultural background has unfortunately been lost. In order to fully and more readily understand Taoist expression, everyone should be somewhat familiar with Taoism's use of the following symbols:

Bamboo 竹

Bamboo (*zhu*) is revered by Taoism as a symbol of longevity as a result of its extreme adaptability. Bamboo adjusts to many climatic conditions, and can tolerate some degree of being cut, burned, trampled, etc. It accepts many types of conditions and continues to rapidly grow. Bamboo is also used as a Taoist artistic device simply because it is beautiful and often quite evocative to the Chinese artistic mind.

Bats 蝠

Sound plays an important role in the Chinese language, and homophonic connections are often deemed to be significant. The Chinese word for bat, *fu*(3), rhymes with the Chinese word for fortune, *fu*(4). Traditional Chinese wisdom thus holds that bats carry good fortune with them. Whereas bats often have an evil association in the West (think of Dracula!), bats are considered quite lucky in Taoism. That is why a demon-slayer like Zhong Kui is almost always depicted with bats, as he is a bringer of good luck.

Beards 鬍鬚

Taoists are typically depicted with beards (*huxu*), and most Taoist beards are thin (sometimes sparse), black, and well groomed. Some beards are wild and unkempt, and are meant to suggest a sort of primal power, or perhaps the idea that the wearer somehow exists on the edges of polite societal rules. A deity like *Zhang Daoling* is often depicted with this sort of beard. Beards can also be red, and this is meant to depict fierceness. *Wang Lingguan* is often depicted with such a red beard. Long white beards indicate age and wisdom. *Laozi* is sometimes shown with a beard of this type.

Big Bellies 大腹部

Traditional China was wracked with severe and recurring famines. The average Chinese person was quite thin. A large and robust physical frame, complete with a round, protruding belly (*da fubu*), was thus a symbol of a unique and special individual. A big belly represents power, affluence, and strength and should not be construed as being the result of ill health, sloth, or ineffectiveness. Many Taoist deities, especially those connected with martial arts or other feats involving human, physical strength, are commonly depicted with very large bellies.

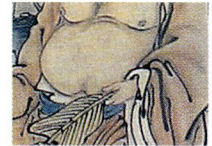

Cauldrons 鍋

Cauldrons (*guo*) represent either the creation of medicine or engagement of the alchemical process. If a Taoist deity is depicted alongside a cauldron, he or she will either be a famous healer such as *Sun Simiao*, or someone who is famous for their alchemical knowledge and prowess such as *Ge Hong*.

Chaoban 朝板

Anyone who sees ceremonial images of Taoist deities will undoubtedly see many such deities holding a pointed slab with both hands in front of their chests. These deities are holding a *chaoban*, an 'audience tablet,' indicating that the deity is in audience before a more potent deity. Taoists today utilize *chaoban* whenever they are in ritual audience with deities.

Cranes 鶴

The Crane (*he*) is thought by Taoists to represent pure *yang* energy. This is reflected in the crane's typical depiction of having a reddish head. Having alchemically transmuted itself into pure *yang* energy, the crane is considered to be immortal, and to possess the wisdom of an immortal. Thus when a Taoist achieves immortality, he or she is thought to ascend to heaven on the back of a crane. A single crane thus usually represents immortality, while a pair of cranes is sometimes thought to represent the Taoist deity *Wenchang*.

Deer 鹿

The deer (*lu*) is a traditional Taoist symbol of immortality. Given its powerful and graceful physique, the deer is considered to be a master of alchemical techniques. It is often depicted with a mushroom of immortality in its mouth. Moreover, the Chinese word for deer is a homophone for the salary of a government official. Thus Chinese culture considers the word for deer to be quite lucky, and believes that it will bring fortune with use.

Dragons 龍

The dragon (*long*) is a complex traditional symbol. It can be used to represent the principle of heaven or that of the Chinese Emperor. It is a common background motif throughout traditional Chinese art. In Taoism the dragon most often represents *yang* energy, and is most often depicted amidst clouds and water, which both represent a very *yin* environment. In terms of alchemy, dragons are associated with the trigram *Li* – fire. They also denote the eastern direction, the liver, the spring season, and the element of wood.

Eight Treasures 八寶

In all likelihood, the Eight Treasures (*ba bao*) were originally more famous Tibetan Buddhist symbols, consisting of the wheel of law, conch shell, umbrella, canopy, lotus, jar, pair of fish, and the endless knot. Taoism, probably in relation to these famous symbols, developed its own Eight Treasures. Each treasure is associated with one of the deities known as the Eight Immortals, and includes: fan (*Han Zhongli*), sword (*Lü*

Dongbin), gourd & crutches (*Li Tieguai*), castanets (*Cao Guojiu*), flower basket (*Lan Caihe*), bamboo tube-like musical instrument with protruding rods (*Zhang Guolao*), flute (*Han Xiangzi*), and lotus blossom (*He Xiangu*). These Eight Taoist Treasures are commonly used as an artistic background motif.

Eyebrows & Fingernails 眉毛 & 指甲

Eyebrows (*meimao*) and fingernails (*zhijia*) are used to denote Taoist age, experience, and wisdom. One way to convey a Taoist's high level of cultivation is to depict him or her with exceedingly long or bushy eyebrows, which are usually a stark white color. Immortals are often depicted in this fashion. The identical ideas are expressed with extremely long fingernails, although this practice will also have a cultural basis, as China's aristocracy historically favored long fingernails.

Foreheads 額

You may see Taoists depicted as having exceedingly large, rounded foreheads (*e*). This type of forehead is not merely large – it is not natural to mankind. You will certainly know it if you see it. It is a sign of immortality and tremendous wisdom.

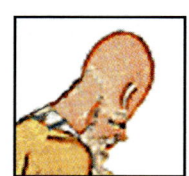

Gourds 葫蘆

The gourd (*hulu*) is a frequent symbol in Taoist art. Taoists consider its typical hourglass shape to be reminiscent of heaven and earth and the relationship that binds them. Immortals such as *Li Tieguai* or *Lü Dongbin* often carry such gourds. This represents their ability to create and dispense magical potions and vapors, as well as their ability to trap harmful spirits.

Lotus Blossoms 蓮花

Although the lotus (*lianhua*) is primarily a Buddhist symbol, it can be quite common in Taoism as well. The Lotus germinates in mud, and its tall stalk reaches out from the mud towards the heavens. Its bloom is regarded as a thing of beauty throughout Asian cultures. The Lotus Blossom itself is thus taken as a metaphor for the spiritual quest.

Mushrooms 靈芝

A mushroom in Taoist art of literature is almost invariably a *lingzhi* mushroom, which is also called the Mushroom of Immortality. Only someone with the appropriate destiny can

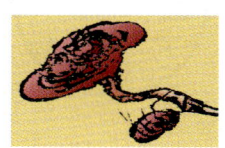

hope to find such a mushroom, and eating it will provide him or her with a type of immortality.

Nakedness 裸體

No Taoist deities are depicted in a totally naked state (*luoti*), but some are depicted as shirtless or bare-chested. This semi-nakedness usually represents a Taoist's unwillingness to conform to society's norms. *Han Zhongli* is often depicted in a bare-chested fashion.

Oxen 牛

The ox (*niu*) is usually used in reference to Laozi, who rode beyond society's western edge on the back of an ox. Oxen could be symbolic of *Laozi* himself, and could be symbolic of *Laozi's* Taoist attainment.

Peaches 桃花

Peaches (*taohua*) always represent the 'Peaches of Immortality.' These peaches are the property of the Queen Mother of the West, and a taste of one peach will confer upon the taster a level of Immortality. These peaches figure prominently in a great deal of Taoist mythology and art.

Phoenix 鳳

The phoenix (*feng*) is a complement to the dragon, and is broadly used throughout all traditional Chinese art. It represents the earthly counterpart to the heavenly dragon, as well as the female Empress counterpart to the male Emperor. In Taoism, the phoenix is always a symbol of extreme *yin*, and as such would be associated with the trigram *Kun* – water.

Pill of Immortality 仙片

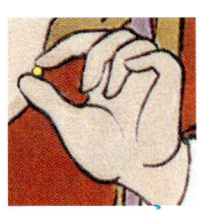

Taoists are often depicted holding a small pill between the thumb and forefinger of one hand. This is a 'Pill of Immortality (*xian pian*).' This pill represents the height of the Taoist alchemist's art, and the consumption of one pill will turn a human into an Immortal. These pills thus represent alchemy or immortality.

Pine Trees 松樹

Taoism sees the pine tree *(songshu)* as a symbol of longevity through a simple tenacity. The pine tree clings with all its might to steep mountain slopes, and braves all types of inclement weather. Its hardiness enables it to reach an extended age with great beauty.

Shou 壽

Literally the character for 'long life,' Shou has gradually assumed an almost talismanic importance to Taoists. Taoists believe that the writing of this character will assist one in attaining long life. The character has thus been artistically adapted into many ornamental shapes, and is an extremely common background motif in Taoist art.

Tigers 老虎

The tiger *(laohu)* is in some sense the complement to the dragon. The tigers most often represents *yin* energy. In terms of alchemy, tigers are associated with the trigram *Kan* – water. A balance between *yang* dragon (*Li* – fire) and *yin* tiger (*Kan* – water) is a prerequisite for transmutation into the balanced tao. The tiger also denotes the western direction, the lungs, the autumn season, and the element of metal.

Turtles & Snakes 烏龜 & 蛇

A common motif in Taoist art is a snake *(she)* wrapped around a turtle *(gui)*. The head of the snake is usually looking back towards the turtle. This is the symbol of a particular Taoist deity, the *Dark Emperor of the North*. Both the snake and the turtle represent the *yin* energy of the northern direction, and their partnership represents the pure *yin* qualities exhibited by this deity.

Weaponry 武器

Many Taoist deities carry weapons *(wuqi)*, such as *Lü Dongbin* (sword), *Guan Gong* (halberd), or *Zhong Kui* (sword). The most important point to remember is that these weapons are not meant to represent martial mastery, but instead represent spiritual or energetic mastery. *Lü Dongbin* may use a sword to perform exorcism, but the sword is just a tool representing his spiritual power.

TAOIST CULTURE

Whisks 撣子

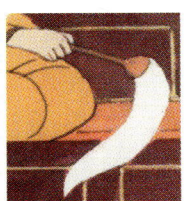

Taoist deities sometimes carry whisks (*danzi*), normally made of horse hair. These whisks symbolize the gentle brushing away of spiritual, energetic, or meditative blockages, as if they were mere flies. It can also represent the effortless brushing away of illusions. *Laozi, Lü Dongbin,* and the *Great Purity* are all often depicted as carrying whisks.

Yin & Yang 陰陽

Yin and *Yang* are the two opposing energies that form the building blocks of all things within the Taoist concept of the universe. There is a continuous interaction between the two, which Taoists see as a constant and predictable ebb and flow from one to the other. A *yin-yang* symbol represents this flow of the tao, or an individual's union with this flow. For more information, see Chapter 4.2 – *Yin & Yang*.

It is important to note that much of the iconography discussed above is not limited to Taoism. Some of these symbols are used throughout traditional Chinese culture, and may have equal fluency in terms of Buddhism, Confucianism, or in matters reflecting Chinese court life. But Taoism does use these symbols, and in order to fully understand and appreciate Taoism we should be familiar with them in their Taoist context.

4.8 Architecture 建築學

Before we can examine the basic tenets of Taoist architecture (*jianzhuxue*), we should first define the basic terminology of Taoist structures. When on a Taoist pilgrimage, or even when reading Taoist books or examining Taoist photos, you will be confronted by a large number of terms denoting a Taoist 'temple' of some sort. The most common terms are:

Ci 祠

Benevolence
Ren

Ancient Seal Script

Ci is a highly ambiguous term, referring to either Taoist or Confucian single buildings or complexes. *Ci* is commonly rendered as a 'veneration temple,' typically used for paying respect to local heroes, important ancestors, or even minor folk deities, but not to major, generally recognized deities. On very rare occasions, a Buddhist structure will include a *Ci* just within its outermost enclosure.

Dian 殿

Dian is commonly used in all Chinese religious traditions, and is typically translated as a 'hall'. It implies a single hall with comparatively high status (as evidenced by architectural features). A *Dian* may be free standing, or may be a part of a larger structure like a *Guan*, *Gong*, *Si*, or *Ci*.

Dong 洞

A *dong* is a cave or grotto used for religious purposes or for worship. *Dong* also frequently refers to sometimes elaborate temples that have been built onto the front of natural caves.

Gong 宮

Gong literally means 'palace,' and signifies a degree of historic, Imperial support. *Gong* also, however, refers to royal palaces. A good rule of thumb is: if a *Gong* is not a royal palace, then it is a Taoist monastery. *Gong* does not imply any minimum level of size or grandeur, and does not necessarily carry a higher status than a *Guan*. A *Gong* is usually a complex and is rarely (if ever) a single structure.

Guan 觀

Guan is the most common type of Taoist structure, and is never used to refer to anything but a Taoist structure. It is typically rendered as 'monastery,' although some people prefer 'abbey' so as to distinguish it from Buddhist 'monasteries.' *Guan* is also sometimes artistically translated as the slightly archaic 'belvedere' in light of the associated meaning of 'looking' or 'viewing' inherent to both the Chinese and English terms. A *Guan* is usually a complex is rarely (if ever) a single structure.

Miao 廟

Miao is a significantly ambiguous term. It is often rendered as a Taoist 'temple,' but can also refer to a larger Taoist complex (similar to a *Guan* or a *Gong*). *Miao* can also refer to Confucian structures, but rarely (if ever) refers to Buddhist structures.

Longevity
Shou

Oracle Bone Script

Si 寺

Si is the Buddhist version of a Taoist *Guan*. Occasionally a Taoist temple will be called a *Si*, invariably as a result of religious blending, historical quirk, or popular misconception. It is generally safe to assume, however, that a *Si* is a Buddhist structure.

Tang 堂

Tang is also commonly used in all Chinese religious traditions, and is typically translated as a 'hall.' It implies a single hall with comparatively lower status (as evidenced by architectural features). A *Tang* may be free standing, or may be a part of a larger structure like a *Guan*, *Gong*, *Si*, or *Ci*.

Yuan 院

Yuan literally means 'interior courtyard,' and is used in all Chinese religious architecture. It refers to a single structure that surrounds an interior courtyard, and it is typically translated as 'temple' or even 'monastery.' A *Yuan* is usually a part of a larger complex.

It is important to remember that even these basic terms are sometimes incorrectly applied. Titles confer status, and some Taoist structures have been awarded higher status for reasons that are no longer clear or evident to modern Taoists. Circumstances also change over the centuries. For example, an old, freestanding Taoist *Dian* may be incorporated into a new Taoist *Guan*, and may give its older but relatively humble name to the newer complex.

Taoist Architectural Principles

Almost all Taoist structures adhere to a set of general principles. Many of these principles, however, apply to a wide variety of traditional Chinese religious buildings and not specifically to Taoist structures. To the unobservant, there are often few architectural details to distinguish a Taoist site from a Buddhist site. Only when one begins to understand the history of a given site, or can determine the deities to whom a site is dedicated, or can understand place names or the messages that are

Taoist Manual

Elaborate Roofline
Wudang Mountain
Hubei Province

depicted in temple murals or iconography, can one really know the true religious affiliation of a Chinese religious site. Nonetheless, almost all Taoist structures adhere to the following guidelines:

Wooden Structure

Most Taoist structures are built around a wooden frame. This frame serves to bear the entire weight of the structure through the use of columns, and thereby eliminates the need for weight-bearing walls or partitions. There are thus no restrictions in terms of the number or placement of doors or windows. In order to protect these wooden frames from excessive moisture, they are built upon elevated foundations (mostly made from stone).

Roofing

Taoist structures are also covered with sloping roofs utilizing large overhangs and usually upturned corners. The overhang serves to protect the structure by directing rainfall away from the wooden frame, while the upturned corners serve to allow a greater degree of sunlight into the building. These roofs are traditionally covered with glazed tiles. The corners of these roofs frequently contain a series of decorative glazed pottery figures, the origin of which is uncertain but which may have originated as a means to ritually prohibit lightning strikes.

Three Purities Hall
Palace of Eternal Joy
Shanxi Province

Roof Bracketing
Heng Mountain
Hunan Province

Symbolic Bracketing

Taoist bracketing originated as a structural device used to cushion the tops of columns as they met the roof. Structural bracketing developed as techniques were discovered to enable the construction of larger and grander buildings. While bracketing eventually lost its structural usefulness, it remained symbolically important. Buildings were graded according to their status, and the type of bracketing they were allowed to use reflected that status.

Open Interior

Taoist structures are designed to be open spaces. The use of mostly external columns allows for the creation of an open floor plan, which helps to create a more solemn, religious atmosphere. Interiors are often broken into separate areas in situations where more than one altar is to be housed.

Painting

Wooden frames and columns require painting in order to protect them from moisture and insects. Thus all the exposed wooden elements of a Taoist structure will be painted. Columns are typically painted a warm red or vermilion, while bracketing and other architectural members are often painted in a brocade-like, polychrome style called *caihua*.

Caihua

4.9 Nature 大自然

Taoists often, but not always, prefer to live amidst tremendous natural scenery. Their motivations for this are myriad.

First and foremost, such a deeply introspective and meditative lifestyle works best if one can remove oneself from the distractions of a harried, noisy, fractured, urban existence. A car horn or a siren can easily disturb a Taoist in ways that a bird or the wind cannot. There are also energetic considerations. Anxiety, pressure, and time restrictions all serve to negatively impact one's energy system. Rushing to catch the last train home is something that a Taoist would avoid at all costs, as it can easily result in an unsettled heart/mind, and can manifest itself in energy-impeding muscular knots, decreased energy flow along particular meridians, and associated negative consequences. Our typical urban environments also promote poor

Caihua Painting Ornamentation
Heng Mountain
Shanxi Province

energy in other ways as well. We are almost constantly confronted with pollution, toxicity, unhealthy food, unclean water, etc. Poor quality fuel invariably leads to a poor quality engine! Finally, removal from nature can also rob us of a tremendous opportunity for energetic and spiritual grounding. A brief walk in the hills or through the woods does more good for us than we can know!

Taoists traditionally tried to overcome or avoid these problems by living in remote areas of great natural beauty. They avoided all the negatives associated with our typical Western lives. This was an important factor in helping Taoists to deepen their practices and to prolong their lives.

If you have the opportunity to quit your job and leisurely move into a cabin in the world's most beautiful valley, I heartily recommend that you do just that! But what about the rest of us, those who must continue to work normal jobs and live in communities where we can educate our children? The most important point is to not completely neglect this Taoist drive towards harmonious interaction with nature. Make sure that you spend adequate time grounding yourself in the beautiful spirit of Mother Nature. In doing so you will be connecting with your Taoist forebears, improving your energy, learning important lessons regarding your practice, and hopefully enjoying deep peace and happiness.

4.10 Clothing 衣服

Taoists have a surprisingly wide variety of traditional clothing options, and they frequently seem to delight in establishing a unique yet traditional style for themselves. Nonetheless, almost all Taoists recognize a somewhat standard uniform, as follows:

    Undershirt: White cotton
    Pants: Black/blue, cotton, loose, drawstring
    Socks: White, calf-length
    Shoes: Felt or cotton slip-on loafers
    Robe: Black/blue, cotton, butterfly closure

The t-shirt is tucked into the drawstring pants. Pant legs are folded tight around the ankle, and are tucked inside the socks, which are pulled up high along the calf. Wide pant legs billow out from above the socks. The tongue area of a Taoist's specialized loafers is often quite reduced so as to expose the sock on the top part of the foot. Over the t-shirt the Taoist wears a robe. Some robes close along the front, and some close along the side (much like the difference between single and double breasted men's suits in the West). Sleeves can be narrow, or can be extremely wide so as to be able to hide one's hands. Robes can also vary from waist-length to ankle-length. In colder areas, layered clothing (such as sweaters or long underwear) is added as needed as long as it is minimally visible.

This basic uniform is remarkably consistent from tradition to tradition. Whereas Complete Perfection Taoists wear only this uniform at all times, more relaxed Orthodox Unity Taoists wear this uniform while performing Taoist activities or while in a formal or Taoist environment. Complete Perfection female Taoists also wear this same uniform at all times.

No traditional Taoist, however, would ever ignore his or her hair or forget to wear a hat. Complete Perfection Taoists, both male and female, never cut their hair. They instead allow their hair to grow naturally long, oil it, and comb it upwards into a large 'topknot' which they fasten with a wooden or stone pin. Orthodox Unity Taoists cut their hair into normal, modern hairstyles, although they sometimes wear symbolic (i.e., fake) topknots on important occasions.

Since a traditional Taoist wears a large topknot on top his or her head, it is only natural that hat styles accommodate this large protrusion. One popular style has a flat or ridged mortarboard angled downwards towards the wearer's face. The height in the rear of the hat can accommodate the Taoist's topknot. Along the band of the hat that rests on the wearer's forehead is typically a piece of jade, which is thought to energetically benefit the third eye area. Many deities, including the Jade Emperor and Lü Dong Bin, are typically seen wearing versions of this hat.

Another popular style of hat is a rounded version, the rim of which arcs slightly and rises to the front and the rear. There is a hole in the center of the hat, through which the Taoist's topknot protrudes.

Another hat style, worn primarily by deities in Orthodox Unity Taoist art, is called the Golden Crown. It is normally depicted as a delicate golden piece worn around the topknot. High-ranking Taoists may wear such a hat for important ceremonial or ritual purposes, but most Taoists do not wear them. You should, however, be familiar with their appearance.

Now that we know how a traditional Taoist dresses, what are modern Westerners to do? Most Westerners will not be able to dress solely in traditional Taoist garb.

Wearing Taoist Socks

The most important rule when working with your Taoist altar is to dress comfortably, without any significant restrictions (tight collar, uncomfortable dress shoes, pinching undergarments, etc.). You should not wear any exposed white clothing, as white is the color of death. You should also try to dress in all natural fiber clothes, and to wear as little wool or leather as possible Taoists follow this restriction because certain animal products can carry their own energies, and not out of an ethical reluctance to participate in the death of animals. That is why, for example, Taoists willingly use silk products despite the fact that silk production necessarily involves the death of silkworms. You should also wear as little metal as possible, as metal can easily impact your body's subtle energies.

Golden Crown

When engaging in major ritual activity (a standard that your own intuition should define), you should not wear any wool or leather at all. It would also be beneficial to wear a hat, as a Taoist would generally not undertake any ritual or heavenly interaction with an exposed head.

4.11 Conduct 戒律

Traditional Taoist codes of conduct, called precepts (*jielü*), are extensive and complex. Although the Taoist spirit may be free, Taoist conduct is quite regulated. Once accepted, these all-encompassing precepts are meant to be followed without exception. While perfect adherence is not always possible, it is left to one's official Master to determine how much leeway any disciple should be allowed. Repeated violations of precepts could cause a Master to disavow a disciple, or a temple to expel a Taoist.

As an example, early Orthodox Unity Taoists adhered to three ranked sets of nine precepts each:

Song Mountain
Hebei Province

Orthodox Unity Precepts

1. Do not delight in deviance. Delight is the same as anger.
2. Do not waste your essence and pneumas.
3. Do not injure the ascendant pneumas.
4. Do not consume beasts that contain blood, delighting in their flavor.
5. Do not envy the achievements and fame of others.
6. Do not practice false arts or point to any shape and call it the Dao.
7. Do not neglect the law [i.e., the doctrine and ritual practices] of the Dao.
8. Do not act recklessly.
9. Do not kill or speak of killing.
10. Do not study deviant texts.
11. Do not covet glory or seek it strenuously.
12. Do not seek fame.
13. Do not be deceived by your ears, eyes, or mouth.
14. Place yourself in a humble position.
15. Do not slight [the Dao] or become agitated.
16. Consider carefully all undertakings and do not be flustered.
17. Do not pamper your body with good clothes and fine foods.
18. Do not allow [your emotions and vital forces] to overflow.
19. Do not, through poverty, seek strenuously after wealth.
20. Do not commit any of the various evil acts.
21. Do not overly observe the interdictions and taboos.
22. Do not pray or sacrifice to demons and spirits.
23. Do not be obstinate.
24. Do not consider yourself inerrant.
25. Do not contend with others over right and wrong. When you meet the contentious, flee them.
26. Do not proclaim [yourself to be a] Sage or contribute to the fame of the mighty.
27. Do not delight in arms.

(Stephen Bokenkamp, *Early Taoist Scriptures*)

Complete Perfection Taoists adhere to a different set of ten precepts:

Complete Perfection Precepts

> Do not be disloyal or unfilial, without benevolence or good faith. Always exhaust your allegiance to your lord and family, be sincere in your relation to the myriad beings.
>
> Do not secretly steal things or harbor hidden plots, harm others in order to profit yourself. Always practice hidden virtue and widely help the host of living beings.
>
> Do not kill or harm anything that lives in order to satisfy your own appetites. Always behave with compassion to all, even the multitude of insects and worms.
>
> Do not be lascivious or defile yourself, defile or debase the numinous energy. Always maintain chastity and be without shortcomings or blame.
>
> Do not defeat others to gain yourself or leave your kith and kin. Always use the tao to help others and support the nine clans living in harmony.
>
> Do not slander or defame the wise and virtuous or boast of your own skill to elevate yourself. Always praise the beauty and goodness of others and never fight about your own merit and ability.
>
> Do not drink liquor beyond measure or eat meat in violation of the prohibitions. Always maintain a harmonious energy and peaceful nature, do your duty in purity and emptiness.
>
> Do not be greedy and acquisitive without ever being satisfied, accumulating wealth without ever being generous. Always practice moderation in all things and show sympathy for the poor and the destitute.
>
> Do not have any relations with the unwise or live amongst the unclean or defiled. Always rise to overcome yourself and live in purity and emptiness.
>
> Do not speak lightly or make fun of serious matters, be agitated in language or abuse perfection. Always maintain seriousness and speak humble words, making the tao and its virtue your main duty.

(Livia Kohn, *Daoism and Chinese Culture*)

Hua Mountain – Shaanxi Province

Note that the precepts of both Orthodox Unity and Complete Perfection Taoism are not outlining the methods of either becoming a Taoist or gaining Taoist accomplishment. They generally concentrate on detailing how a Taoist should act and not how a Taoist should go about becoming some sort of expert or 'master.'

The precepts of both traditions, however, represent the cultural and lifestyle pledges demanded of Taoists who have been initiated into them. If you feel a significant connection to one of these Taoist traditions, you should attempt to follow its precepts as closely as possible. If you have not yet reached any conclusions regarding your possible preference, you should simply keep in mind that to be a Taoist is to accept a continuous quest for self-improvement. A Taoist seeks to bring to each moment an awareness of his or her practice. Eventually as your practice grows deeper, stronger, and more internalized, your awareness of it may fade. In the meantime, the following are some general guidelines for your daily conduct:

A Practitioner Should Be:	A Practitioner Should Not Be:
Sincere	Contentious
Truthful	Gossipy
Simple	Materialistic
Kind	Aggressive
Sympathetic	Competitive
Generous	Envious
Content	Exclusionary
Humble	Evangelical
A Student	A Master

Remember, your ultimate goal is not to force yourself to adhere to any precepts or to encourage positive traits or to suppress negative ones. You should instead work diligently to refine yourself until your goals regarding conduct are natural and internalized. If you can adhere to these suggestions in your daily life, you will have succeeded in going quite far along your Taoist path!

Taoist Manual

Taoist Greeting

It is also important to understand how Taoists typically greet each other. Taoists do not shake hands, shout 'hello' from a distance, hug each other, or clap each other on the back. Taoists are often reserved and quiet, and their greetings reflect these personality traits.

Upon seeing another Taoist or Student/Practitioner (of either gender, of any age, etc.), a male should place his hands in front of his heart or throat with right fist covered by his left palm, making a symbolic *taiji* symbol. This greeting, which requires no words, is sufficient in most situations. If a male wants to express a deeper, more sincere, or more formal greeting, he should immediately follow the greeting described above by bowing slightly forward from the waist, simultaneously dropping his attached hands to his waist. He can then stand erect, raise his hands back to his heart of throat, and release. The lower the bow, the more expressive or formal the greeting will be.

Both the informal and formal greetings are the same for women, except that women should reverse their hand positions, with the left fist being covered by the right palm.

There are several terms by which friendly Taoists refer to each other. Some, like Daoyou ('friend in the tao') or Tongdao ('friend on a common path'), are quite common. It is important to realize, however, these terms imply a common status between both parties. Unless you have been initiated as a Taoist, you should not use these terms in reference to an initiated Chinese Taoist. To do so would be overly familiar and less than humble.

Daoyou

5
Continued Study

5.1 Continued Study

This book is not meant to make anyone into a Taoist. No book can possibly achieve that. My only goal is to provide you with an accurate, traditional depiction of what it means to be a Taoist. But once you understand this message, it is solely up to you to move forward along your Taoist path, or to choose some other option for your life. If you opt to continue along your Taoist path, you must realize that you have barely crossed the threshold into the house of Taoism. You still have very far to go, and it will require as much time as you have left allotted to you. I absolutely guarantee that you have the ability to progress very far along this path. The only question is whether you have the desire, the dedication, and the willingness to diligently apply yourself over a very long period of time.

What can you expect from your spiritual path as you dedicate yourself to becoming more Taoist? For one thing, Taoists are, by definition, initiates. At some point in your development (perhaps a point that is still very distant into your future), you will probably need to undergo initiation in order to continue your progress. Initiation will strengthen your connection to the Taoist pantheon, and will make you the rightful possessor of additional Taoist teachings. When the time is right, initiation will undoubtedly make itself available to you.

Study
Xue

Ancient Seal Script

Taoists see all life in terms of energy. You and I are nothing but energy, and we are constantly interacting with other energies. Taoist cultivation techniques are the science of refining energy and controlling interactions between energies. No Taoist is familiar with all techniques. A Taoist can spend a lifetime becoming an expert in these areas, and that may be your fate should you continue on your Taoist path.

Taoists believe that spirits are all around us, and that there is a constant interaction between the human and spirit worlds. This is the focus of Taoist ritual. You will have endless talismans, mudra, and mantra to learn in order to successfully navigate your way through this field of knowledge. Again, a Taoist may spend a lifetime specializing in this arcane field.

The pantheon is also central to the daily activities of Taoists. There are an endless number of deities, and an overabundance of information to be learned about each one. The information we have covered in this book is merely a brief introduction. Each deity has its own history, areas of responsibility, preferences, and circumstances. Some Taoists choose this field as a life-long specialty.

Shifu

As you can probably guess, these aspects of Taoism are all inter-related. A great Taoist knows a good deal about all aspects of Taoism. I have met many great Taoists, but I have never met one who did not meet one crucial criteria: they studied like mad for many decades to attain the knowledge they sought, and they never ceased striving to achieve a deeper understanding. That is precisely the path that I would recommend to anyone who would become a great Taoist!

I should say a final word regarding academic rather than religious training. An academician who specializes in a particular Taoist field is not necessarily a Taoist or even a Practitioner. To understand Taoism is not necessarily the same as believing in or practicing Taoism. That being said, however, the structured and guided intellectual training offered by a serious graduate studies program can be a tremendous aid in learning more about Taoism. Such training can easily lead someone to the point where they can become seriously interested in Taoism as a religious practice. You will have to decide for yourself whether to immediately embark upon your Taoist path, or whether to first undertake academic training. Both paths are valid, and both can lead to the same ultimate destination.

5.2 Selecting a Teacher

At some point along your Taoist path (probably sooner rather than later) you will confront the problem of finding a teacher. You will only be able to make a certain amount of progress until books no longer serve you. At that point, a teacher becomes a necessity. Your first (or next) teacher does not have to be an initiated Taoist. He or she does not really have to be a Taoist at all. Someone can teach you vital information about *taiji quan*, *qigong,* Taoist philosophy, etc. without being a Taoist. Spiritual advancement, and the ability to transfer that advancement, is not limited to Taoists. A non-Taoist cannot be the ultimate teacher on your Taoist path, but can still be a pivotal figure in your spiritual development. The person who initiates you into their lineage is forever your Master (*shifu*), but anyone who passes along knowledge to you is your Teacher (*laoshi*). Take good instruction wherever you can! Each step you take along your Taoist path not only moves you closer to your goal, but also helps to prepare you for the lessons to come.

Laoshi

There are many teachers out there, some of whom are good, and some of whom are not so good. How can you select an appropriate teacher? The trick is to not make a small problem into a large problem. Try to follow these simple guidelines:

1. ***You already possess a solid understanding of Taoist basics. Trust it.*** Do not underestimate your own knowledge. We know that Taoists disagree on many aspects of Taoist practice and knowledge. If a prospective teacher disagrees with your existing knowledge, ask yourself if this disagreement seems reasonable for Taoists. For example, if a prospective teacher tells you that your hands should be in a slightly different posture during *qigong* practice, or that a particular deity exhibits different characteristics than you had thought, he may be right (even if such advice contradicts something in this book!). If a prospective teacher tells you that devotion to the spirits of the pantheon is not an important part of Taoist practice, you should immediately look for another teacher.

2. ***Avoid 'Flamboyant Personalities'*** as such traits are indicative of an unrefined or inappropriate practice. If a teacher advertises on the internet, or with storefront signs, flyers, etc., he or she is probably not sufficiently advanced or professional. Taoist teachers rarely advertise. If someone easily relates that they are booked for months in advance, or that their students or clients include many impressive people, take this as a warning to find a different teacher, as serious spiritual teachers would find such revelations to be utterly worthless.

3. ***One of the most important factors in accepting a spiritual teacher is the energetic connection between teacher and student.*** If you have been practicing the activities described in this book, you should have a fairly good sense of intuition. Does a prospective teacher 'feel' right to you? You should feel completely at ease with a potential teacher from the moment you meet. If you do not, for any reason, respectfully walk away. Even a great Taoist would not be a suitable teacher for you if the two of you do not possess the appropriate energetic connection.

4. ***Your teacher is not a deity.*** Taoists, even great Taoists, are also human beings. No one is perfect. No Taoist has fully acquired all possible knowledge. While some teachers may expect to be treated as if they were deities, I have never met a Taoist who exhibited this quality. Taoists are usually humble, likeable people because they know better than anyone how very human they are. If a teacher expects to be treated as a 'Master,' take that as a sure sign that he or she is not one. Your relationship with your teacher will also become skewed if you begin to treat your teacher as a deity (even if your teacher has not asked

for such treatment). Your teacher should be a gifted, knowledgeable individual who is deeply concerned for your spiritual development. Treat him or her with the respect and love due to such a teacher, and with no more and certainly no less.

Once you have located a teacher with whom you think you would like to study, freely approach your potential new teacher with an attitude of respect and humility. In dealing with your prospective teacher, there are several important points to remember:

1. Make sure that you remain 'open' to spiritual teaching. A teacher can only work within the parameters of the student's life and potential. If you believe that the methods or beliefs of your potential teacher are not effective (or worse!), then it would be best to not waste your time or the time of your teacher.

2. A Spiritual Teacher is not a psychic. Although many good teachers will indeed possess psychic abilities, Taoists (and many good non-Taoist teachers) hold these abilities in low regard. If you are looking for a psychic reading, visit a professional fortune teller and not a spiritual teacher. A serious Taoist teacher will appreciate your focus.

3. Do not take rejection personally. A potential teacher may refuse you as a student simply because he or she sees they cannot provide whatever you need. This does not mean that you cannot find a different teacher who will be able to provide you with excellent guidance. A potential teacher may also react with delay when responding to your entreaty. Again, you should not take this personally. A teacher may be testing your sincerity, secretly requesting time to meditate or otherwise consider your consideration, or may simply want to make sure that you are not involved in an emergency situation that they cannot resolve.

Finally, there are certain things that everyone should absolutely avoid in terms of finding a spiritual teacher:

1. Avoid any teacher who makes you feel inadequate, guilty, fearful, etc. Serious spiritual teachers are non-judgmental, accepting, and supportive. Experienced Taoists exhibit these qualities without fail. If a potential teacher does not exhibit these qualities, quickly and respectfully find a different teacher.

2. Dependency is inappropriate. No legitimate spiritual teacher will stress his or her own holiness or advancement in contrast to your own lack of those qualities, even if your teacher is a Taoist and you are not yet one. Your teacher should realize that everyone is capable of great spiritual achievement. You do

Meditation
Chan

Seal Script

not 'need' any particular teacher, and should not be made to feel like you do.

3. Sexual relations with your teacher are always inappropriate. I cannot sufficiently stress this point. Healthy physical relationships are usually the product of a relationship between general equals. This cannot be the case within the framework of a teacher-student relationship. A serious Taoist teacher should know better than to become physically or romantically involved with a student.

4. Beware of Immediate Acceptance. Just as you should need some time to evaluate a prospective teacher, so should a teacher require some period to evaluate you as a prospective student. It is possible that an insightful teacher will immediately know that you are a great candidate, but that is mostly the work of movies and books. Most productive teacher-student relationships will take some time to develop.

5. Resist a request by to any prospective teacher for an extraordinary amount of money. I have met many accomplished Taoists during my travels and studies, and not one of them has ever charged me anything. Some were willing to pass along a small bit of knowledge to me, and some were not. But none demanded great sums of money from me. A true teacher will be infinitely more concerned with helping people, or with finding an appropriate student, than with earning money. If you intuitively feel that money is too important a part of your potential relationship with a new teacher, trust your instinct. That does not mean that you should feel no financial obligation towards your teacher. You should. A student should support a teacher just as a teacher should guide a student's spiritual development. But if you believe a potential teacher is just too concerned with money, that individual is not an appropriate teacher for you.

5.3 Reading and Internet Resources

There are a countless number of available books on Taoist topics, a number that is growing with each passing day. A fair number of these books, however, are not worthwhile resources for further study. It is a very difficult process today for a beginning practitioner of Taoism to walk unaided into a bookstore and to select a reliable and respected resource. Untrustworthy or misleading works vastly outnumber intelligent and worthwhile ones.

You may also notice that your local bookstore possesses a seemingly infinite variety of translations of the *Dao De Jing*. While a number of these translations are undoubtedly quite reasonable, at least several have been written by authors who work only from the translations of others and not from original source documents. Such efforts are more aptly labeled 'interpretations' than 'translations,' and you should avoid them if possible. For a beginning list of recommended texts, written on a wide variety of specific topics and for a wide variety of intended audiences, please see the bibliography at the end of this book.

The internet is perhaps even more confusing than the bookstore. The internet is a universe unto itself. Most of the Taoist information available on the internet, however, should be taken with at least several grains of salt. The benefit of the internet is that it fosters instantaneous communication and community among widespread groups. The danger of the internet is that no expertise of any sort is required in order to pose as an expert. There are too many Taoism-related internet websites out there that are run by folks who are not terribly knowledgeable regarding Taoism. Caveat emptor!

Here is a quick list of some of worthwhile Taoism-related websites:

Academic Websites

Daoist Studies:
http://www.daoiststudies.org

This website does an excellent job of fostering international scholarly communication about the study of Taoism.

Taoist Studies in the World Wide Web:
http://venus.unive.it/~pregadio/taoism.html

This is one of the most academic websites on the internet dealing with Taoism. It is filled with academic articles and essays, as well as with links to various scholarly associations, translated source materials, etc.

Taoism by Russell Kirkland:
http://www.uga.edu/religion/rk/basehtml/home.html

As a Book Review Editor for the *Journal of Chinese Religions* and a Board Member of the *Society for the Study of Chinese Religions*, Kirkland is a well-respected member of the academic community, and his website posts many of his myriad journal articles, conference presentations, reference work entries, and book reviews.

Eternal, Constant
Chang

Ancient Seal Script

Society for the Study of Chinese Religions ("SSCR"):
http://www.indiana.edu/~sscr/

The SSCR is an academic organization that annually publishes the excellent *Journal of Chinese Religions*. For anyone interested in a serious, intellectual look at Taoism, membership in the SSCR (which is the only way to subscribe to the *Journal of Chinese Religions*) is a must.

Professor Torchinov's Home Page:
http://www.members.tripod.com/~etor_best/ie4.html

The late Yevgeny Torchinov was a Professor at the University of St. Petersburg (Russia), and his excellent website reflects his great knowledge of the Taoist and Buddhist traditions.

Books

Sacred Mountain Press
http://www.smpress.com

Sacred Mountain Press publishes specifically for the international Taoist and Taoistic communities. They are part of a growing trend to make a greater number of important and traditional Taoist materials easily available. Check their website for their latest offerings.

Chinese Art & Culture

China the Beautiful:
http://www.chinapage.com/china-rm.html

This isn't really a Taoist website, but a great place to learn more about traditional Chinese art and culture.

Chinese Language

Zhongwen:
http://www.zhongwen.com

This is perhaps the internet's premier website for learning the Chinese language. There are plenty of online lessons available, and they even have a pinyin (Chinese language in Romanized letters instead of Chinese characters) discussion board for beginners.

Worldwide Language Institute:
http://wwli.com/languages/zhongwen/lesson01/pinyin.html

This website offers detailed lessons in the pinyin system of Romanization. If you are trying to learn pinyin online, this is also a great website!

Emperor, God
Di

Ancient Seal Script

Continued Study

Feng Shui

Geomancy.net:
http://www.geomancy.net

This is perhaps the best overall *feng shui* website on the internet, containing excellent overviews for beginners interested in any number of *feng shui* styles.

Taoist Feng Shui:
http://www.susanlevitt.com/

This website is filled with easy to understand explanations and examples from Susan Levitt's *Taoist Feng Shui: A Handbook of the Authentic Chinese Tradition* and *Taoist Astrology: The Ancient Roots of the Chinese Art of Placement*.

Food and Diet

Yutopian's Cooking Page
http://www.yutopian.com/cooking/

Although you won't find any specifically Taoist material on this website, you can learn how to prepare excellent Chinese meals!

International Sivananda Yoga Vedanta Centers
http://www.sivananda.org

This is a website dedicated to a particular yoga lineage, but the dietary and lifestyle principles it advocates are quite similar to those of Complete Perfection Taoism.

International Community

The United States Taoist Association
http://www.ustaoism.org

The U.S. Taoist Association ('USTA'), which is recognized by the China Taoist Association, promotes greater popular understanding of traditional Taoism, lobbies when necessary for Taoism-friendly policies and ideas, and interacts with foreign Taoist Associations in order to create a more vibrant and effective global Taoist community. Membership is free!

The Taoist Restoration Society:
http://www.taorestore.org

The Taoist Restoration Society ('TRS') is a nonprofit organization helping to preserve and restore China's Taoist heritage. Donations go towards charitable projects in China's Taoist communities, such the restoration of ancient sites, the subsidization of elderly Taoist masters, the promotion of research and scholarship, etc. This website is filled with copious amounts of information, as well as active discussion boards.

The British Taoist Association:
http://www.taoists.co.uk

This is the website of the British Taoist Association, a non-profit organization associated with Taoism's Complete Perfection Dragon Gate tradition. The BTA runs a center in England, complete with classes and community, and publishes a quarterly pamphlet called the *Dragon's Mouth*.

The Taoist Society of Brazil:
http://www.taoismo.org.br

This is a Portuguese-language website of an active and dedicated Taoist organization headquartered in Rio de Janeiro.

Siu Tao:
http://english.siutao.com

'Siu Tao' means 'Student of Taoism,' and this website does an admirable job of helping Indonesians to earn that title.

Taoist Mission (Singapore):
http://www.taoism.org.sg

The Taoist community is quite strong in Singapore, and this is the main English-language website of that community. There is some general information on Taoism, but the website primarily focuses on the activities of the local Taoist community.

Taoist Culture & Information Centre:
http://www.eng.taoism.org.hk

Run by a Hong Kong Taoist Temple, this website is dedicated to the dissemination of information on Complete Perfection Taoism. Their website contains a great deal of information on Taoist belief and practice, but much of this information has not yet been translated into English.

Qi: The Journal of Traditional Eastern Health and Fitness
http://www.qi-journal.com

This is the very informative online version of Qi's monthly magazine. It is an excellent source of information on a variety of Taoism-related activities, but it sometimes doesn't understand that that those activities don't define Taoism.

Treasure
Bao

Ancient Seal Script

Continued Study

Chad Hansen's Chinese Philosophy Page:
http://www.hku.hk/philodep/ch/Daoindex.html

The Taoism page of this website is well worth a visit, although it consistently confuses the concept of tao with that of Taoism.

Qigong

Ken Cohen's Qigong Research & Practice Center:
http://www.Qigonghealing.com

This is an excellent website for anyone interested in learning more about either Taoist or medical *qigong*.

Qigong Association of America
http://www.qi.org

This website includes a host of interesting articles and practitioner listings. It does tend to advocate some controversial positions (*qigong* should be regulated by the government according to standards supplied by the Qigong Association of America!), but it is still worthwhile.

Traditional Chinese Medicine

Acupuncture.com
http://www.acupuncture.com

This is a large, comprehensive site covering all major aspects of traditional Chinese healing practice. Information is divided into 'consumer,' 'student,' and 'practitioner' levels, making it fairly simple to seek out useful information for one's particular circumstances.

Yi Ching

Yi Ching Bookmarks:
http://www.zhouyi.com

This website contains the largest number of Yi Ching links on the internet. This is just a collection of links, however, and you should exercise appropriate caution.

Destiny
Ming

Oracle Bone Script

Reconstruction Supplies — Chaoyang Temple — Datong City, Shanxi Province

5.4 Taoist Pilgrimage

At some point, everyone's Taoist path will lead them to one (or more) of China's Taoist communities. You may study with brilliant teachers and apply yourself very conscientiously to those studies, but eventually you will need to make a pilgrimage (*chaosheng*).

Making such a trip will allow you to witness for yourself the birthplace of the tradition you are attempting to follow. Such an experience cannot help but provide one with a deeper understanding of Taoism. You can read about Taoism and hear about Taoism until you are old, but nothing will replace the opportunity to *see and feel* Taoism as it is traditionally practiced. I have told you of the incredible beauty of the Taoist morning prayers. My poor explanation will simply evaporate once you have the experience of rising with the sun and chanting to the gods with a group of Taoists as the morning steam rises with streams of fresh incense.

When to Go

I recommend, however, that people delay making pilgrimages for as long as they can, until such time as they can absolutely make no further progress without a pilgrim's experience. Travel to China can be difficult. Travel to remote China can be physically and spiritually exhausting. At your average Taoist community, no one speaks English. Rural Chinese people (most Taoist communities are in rural or extremely rural areas) generally speak only Chinese, and frequently only a non-standard Chinese. A year or two of Chinese language study will not suffice in these areas. Most people will definitely need a guide or translator.

Most guided tours cannot provide one-on-one translation. When a Taoist speaks to your group, his or her words will be translated (and often poorly translated). When you are off wandering by yourself or with one or two friends (precisely when you can have the most enriching experiences!), you will generally be without any capacity to speak to anyone. You will see things and not be able to gain an understanding of what you are seeing. Even in a group with a translator, any individual is usually not allowed to dominate with endless and specific questions. A lack of comprehension can blind one to the beauty that surrounds them.

朝聖

Chaosheng

It is generally more worthwhile to make a pilgrimage once you have achieved a sufficient basic understanding of Taoist devotion, ritual, practice, and culture. The more Taoist knowledge you acquire prior to your trip, the more you will benefit from the experience. Then when you see familiar things being done, you will intuitively understand them. The Taoists will surely notice your understanding, and some important communication can take place regardless of language difficulties.

It is also important to note that conditions in rural China are also not up to Western standards. Toilets are often no more than exposed, public holes in the ground with slats of wood thrown over the top. Every time you put them to use you will pray very, very hard to the *Great Jade Emperor* to provide those ancient slats with the strength to last another day. Conditions can be filthy in rural China. Some people will never, under any circumstances, want to look into a kitchen. If they do, they may never eat again. I have awoken to find rats the size of large cats sitting near my head staring at me. Rats are, unfortunately, quite common. Chinese culture can also require some adjustment from Westerners. Pushing is so accepted that it is not even noticed. No one would ever wait in a line when they can just push right up to the front. Overt and continuous staring, at extremely close and uncomfortable distances, is not considered rude. Spitting is constant, location be damned. Rural people will spit indoors, on floors, on walls, etc. My point is that an advanced pilgrim will not notice these things. He or she will be too engrossed by the spiritual power and beauty that they have come to witness and share. A beginner who has gone on a pilgrimage too soon, however, may well be overcome by these difficulties. Such an experience can overwhelmingly impact one's

Continued Study

Typical Taoist Bathroom

ability to continue on a Taoist path. I have seen this unfortunately happen to many good and sincere people.

How to Go

When you do go on a pilgrimage (as I said, I believe everyone on a Taoist path will have to go at some point), the manner in which you act and handle your experience will determine to a large extent how valuable that experience is to you. You will be a foreigner in a strange place, dealing with strange people to whom you will be equally strange. Yet common beliefs will somehow bind you.

The following are some good tips to help you maximize the richness of your pilgrimage:

Be as flexible with your schedule as possible

Rural Taoists have a vastly different concept of time than do most Westerners. A highly developed awareness of time can only injure your energy. Temple bells sound whenever Taoists' attention is required. You should be flexible as well. 'In a minute' or 'later' should never be taken as a literal statement. 'Tomorrow' might not even have a defined meaning. Moreover, there is not much to do as a visitor to a typical Taoist temple. One wanders through beautiful areas, talks with new friends if and when one meets them, eat and sleeps when one can, etc. There are few activities, and a mostly open schedule. If you are easily bored, or if you generally like to have a well-planned itinerary, Taoist pilgrimage may not be your preferred vacation.

Saint
Sheng

Ancient Seal Script

Be polite, not obsequious

Taoist culture is very polite, and you should follow that custom. Stand aside and let Taoists or senior citizens pass by, or pass through a doorway. Never touch anything unless invited to do so. Avoid too much direct eye contact (a Western habit!). These are all examples of the politeness you should exhibit. Yet I have seen people fall down on the knees before Taoists in an uncalled for display of reverence. It created an uncomfortable situation for everyone. These are Taoists, not gods. They are to be respected, not worshipped.

Balance your desire to ask questions with your need to stay inwardly focused

Taoists are rarely chatterboxes. Taoism causes people to delve inward, not outward. There are no great Taoist proselytizers. Therefore pick and choose your questions well. You do not want to monopolize a Taoist's time, and you do not want to communicate to anyone that you lack sufficient inward focus. Yet you are on a pilgrimage to learn as much as you can about traditional Taoism, and questioning a teacher is one valid way to accomplish that task.

Participate, but know your place

A Taoist temple can be a very intimidating place. It can be very difficult for some Westerners to participate in religious activities. Try to get over any self-consciousness you may feel. If you visit a temple with a shrine to your favorite deity, you should feel free to make an offering at the altar. Chinese people will gather around to watch the strange foreigner, and the resident Taoist himself may give you a funny look. Don't be dissuaded from any similar activities. But you must also be aware of other participants. Some activities are really restricted to initiates, and you should do your best to respect those restrictions.

Do not ask to stay!

No matter how much you may fall in love with a particular temple or teacher, do not ask if you can stay or if you can become a disciple. First and foremost, it would be illegal for any temple to agree. The Taoists at that temple would find themselves in a great deal of trouble with the authorities were they to agree. But don't worry about this, as no one will agree. It would also be quite contrary to Taoist tradition (no matter what we may have seen on television!) to accept a disciple so lightly. The mere question will undoubtedly create an uncomfortable atmosphere for the Taoist you're hoping to engage! Since there is no chance of success, you are better off focusing on making your pilgrimage (and the relationships and impressions that you form therein) the most they can be.

Be respectful in everything you do

You may witness other tourists, Chinese people, or even Taoists themselves who are not seemingly acting in a respectful manner towards a temple or a Taoist practice. Do not follow the crowd. Conduct yourself at all times like a respectful pilgrim, no matter what anyone else does. You are not only representing yourself, but in the eyes of the local Taoists and populace at any given community, you are representative of all foreign pilgrims. In China people often simply throw trash on the ground, especially in high, remote, mountainous Taoist communities. Whatever you carry in, carry out. Your back may become sore, but your spirit will remain strong. Even if others disregard traditions or fail to act in a responsible or respectful manner, you will know better. Local people may be unaware of their transgressions, but we should nonetheless act with all the respect we can manage. In showing respect for the Taoism we encounter as pilgrims, we are showing respect for ourselves and for our own traditions as well.

Do Not Photograph Altars

Although you may freely photograph temple grounds or even the outside of temples, you should never photograph an altar. It is offensive to the altar's resident deity and to the temple's resident Taoists to have visitors (and especially uninitiated visitors) intrusively impact the energy of an altar in this way. Be thankful for the opportunity to see and experience a temple's altar, and resist the natural urge to desecrate it with photography of any sort. Resist this urge even though you will probably see many local Chinese tourists who are ignorant of this prohibition. Even if a local Taoist agrees to let you photograph an altar (as a courtesy to a foreign guest), you should not do so. You may, however, freely sketch altars.

Do Not Photograph Taoists without Permission

You should similarly refrain from photographing Taoists without first requesting their permission. Many Taoists will happily agree to such a request. Some, however, do not like to feel that they are on display and may therefore refuse. Either way, you should respect their decisions.

Females – A Note of Caution

The same prohibitions that we observe at our own altars should be doubly enforced while you are a pilgrim. Just as with your own altars, females should refrain from entering the altar area of any Taoist temple (not the complexes themselves, but rather the specific altar areas of the temples) while experiencing their menses. At that time your energy requires rest, and should not interact with the energy of a Taoist ritual. We may not understand or agree with such rules, but as guests we should respect them. This holds true even if others do not show the same respect (and most Chinese visitors to Taoist temples will not be aware of this prohibition!).

Open Wounds

For the same reasons described above, anyone with an open flesh wound should avoid altar areas.

Where to Go?

There are innumerable Taoist sites in China. Researchers are always attempting to compile a complete list, but I have never seen one. The following are brief descriptions of great destinations with tremendous Taoist history and (mostly) current, active Taoist presences:

Taoism's Five Traditional Holy Mountains
Tai Mountain (Shandong Province) 泰山

Sunrise
Tai Mountain
Shandong Province

Tai Mountain, the easternmost of Taoism's five traditional holy mountains, has long been viewed as the most important of all the Chinese Taoist mountains. The first Qin Dynasty Emperor, Qin Shi Huang Di scaled Tai Mountain after reuniting China in 221 B.C. in order to give thanks to the resident deities. The religious history of Tai Mountain thus vastly predates Christianity! Taoists have resided on Tai Mountain for almost as long. Tai Mountain was declared a 'World Heritage Site' by UNESCO during the 1980's. It turns out this was quite a mistake. Tai Mountain is very famous for having an exceedingly long and arduous climb to its fabled peak. The stone staircase can take all day to climb. Early Taoists built the original staircase along various energy lines. The energy of the climb would thus impact pilgrims as they reached important religious sites. Since the UNESCO decision, the Chinese government has heavily promoted non-religious tourism at Tai Mountain. The ancient pathway was significantly altered to make the climb easier, without regard to the plans of the original Taoist builders. A cable car was added, so that Chinese revelers could make an overnight trip to the summit in order to watch the sunrise. At any time, expect a huge crowd of people (not pilgrims!) along the path and all over the mountain. The peak is littered with filthy motels and sleazy karaoke bars. But no place is richer in Taoist history. There are plenty of temples and Taoists. The collection of stone calligraphy tablets ('stele') along the mountain is utterly fabulous. And the sunrise could be world's absolute finest. I once purchased a pair of stone exercise balls from a beggar sitting along the steps of Tai Mountain, only to have

CONTINUED STUDY

Sleeping Monastery
Heng Mountain
Shanxi Province

him tell me in heavily accented Chinese many true and unknowable facts regarding my family and life back in the U.S. You might want 2-3 days (excluding travel time) to explore Tai Mountain if you are walking.

Heng Mountain (Shanxi Province)
恆山

Heng Mountain is the northernmost of Taoism's five main holy mountains. Located deep in China's coal country, Heng Mountain is at turns blackened with soot and outstandingly beautiful. There's not much non-local tourism here, and you can find some private moments. Some of the temples, like the Hanging Temple, the Immortals' Room, and the Sleeping Temple, are simply outstanding. You can find the hoof prints from Zhang Guolao's magical donkey, and one of the main ingredients for Immortality Pills (a five-colored stone) was said to come from a lost mine on this mountain. Although the mountain is beautiful and rich in Taoist culture, the Taoist presence here is relatively weak. This area was virulently communist, and only in the last few years have Taoists openly returned to Heng Mountain. Upon my last visit there were a group of 10-12 Taoists living in the temples there (both male and female Taoists). Moreover these Taoists were followers of Wang Li Ping (as described in Thomas Cleary's *Opening of the Dragon Gate*), and as such were held in extremely low regard by more mainstream Taoists. I understand they have since left the area. Nonetheless, any return of Taoists to Heng Mountain should be celebrated. You might want 1-2 days to explore the mountain itself, plus whatever time you might want to explore the surrounding area (much of which is fascinating).

East Peak Pavilion
Hua Mountain
Shaanxi Province

Hua Mountain (Shaanxi Province)
華山

Hua Mountain is the westernmost of Taoism's five main holy mountains. First let me say that recent fictional accounts concerning an alleged Taoist from Hua Mountain named Kwan Saihung are just that – fiction. People who go there hoping to find this fictional Taoism are going to be sorely disappointed. People who visit Hua Mountain in search of authentic Taoism, however, will be truly delighted. Hua Mountain, like Tai Mountain, could take all day to climb. There are five peaks, each one of which is a fantastic natural sight. There are plenty of temples, but walking from one peak to another requires great strength! Moreover, there are plenty of exceedingly dangerous paths on this mountain. Be prepared. Hua Mountain is unfortunately under the predominant control of a local tourism bureau and not the local religious affairs bureau. This means that Taoism is dampened in favor of tourism. A cable car has also been installed so that the often drunken masses can see the sunrise without having to climb! One famous temple on each peak is operated by the local government purely as a karaoke bar, restaurant, etc. If you stare at the mountain long enough, however, you will start to notice the Taoists wandering about. I have met many great Taoists here. In fact, I was once offered as my wife the daughter of a monastery cook. The cook was a wonderful man, but as his daughter was probably about 12 years old, I politely declined. Expect large crowds of mostly non-pilgrims throughout the summer. Expect no one in the winter, but it will be too cold for you, too. You may want 4-5 days to explore this gem of a mountain.

Middle Monastery
Heng Mountain
Hunan Province

Heng Mountain (Hunan Province) 衡山

Heng Mountain (a different Heng than the northern Heng!) is the southernmost of Taoism's five main holy mountains. Although Heng Mountain is indeed a beautiful place, it does not possess the knock-out beauty of Hua Mountain or Tai Mountain. But it is home to a large and thriving community of Taoists. There are actually three communities: at the base of the mountain, at the mid-point, and at the peak. The base community lives in a tremendous and recently rebuilt temple complex. The rebuilding cost was several million dollars, raised mostly from Hong Kong donors. The restoration, overseen by a powerful Abbess, was a huge success. The middle community lives in a normal, modest monastery, which despite having been rebuilt in the 1980's in less glorious fashion, evokes ancient times. The peak, the holiest point of any Taoist mountain, houses both Taoists and Buddhist temples, and is significantly less serene than the lower communities. Expect a crowd at the peak, especially on weekends. There are also surrounding valleys that are very picturesque and well worth exploring if you have the time. I was once walking along a path at dusk with a young local Taoist who was a very good friend of mine. We saw a person dressed in red walking along a ridge

Summit Temple
Song Mountain
Hebei Province

above us who disappeared in a flash. My Taoist friend insisted this was a famous local deity, and I could not have been happier to agree! You may want 1-2 days to tour this mountain, excluding travel time.

Song Mountain (Hebei Province) 嵩山

Song Mountain is the most central of Taoism's five main holy mountains. The mountain itself is beautiful, wooded, and empty. If you bring some water and some snacks, it will afford you a wonderful hike. There are no people on the mountain (except for some local farmers) because there are also no active temples on the mountain. Just down the mountain and to the west a mile or so is the Shaolin Temple. Shaolin, in addition to being a purely Buddhist temple staffed mostly with non-religious acrobatic actors in religious garb, also receives more than one million visitors per year. There is a bit of a 'third-world Disneyland' feel to Shaolin. A must for local tourists is the Chinese army-managed shooting range on the hills directly behind Shaolin. Although Shaolin is famous, a much better use of your time is to visit the extremely large, purely Taoist temple at the foot of Song Mountain. Because of its proximity to Shaolin, it receives very little attention while offering a much more traditional, more Taoist experience. The grounds are vast and are awe-inspiring. The statuary is particularly impressive. While the Taoists are numerous, they are also quite poor. That means all but the very oldest and most senior must work in the fields all day long. Most don't seem to mind, and appear to be quite content. I understand there is a problem in retaining young disciples, who often don't want to work that hard in the fields. One full day may be sufficient to tour this mountain for most people, excluding travel time.

OTHER MOUNTAIN/RURAL SITES

Wudang Mountain (Hebei Province) 武當山

Wudang Mountain is the most famous of the Taoist mountains not belonging to the traditional list of five (it is actually even more famous than some of its traditionally more revered brethren). It is the seat of Taoism's Dark Emperor of the North cult, and as such is home to a fantastic martial arts tradition. The 'mountain' is actually a series of countless peaks. The landscape is lush and wet, and fog frequently obscures the sights but adds to the intense, eerie beauty of the place. Only one of Wudang Mountain's five traditional complexes, the Purple Empyrean Palace (the Zixiao Gong), still stands. But this could be global Taoism's single most impressive complex. The Palace (a

Zixiao Palace
Wudang Mountain
Hebei Province

complex unto itself) is large, traditional, and filled with bustling religious activity. While there may be as many as one hundred Taoists, there are also a good many tourists from throughout SE Asia. The complex has recently undergone significant repairs, which appear to be excellent. The surrounding peaks and ruins make for great exploration. Most tourists stay in the tourism-oriented village down the mountain a bit. The village is crowded, unbelievably noisy, and filthy, but shouldn't be the focal point of anyone's trip. Beware of rampant scalping of foreign tourists. You may want 3-4 days to tour this mountain, with additional days allotted for traveling to and from this very remote mountain.

Qingcheng Mountain (Sichuan Province) 青城山

Qingcheng Mountain (literally 'Green Wall Mountain'), so named because it is so lush with vegetation, is a beautiful and picturesque place. The Taoist complex there is immense and traditional, and escaped major damage during the Cultural Revolution. There are many, many Taoists who live at Green Wall Mountain. The local religious authorities, however, can be quite difficult. They maintain a very communist attitude towards most policy, while they simultaneously run a variety of new commercial enterprises from the mountain. You should expect the Taoists here to be somewhat more rigid in their dealings with foreigners. That being said, this mountain is the very birthplace of Taoism, and has produced numerous important Taoists in recent history. You should also expect to stay in a sanctioned motel and eat at sanctioned restaurants. The view, the history, and the large Taoist presence make it all tremen-

Yuanfu Temple
(Post-renovation)
Mao Mountain
Jiangsu Province

Yuanfu Temple
(Pre-renovation)
Mao Mountain
Jiangsu Province

dously worthwhile! You may want at least 2-3 days to explore this immense mountain complex, which is easily accessible from Chengdu (the capital of Sichuan Province).

Mao Mountain (Jiangsu Province) 茅山

Mao Mountain has rebounded nicely from repeated and total destruction over the last 150 years. Three of the five traditional complexes on Mao Mountain have been substantially rebuilt. Located within a restricted area similar to a Western national park, the area is beautiful. Traditional farming still occurs within the area, but logging and myriad other activities are forbidden. The main Mao Mountain complex is again home to a large number of Orthodox Unity Taoists who are studying the traditional Mao Mountain Taoism. Another of the complexes, the Yuanfu Temple, is now the home to the world's largest statue of Laozi. Is this statue an affront to traditional Taoism, or is it a bold move into modernity? Only time will tell. But the statue is indeed impressive. Another complex, the Qianyuan Temple, is home to a devoted group of female Taoists. All three complexes have their charms, and are well worth a visit. You may want 1-2 days to tour this mountain, which is a drive of several hours from Shanghai.

Dragon Tiger Mountain (Jiangxi Province) 龍虎山

Three Purities Temple
Dragon Tiger Mountain
Jiangxi Province

Dragon Tiger Mountain is the ancestral home of the Celestial Masters, the primary leaders of Celestial Master Taoism. Over the years various Dynasties supported Dragon Tiger Mountain and the complex there became immense, and filled with Taoist treasures. For most of the last 1,000 years of Imperial rule in China, there was probably no more powerful figure in the Jiangxi Province area than the Celestial Master! The complex itself is a joy to explore. There are endless rooms and passageways, and most are filled with great historical interest. The complex was destroyed during the 1920's by a Chinese warlord who was a professed Christian. In one room destroyed by the General's army the Celestial Masters had countless sealed jars, in which they claimed were the captured spirits they had exorcised over the centuries. All the jars were broken! The Celestial Master fled to Taiwan in 1950, and his nephew remains there today as his appointed heir and the current Celestial Master. In the late 1980's, however, as China was developing a more commercial outlook, the government installed a grandson of an earlier Celestial Master as the leader of Dragon Tiger Mountain. How was this person selected? The authorities conducted a foot race up a steep mountain peak, and this man beat his competing relatives to the top. Since that time he appears to have lost his political standing, and is no longer in a position of authority. You may need one long day to tour this mountain, but since it is so remote you may as well take two.

Lao Mountain
Shandong Province

Lao Mountain (Shandong Province) 嶗山

Roughly fifteen miles east of the port city of Qingdao is Lao Mountain, a traditional home to Taoists for many centuries. The Palace of Supreme Purity, one of the main Taoist sites on Lao Mountain, was originally built in 140 B.C.! Many individual temples are well preserved, and the Taoist presence is quite strong at this site.

The Palace of Eternal Joy (Ruicheng, Shanxi Province) 永樂宮

The Palace of Eternal Joy (the *Yongle Gong*) is one of Taoism's most famous sites. Originally a temple complex originally dedicated to *Lü Dongbin,* the Palace of Eternal Joy was originally located in Shanxi Province's Yongle County. Built during the Yuan Dynasty (1260-1368), the entire complex was moved to its present location (Ruicheng City) during the 1950's when Yongle County was permanently flooded by the creation of a new hydroelectric dam. The walls of the Palace of Eternal Joy are covered with tremendous painted murals depicting Yuan Dynasty Taoism. These fantastic murals are among the most photographed and noted examples from all of Taoist art. While the Palace of Eternal Joy is absolutely worth a visit by anyone interested in Taoism or in Taoist art, Ruicheng City is unfortunately quite remote. It will take significantly more time to reach the Palace of Eternal Joy than it will to tour it!

Qian Mountains (Liaoning Province) 千山

About fourteen miles east of the industrial city of Anshan, in the Qian Mountains, is the Temple of In-

Front Gate
Temple of Infinity
Liaoning Province

finity. It is a large complex founded in the early Qing Dynasty (1677), and includes many sites spanning a number of peaks.

Luofu Mountain (Guangdong Province) 羅浮山

Located about forty-five miles east of the capitol city of Guangzhou, Luofu Mountain is one of the many sites where the famous Taoist Immortal Ge Hong lived and practiced his alchemy. Several sites relating to Ge Hong are still maintained.

Louguan Terrace (Zhongnan Mountain, Shaanxi Province) 樓觀臺

Louguan Terrace is essentially a complex dedicated to Laozi. Taoists believe that Laozi spent time here involved in immortality cultivations, and that he is actually buried at this site. Various sites connected to Laozi, including his burial site, his alchemical furnace, and a spot where Laozi once hitched his ox, are clearly marked. Although the Louguan Terrace is not a large site, it is very remote and will thus require several days to visit.

Urban Sites

White Cloud Monastery (Beijing City) 白雲觀

Ancient accounts of the White Cloud Monastery always include some reference to its far distance from Beijing. If night fell, or if the weather became difficult, travelers were invariably stuck there until morning. A modern visitor might be surprised to find the Monastery in the middle of downtown Beijing's southwest corner! The White Cloud Monastery dates back to the Yuan Dynasty (1271-1368), and in many respects is China's single most important Taoist site. It is both the headquarters for Complete Perfection Taoism (a historical designation) as well as headquarters for the China National Taoist Association (the governmental entity charged with the administration of Taoist affairs throughout the country). As such, the White Cloud Monastery is a rich, historical treat worthy of visitation, but it is also a highly politicized government center. My view is that if you have extra time in Beijing, you might want to go for a visit. But if you are already planning a visit to more receptive places, then it is not an absolutely necessary part of your itinerary.

If you do visit, be aware that amidst the countless temples and isolated pathways are a variety of government bureaucrats. Some of them will be wearing Taoist robes, posing as Taoists. There are a good number of legitimate Taoists, but many of them are

Ge Hong's Furnance Site
Luofu Mountain
Guandong Province

Laozi's Tomb
Louguan Terrace
Shaanxi Province

less than friendly, in part because they never know who is watching them. If you happen to visit on a Taoist holiday, expect a pleasant crowd. An afternoon is plenty of time for most people to explore the White Cloud Monastery.

Fire God Temple (Beijing City) 火神廟

Not far from the White Cloud Monastery, on what is known as Finance Street in the heart of Beijing's nascent financial district, is the Fire God Temple (Houshen Miao, also known as Finance Street Temple). This is a small, somewhat run-down temple staffed by 2-3 Taoists. It is unique, however, in that it is a small oasis of Traditional Taoist culture in an area of modern office buildings and high finance. The interior of the main hall is decorated with Taoist scrolls donated by the Taoist Restoration Society. As this site is so close to the White Cloud Monastery, it is worth touring if you are in the area.

White Cloud Monastery (Shanghai City) 白雲觀

Unconnected to its namesake temple in Beijing, Shanghai's White Cloud Monastery is an active Orthodox Unity Taoist center. Located in a densely residential area, a good portion of which once belonged to the monastery grounds, this small complex has a variety of nice temples centered around a large interior courtyard. Perhaps because the monastery is located in what is probably China's most cosmopolitan city, the local Taoists are not particularly warm or welcoming towards foreign visitors. White Cloud Monastery is nonetheless host to frequent ceremonies and public rituals, and is worth a visit if you are in the area.

Front Gate
White Cloud Monastery
Beijing City

Lü Dongbin Temple
White Cloud Monastery
Beijing City

Temple of the Eastern Mountain (Beijing City)
東岳廟

In the northeast quadrant of old Beijing is the Temple of the Eastern Mountain (dedicated to the God of Tai Mountain). This Temple was once the headquarters of Taoism's God of Tai Mountain cult. Closed during the Cultural Revolution but spared destruction, this historic Temple has recently reopened as a Museum for Folk Cultures. The museum itself is nearly worthless, but it is a rare treat to be able to visit this important and ancient site.

Chaoyang Temple (Datong City, Shanxi Province)
朝陽寺

In the heart of downtown Datong (the capitol of Shanxi Province) is the cozy Chaoyang Temple. Unknown even to many Datong residents despite its central location, the Chaoyang Temple has operated as a Nunnery for many decades. It remained in silent operation throughout most of China's turbulent modern history. Recently renovated with the assistance of the Taoist Restoration Society, this temple now houses a small group of female Taoists. The various shrines have been opened by a Taoist ritual master, and the Temple exhibits a profound warmth. If you are in Datong, you will probably be quite close to this Temple, and it is well worth a visit.

City Deity Temple (Shanghai City) 城隍廟

In the heart of Shanghai's downtown area is the Temple for the Shanghai City Deity (the *cheng huang miao*). Formerly a very large and prosperous temple, and the most famous of

China's City Deity Temples, this site fell into serious disrepair during China's communist era. As the Shanghai economy recovered in the 1990's, and as China's society liberalized, the Shanghai City Deity Temple was renovated. It is again a bustling hive of activity, with constant crowds leaving offerings and making prostrations.

Mazu Temple (Tianjin City) 媽祖廟

This temple was once the headquarters of China's extensive and powerful Mazu cult. The Qing Emperor and his court would make the trek from Beijing to Tianjin every year on the date of the Mazu festival. Western powers invaded China in 1900, however, and ransacked this historic temple. The temple was not restored for almost 100 years, and is now an immense outdoor market that includes several small shrines. A visit to the Mazu Temple is less of a religious experience than a historical one, but you will definitely find it fascinating.

Finance St. Temple
Beijing City

The Eight Immortals Temple (Xian, Shaanxi Province) 八仙庵

Anyone who goes to visit Hua Mountain must pass through Xian, the capital city of Shaanxi Province. While in Xian, you should definitely pay a visit to the beautiful Eight Immortals Temple. This urban complex has a large resident number of Taoists and ancient temples. You should expect a crowd at almost any time. If you visit during the summer months, bring insect repellent as mosquitoes seem to love this temple as much as you will!

Chongyang Temple (Xian, Shaanxi Province) 重陽觀

Several miles southeast of Xian is the Chongyang Temple, reportedly built over the grave of Wang Chongyang, the founder of Complete Perfection Taoism. Complete Perfection Taoists regard this as one of the most important of Taoist temples. The stone stele at this site are fabulous.

The Purple Sheep Palace (Chengdu, Sichuan Province) 青羊宮

If you are going to visit Qingcheng Mountain, you must pass through Chengdu, the capital city of Sichuan Province. In Chengdu, you should certainly make time to visit the Purple Sheep Palace. This large and ancient complex is often crowded with worshippers, and includes a variety of beautiful temples. The complex also houses large and excellent outdoor teahouses, and can probably be toured in an afternoon.

Temple Well
Eight Immortals Temple
Shaanxi Province

Courtyard Waterway
Jin Shrines
Taiyuan City, Shanxi Province

Jin Shrines (Taiyuan, Shanxi Province) 金祠

The Jin Shrines (*jin ci*) is located roughly one hour's drive south of Taiyuan City (the capital of Shanxi Province). It is a large and picturesque Song Dynasty complex that contains about one-third Buddhist structures. The Sage Mother Hall, the focal point of the entire complex, is an excellent example of Song Imperial architecture, and contains fantastic statuary. While there is no active religious presence at the Jin Shrines, the complex itself is a Taoist historical wonder.

Geling Monastery (Hangzhou, Zhejiang Province) 葛嶺道院

This small but quaint complex is built along the incredibly scenic banks of Hangzhou's West Lake. The Taoist Immoral *Ge Hong*, author of the famous 'Master Who Embraces Simplicity,' spent years performing personal cultivations at this site. The elevated teahouse at the Red Plum Pavilion offers exceptional vistas of the West Lake. If you are in Hangzhou, the Geling Monastery should definitely be on your itinerary, and can be visited quickly and easily if need be.

Mysterious Secret Temple (Suzhou, Jiangsu Province) 玄妙宮

The Mysterious Secret Temple (*xuan miao gong*), on Guanqianjie Street in Suzhou City, was originally built during the Western Jin Dynasty (276 A.D.). The site was renovated in 1371, 1956, and 1980, although only two of the original thirty-one halls now remain. Nonetheless, if you are in the beautiful city of Suzhou, this site is well worth a visit.

Ba Da Shan Ren Museum (Nanchang, Jiangxi Province) 八大山人博物館

In the far southern end of Nanchang City is a museum honoring the well-known Ming-Qing Dynasty artist *Ba Da Shan Ren* (literally, '8 Great Mountain Man') (1626-1705), a 16th generation descendent of the first Ming Dynasty Emperor. *Ba Da Shan Ren's* real name was Chu Ta, a name which he renounced as part of his rejection of the new Qing Dynasty. Rather than serve the new ruling house, *Ba Da Shan Ren* retired as a recluse to the exquisite temple which now houses this museum. He eventually became a Taoist, and is well known for his ink-wash paintings in the *Xieyi* Style (a freehand brushwork style characterized by spontaneous expression and bold outlines).

Red Plum Pavilion
Geling Monastery
Hangzhou City,
Zhejiang Province

Xu Xun Temple
Ba Da Shan Ren Museum
Jiangxi Province

The *Ba Da Shan Ren* compound is an elegant, ancient collection of temples, buildings, gardens, and lakes (man-made). Temples and other buildings are all connected via zigzag corridors, and are separated by beautiful recessed stone garden areas. The gardens and dispersed artwork all invite peaceful wandering. It is easy to see how Taoists and recluses found serene refuge in this beautiful place. *Ba Da Shan Ren* was buried in the garden area upon his death, and visitors can pay their respects at his burial mound.

The Eternal Spring Monastery (Wuhan, Hubei Province)
長春觀

Another worthwhile urban site is the Eternal Spring Monastery. If you are ever in Wuhan, you should make time to visit this Taoist site. It is a large and traditional complex that stands out like a sore thumb from its urban and industrial surroundings. The murals depicting Laozi in the Hall of Supreme Purity are quite beautiful. This complex is easily accessible and can be toured quickly and easily if need be.

The Palace of Supreme Purity (Shenyang, Liaoning Province)
太清宮

This small urban complex has been so encroached upon that it feels almost claustrophobic! It is nonetheless a traditional and active Taoist site, and includes a variety of temples.

As with most urban temples, crowds are commonplace, especially on weekends or holidays. If you happen to find yourself in Liaoning Province, you should spend a few hours examining Taoism in this far northeastern outpost.

The Green Pine Monastery (Hong Kong) 青松觀

For those people who find themselves in Hong Kong with a few hours to spare, but not with sufficient time to make a difficult side trip into mainland China, The Green Pine Monastery (*Qing Song Guan* in Mandarin, *Ching Chung Koon* in Cantonese) is an excellent destination. Founded by the recently deceased Abbot *He* in 1950 (immediately after fleeing China's new communist government), The Green Pine Monastery is 'reformed' Complete Perfection institution. Members of this religious community do not renounce society or adhere to the strict Complete Perfection code of conduct. The main temple, however, is quite traditional and is dedicated to *Lü Dongbin, Wang Chongyang,* and *Qiu Chuji* (among the foremost of Complete Perfection Taoism's founders). The complex also includes residential homes for the elderly, a large and fantastic bonsai garden, and a nice vegetarian restaurant. The Green Pine Monastery is in Hong Kong's New Territories, and is about forty-five minutes from Hong Kong itself. Several hours should be sufficient to tour this complex.

Photo Commemorating
Premier Zhou Enlai's Visit
Ba Da Shan Ren Museum
Jiangxi Province

Chen Xiang Rock — West Peak, Hua Mountain — Shaanxi Province

Three Purities Temple — Dragon Tiger Mountain — Jiangxi Province

Bibliography

Andersen, Poul, *The Demon Chained Under Turtle Mountain: The History and Mythology of the Chinese River Spirit Wuzhiqi*, Berlin: Verlag, 2001.

—, *The Method of Holding the Three Ones: A Taoist Manual of Meditation of the 4th Century AD*, London: Curzon Press, 1980.

Beinfield, Harriet, and Korn, Efrem, *Between Heaven and Earth: A Guide to Chinese Medicine*, New York: Ballantine Books, 1992.

Bokenkamp, Stephen, *Early Taoist Scriptures*, Berkeley: University of California Press, 1997.

Cheng Manchao, *The Origin of Chinese Deities*, Beijing: Foreign Languages Press, 1995.

Cohen, Kenneth S., *The Way of Qigong: The Art and Science of Chinese Energy Healing*, New York: Ballantine Books, 1997.

Csikszentmihalyi, Mark, and Ivanhoe, P.J., Eds., *Religious and Philosophical Aspects of the Laozi*, Albany: SUNY Press, 1999.

Fu Yuantian, Ed., *Album for Taoist Deities and Divine Immortals* (Collector's Version), Beijing: Hua Xia Publishing House, 1994.

Graham, A.C., *The Book of Lieh Tzu: A Classic of the Tao*, New York: Columbia University Press, 1990.

Henricks, Robert, *Lao Tzu's Tao Te Ching*, New York: Columbia University Press, 2000.

Hsu, Fun-yuen, *T'ai Chi Ch'uan: An Investigation into the Methods of Practice*, Chicago: Hsu Fun Yuen Tai Chi Academy, 1992.

Kingston, Karen, *Creating Sacred Space with Feng Shui: Learn the Art of Space Clearing and Bring New Energy Into Your Life*, New York: Broadway Books, 1996.

Kohn, Livia, *Daoism and Chinese Culture*, Cambridge: Three Pines Press, 2001.

—, Ed., *Daoism Handbook*, Leiden: Brill, 2000.

—, *God of the Dao: Lord Lao in History and Myth*, Ann Arbor: Center for Chinese Studies, The University of Michigan, 1998.

—, Ed., *The Taoist Experience: An Anthology*, Albany: SUNY Press, 1993.

—, *Taoist Mystical Philosophy: The Scripture of Western Ascension*, Albany: SUNY Press, 1991.

—, Ed., *Taoist Meditation and Longevity Techniques*, Ann Arbor: Center for Chinese Studies, The University of Michigan, 1989.

Kwok, Man Ho and O'Brien, Joanne, *The Eight Immortals of Taoism: Legends and Fables of Popular Taoism*, New York: Meridian Books, 1991.

Lagerwey, John, *Taoist Ritual in Chinese Society and History*, New York: Macmillan Publishing Company, 1987.

Lam, Kam Chuen, *The Way of Energy: Mastering the Chinese Art of Internal Strength with Chi Kung Exercise*, London: Gaia Books, 1993.

Levitt, Susan, *Taoist Feng Shui: The Ancient Roots of the Chinese Art of Placement*, Rochester: Destiny Books, 2000.

—, *Taoist Astrology: A Handbook of the Authentic Chinese Tradition*, Rochester: Destiny Books, 1997.

Li Yangzheng, Ed., *Famous Centres of Taoism*, Beijing: China Taoist Association, 1987.

Liao, Waysun, *T'ai Chi Classics*, Boston: Shambhala Books, 1993.

Little, Stephen, et. al., *Taoism and the Arts of China*, Chicago: The Art Institute of Chicago, 2000.

—, *Realm of the Immortals: Taoism in the Arts of China*, Cleveland, Cleveland Museum of Art, 1988.

Mair, Victor, *Wandering on the Way: Early Taoist Tales and Parables of Chuang Tzu*, New York: Bantam Books, 1994.

—, *The Classic Book of Integrity and the Way*, New York: Bantam Books, 1990.

Robinet, Isabelle, *Taoism: Growth of a Religion*, Stanford: Stanford University Press, 1997.

—, *Taoist Meditation: The Mao Shan Tradition of Great Purity*, Albany: SUNY Press, 1993.

Saso, Michael, *Taoist Master Chuang*, Boulder: Sacred Mountain Press, 2000.

—, *The Gold Pavilion: Taoist Ways to Peace, Healing, and Long Life*, Boston: Charles E. Tuttle, 1995.

—, *A Taoist Cookbook: With Meditations from the Laozi Daode Jing*, Boston: Charles E. Tuttle, 1994.

—, *Blue Dragon, White Tiger: Taoist Rites of Passage*, Washington, D.C.: The Taoist Center, 1990.

—, *Taoism and the Rite of Cosmic Renewal*, Pullman: Washington State University Press, 1990.

Schafer, Edward H., *Mao Shan in T'ang Times*, Boulder: Society for the Study of Chinese Religions, 1989.

Schipper, Kristopher, *The Taoist Body*, Berkeley: University of California Press, 1993.

Steinhardt, Nancy, *Traditional Chinese Architecture*, New York: China Institute of America, 1984.

Strickmann, Michel, *Chinese Magical Medicine*, Stanford: Stanford University Press, 2002.

Veith, Ilza, *The Yellow Emperor's Classic of Internal Medicine*, Selangor Darul Ehsan, Malaysia: Palenduk Publications, 1997.

Watson, Burton, *The Basic Writings of Hsun Tzu, Mo Tzu, and Han Fei Tzu*, New York: Columbia University Press, 1967.

Wilhelm, Richard, *Understanding the I Ching*, Princeton: Princeton University Press, 1995.

Also from Sacred Mountain Press:

Taoist Master Chuang

ISBN: 0-9677948-0-3
LCCN: 00-90198

The fantastic story of Chuang-Ch'en Teng-Yün, a 35th generation Taoist Master, as told by Master Chuang's own disciple, the Taoist scholar Michael Saso. Saso masterfully recounts Master Chuang's previously secret teachings on Taoist history, exorcistic thunder magic, ritual, and practice. A must for any Taoist library!